Shikari Sahib

SIGNED BY THE
AUTHOR.

Shikari Sahib

by

Peter Byrne

From the pen of an ex-white hunter, an in-depth look at the legendary career of the India domiciled Irishman, Jim Corbett, the great man-eating tiger hunter of North India, and at the world of man-eating tigers and leopards, and the terror they instill in people.

With pictures taken in the man-eating tiger country of North India and Western Nepal at the sites of the great hunts, as well as of people who knew Corbett and were associated with him, including relatives of the victims of the man-eaters

PILGRIMS

PILGRIMS PUBLISHING
Varanasi ◆ Kathmandu

Shikari Sahib
Peter Byrne

Published by:
PILGRIMS PUBLISHING

An imprint of:
PILGRIMS BOOK HOUSE
B 27/98 A-8, Nawabganj Road
Durga Kund, Varanasi-221010, India
Tel: 91-542-314059, 314060, 312456
E-mail: pilgrims@satyam.net.in
Website: www.pilgrimsbooks.com

Distributed in India by:
PILGRIMS BOOK HOUSE
B 27/98 A-8, Nawabganj Road
Durga Kund, Varanasi-221010, India
Tel: 91-542-314059, 314060, 312456
E-mail: pilgrims@satyam.net.in
Website: www.pilgrimsbooks.com

Distributed in Nepal by:
PILGRIMS BOOK HOUSE
P O Box 3872, Thamel,
Kathmandu, Nepal
Tel: 977-1-424942
Fax: 977-1-424943
E-mail: pilgrims@wlink.com.np

Cover art by Jeffrey Harvey

ISBN: 81-7769-183-X
Rs.

Printed in India

Dedication

To the people of Western Nepal, and of Kumaon and Gharwal in India, whose courage and fortitude, in the face of the terror that man-eating tigers and leopards impose upon them, cannot but be admired by all who know them.

SHIKARI: (Hindustani) A sportsman. As applied to a native expert, who either brings in game on his own account, or accompanies European sportsmen as a guide and aid—*From HOBSON-JOBSON, The Anglo Indian Dictionary, written and edited by Henry Yule and A. C. Burnell and first published in 1886.*

SAHIB: The title by which, all over India, European gentlemen, and it may be said Europeans generally, are addressed, and spoken of, when no disrespect is intended, by natives—*Also from HOBSON-JOBSON.*

CONTENTS

INTRODUCTION

Stories of man-eating tigers, leopards and lions have always intrigued people, especially hunters, and the question of why this human fascination in such a bizarre subject exists, has a number of interesting answers. Firstly there is the thought of exactly what a man-eater is... which is a large, powerful, member of the cat family that, in a totally emotionless way, kills and eats people; from this thought, undoubtedly, arises reflections on what it might be like to personally encounter one...as a victim.

The thought is terrifying. It is of course, for the average person, a controlled form of terror, and totally vicarious. Because, for the majority of us, having to face a man-eating cat is something that is just not going to happen in our lifetimes. And so why the fear? Personally I think it is based on something deep in our psyche, and, like our fear of falling, and fear of the darkness, has its roots in a time when we lived in the company of large savage animals that, until we used our brains to better them, hunted and killed and ate us. Being killed was bad enough. But being eaten was horrible and in those prehistoric days we need only to have heard the dying screams of one of our companions, with the teeth of some giant beast in his throat, just once, to be genetically conditioned into passing our terror down in the form of instinctual fear. It is still with us today, so that when we read of a human being killed and eaten by a big cat, we cannot but shudder and think, there, but for the grace of God, goes I.

This, I believe, is why we have a fascination with man-eaters and why one man, Jim Corbett, of India, the great man-eater hunter who is the centerpiece of this book, is, for the courage and endurance he displayed in going after them, of immortal memory. For this one man, Corbett, went after more man-eaters than anyone in history and in doing so risked his life to a degree that almost belies belief.

Jim Corbett, an India domiciled Irishman, was born in the old British hill station of Naini Tal, in the United Provinces of north India, in 1875. He was one of seven children. His father was postmaster at Naini Tal for a number of years and his family history in India stretches back through the British Raj to beyond the days of the Mutiny. He developed an interest in natural history and hunting as a boy and, in later life, when he turned his attention to man-eating tigers and leopards, went on to become the greatest hunter and naturalist that Asia has known.

A number of books have documented in great detail the history of Corbett's family and they are listed in this book's Bibliography. Principal among them are, UNDER THE SHADOW OF MAN-EATERS, by Jerry Jaleel and Martin Booth's CARPET SAHIB, the latter being the name by which Corbett was known to the villagers of north India. Because of this adequate documentation of his family, and his social life, and because my real interest in the man was and is in his hunting techniques and abilities, and additionally because these have never been truly documented until now, this book centers on his great hunts, touching only briefly on his family background. However, as seems appropriate, it does include many of the people of his day, his friends and hunting companions, both Britishers and hill people, who were directly associated with him through his years in India.

As an ex White Hunter in the far west of the Kingdom of Nepal, in an area that bordered on to Kumaon and Gharwal, Corbett's hunting territory, and also having hunted tiger in Kumaon, I believe that I am able to bring rare insights to a book about Corbett. Drawing from my own experiences with the big cats, both leopard and tiger, I am also able to provide answers to some of the questions that Corbett's hunting raises and to throw light on some of the mystique that still surrounds his extraordinary abilities.

The reader will quickly see, in my studies of his hunts, and hunting techniques, that I have an enormous admiration for the man, for his integrity, his tenacity and the great courage he exhibited in voluntarily taking the extraordinary risks that he did to bring to bay some of his deadly big cats. But at the same time I do not hesitate to question some of the things that he did—that I as a professional hunter, would never, ever have done-and also to criticize his mistakes some of which, had he not been very lucky, might well have cost him his life. Indeed, I am able to do this latter with authority because I made some of the same mistakes myself, in my own big game hunting career.

An example of one of these, of which Corbett is guilty, deals with the practice of what is called WAAP. WAAP stands for the Wounded Animals Approach Procedure, a skilled hunter's rigid set of rules for approaching large, wounded and potentially dangerous animals. In my last book, GONE ARE THE DAYS, published by Safari Press, Huntington Beach, California, I go into WAAP in some depth and at the book's end, under FINAL NOTES, detail some of the instances where ignoring it has ended in fatal results. During my research on Corbett, one of the most able hunters of his day, I was amazed to find that on one occasion he too bypassed the WAAP rulings as a result of which a wounded man-eater got away, to continue its reign of terror among the hill people.

Research for this book has been spread across two decades. The reason for this is that I felt that if I was really going to write something about Corbett that would be acceptable to both amateur and professional hunters, to naturalists familiar with the Indo-Nepal region and to Corbett fans the world over, that it would need thorough, credible documentation. So, to obtain this, over the course of these years, I personally visited each and every one of the sites of his great hunts, examined them all carefully, compared them in detail with how Corbett described them in his books and, in the villages in their vicinity, talked to everyone I could find who knew about the hunts, or who actually knew Corbett and had an association with him.

I also photographed all of the sites, including, for example, the ravine below Kala Agar where the Chowgarh man-eater lay in wait for Corbett and his men, the great fig tree from which Corbett shot the man-eater of Thak, and the rock on which the dreaded man-eater of Champawat stood at bay and roared its defiance at Corbett and his men. All of the research I undertook could probably have been done in six months. But being forced, like many a man who has to work for his bread and butter, to do mine whenever time allowed, it eventually became spread across twenty years.

Corbett used to tell people that he looked on the tiger as a gentleman of the forests, one the code of which was, essentially, leave me alone and in turn I'll leave you alone. I concur with Corbett on this. I personally consider the tiger a noble beast and I base this statement on a lengthy background of experience.

I have had tiger walk past me at night when I have been sleeping in the open, on the ground, had them see me and move on with hardly a break in their stride. I have bumped into daytime tigers in the deep forests of the Terai of Far West Nepal and have had them more or less tip their hats to me and pass by with nothing more than a hiss or a growl. I have called up tiger and, disconcerted though they may have been to find that the caller was not another tiger, have watched them, on sighting me and realizing this, turn and walk quietly away.

Tigers are gentlemen of the forest, each and every one, and bound by the jungle law and by natural instinct to remain that way. Which they do until something happens to effect the change of personality that turns them from relatively harmless cats into the dark demon of the forest that is the man-eater. That something, which in the case of man-eaters is usually though not always extreme hunger, is what makes the great difference between the man-killing and man-eating tigers and leopards that Corbett hunted, and a normal tiger, the food of which is other animals.

The normal healthy tiger, Corbett's forest gentleman, is one that does not view man as a food source. As such, carrying in its psyche the innate wariness that tells it to leave man alone-the deeply ingrained cautiousness that is the foundation of its gentlemanly behavior-it spends its life being relatively harmless to man. A man-eater, tiger or leopard, is something entirely different.

A man-eating big cat is one that has been incapacitated to a degree that prevents it from catching and killing its natural prey. The incapacitation may be the result of wounds caused by gunshots, injuries from conflict with other animals, including other big cats, or old age. When this happens the cat suddenly finds itself beginning to starve and in this state, driven to desperation, it will eventually overcome its wariness of man-not its fear of man, for tigers fear nothing on the face of the earth-and start looking at him as a source of food. When this happens it quickly finds that a human being, especially a simple villager with no means of defense other than a walking stick, or an umbrella, is very easy to catch and kill. It also learns that a human body provides, in a single killing, an adequate meal. With this realization it finds for itself what is essentially a new career, one that solves the problem of food and opens up for it a way of life that promises survival.

This is fine for the big cat. But it is a different story for the villagers with whom it may have to share the forest and for whom the animal now becomes a menace, a killer striking fear into the hearts of the bravest and one the actions of which may well alter the whole social structure of a region to where inter village communication will cease, villages may be abandoned, daytime journeys can only be done with ample numbers of brave companions and nights are times of terror.

The lurking fear of being killed and eaten by a large, savage animal winds its way through all the stories of Corbett's extraordinary hunts. It can be strongly sensed in the pages of his great books and it was equally evident in the accounts of man-eater depredations told to me, when I did my research for this book, by some of the relatives of the victims of Corbett's killer cats.

But, overpowering through this fear must be, especially when one is faced with it in a no-escape situation, in the one man-eater hunt that I conducted during my hunting career, I learned of another fear and it came upon me as a cold shock when I realized that there could actually be something more frightful than the thought of being eaten by a large, savage animal. There is. It is the sheer terror, the absolute horror, created by the thought of being eaten *while still alive* and in my hunting career I came across one incident where a man-eating tiger's victim almost certainly was still living when the big cat that took him began to eat him.

Some years ago I went to hunt a man-eating tiger in the Girwa Kauriala delta, in West Nepal, an area set between the arms of two great rivers carrying these same names. Just before I arrived in the territory of the man-eater, a villager had been killed by the big cat. The circumstances of the man's death were unusual. He had been attacked by the man-eater while travelling in a buffalo cart-something that a tiger, even a man-eater, will not normally do-taken out of the cart and then carried into the jungle. I was directed to the scene of the killing by a village headman and arriving there with my gun bearer, Pasang Lama, I was immediately able to tell from the sign on the ground what had happened.

I saw where the tiger had waited in ambush for the buffalo cart to come along, where it had launched its attack and, as indicated by the claw marks and blood in the cart, how it had grabbed the unfortunate carter and lifted him bodily out of the vehicle and carried him into a shallow *nullah*.

The tiger's pug marks, their depth, angles and spacing told me all this, and the wretched victim's blood on the cart told me the rest. But in my analysis of the blood sign, and the amount of it that I saw smeared on the cart and on the ground when the tiger jumped down with the man in its mouth, I made a mistake. This was because of the fact that in addition to the droplets of blood on the leaves and grass, there were several dark red gouts of it on the ground and from the size and quantity of these, believing that they came from the victim's throat and neck, I deduced that their source was the man's carotid arteries.

A human being can live for three to four minutes, no more, when blood supply is cut off to the brain and the severing of the carotid arteries does this instantly. Thus I assumed that the man was dead, or at least unconscious, with death but seconds away, when the tiger carried him into the *nullah* and I was somewhat relieved to think that the unfortunate victim's last conscious moments were when he was still sitting happily in his cart, heading for his village, and not while being dragged up a *nullah* to be eaten.

A little later, tracking the tiger up the *nullah*, I saw that my interpretation of the blood sign had been completely wrong because, rounding a corner, a quarter of a mile from where he had been seized, I found the man's umbrella. Again reading the sign, I saw that he had carried it in his hand all this way and the full horror of his last moments was quickly brought home to me when I realized that to do this he must have been conscious all the time the tiger was carrying him up the *nullah*. He may well have been still conscious-the ultimate horror-when the tiger put him down and began to eat him. (The detailed story of this hunt is included in my book, GONE ARE THE DAYS.)

For a hunter, hunting a man-eating tiger, or leopard, makes for one of the most dangerous and challenging sports on the face of the earth. For when a hunter goes into a man-eater's domain, the very first thing he must keep in mind-though of course if he knows what he is doing this is something that will come to mind very quickly-is that the minute he sets foot in there, to hunt his big cat, he is going to be hunted by it in turn. And whereas his intention is simply to find and kill the cat, and perhaps end up with it as a trophy on the wall of his den, the intention of his opponent is quite different.

It does not want to just kill him and it does not want him as a trophy. It wants to eat him. And from the moment it senses its opponent moving within its territory, a man-eater will have a definite plan in mind, one that will include attacking him without warning, incapacitating him and then carrying him-and even if he is a three hundred-pound man, a tiger will pick him up and carry him with ease-to a place where his body will provide it with a nice, undisturbed meal.

It may carry off the hunter while he is still alive, quite oblivious of his vocal and physical protests-if any-about being dragged through the brush to the big cat's dining area. It may also start to eat him while the man is still conscious.

Hunting man-eating big cats is the quintessential sport. Jim Corbett indulged in it for forty years and while in his books he dwells from time to time on his fears and his anxieties, my personal feeling is that he loved every minute of it. Every red-blooded man loves challenge and when the challenge is spiced with danger, even with the possibility of death in one of its most unpleasant forms, that only makes it the more attractive. The true hunter who is given an opportunity to hunt a man-eater, even though he knows his opponent is going to be a big, quick thinking, fast moving, highly dangerous animal with skills in its natural habitat far superior to his own, and who turns down that opportunity, will regret it for the rest of his life.

It was this thought that made me go after the Girwa Kauriala man-eater when I did and I believe that it was probably the same thinking that made Jim Corbett pick up his rifle at the tender age of twenty-six and set out on the trail of his man-eaters. A trail that began with the hunt for the man-eater of Champawat. A trail from which he never turned back.

—Peter Byrne

BOOK ONE

THE MAN-EATER OF CHAMPAWAT.
1907.

CHAPTER ONE

Fifty miles to the north of the White Grass Plains Wildlife Reserve, in far west Nepal, lies the hill district of Dandeldura. The region, set in rolling six thousand foot hills, has many small settlements. One of these is the village of Rupal.

In the late 1800s, a big tigress lived in a large patch of brush east of this village and one day, as the old century was coming to an end, someone, we will never know who, took a shot at her with an inadequate weapon, probably a muzzle loader. The shot smashed the animal's upper right and left canines, teeth vitally needed in the big cats to hold and kill their prey. After a while, when the tigress found herself, because of her injuries, unable to kill wild boar and deer, her natural food, she turned to killing people and became a man-eater. She quickly found this new source of food easy to obtain and over the course of a number of years she became a menace to the people of the Dandeldura district.

The tigress, which quickly became known as the Rupal man-eater, ranged east from the Sarda river, the river that marks the border line between Nepal and the district of Kumaon, in India, as far as the town of Dandeldura. In the beginning she hunted at night and her victims were travelers on the mountain trails, mostly men and women visiting between villages. In time however, as more and more people fell victim to the big cat's murderous appetite, night travelling came to an end. Indeed, even in the villages, the onset of darkness brought closed and locked doors and until the sun rose again out of the eastern ranges and flooded the hills with daylight, not a man, women or child ventured outside of the comparative safety of their houses. Inside the houses they were reasonably safe because, unlike a leopard, a tiger, even a man-eater, will almost never go into a village and, again unlike the leopard, it is unknown for them to physically attack a house.

Accepting this as a set form of behavior on the part of tigers has been challenged by some writers on the subject. In my own opinion, and I speak from experience, it is a form of conduct with them to the point where, even with a man-eating tiger, it can be depended upon to a considerable degree.

Some years ago I took a client, a Mr. C. W. Ennis, from San Antonio, Texas, on a river safari, using rafts, in the Chitwan National Park in south central Nepal. One evening, two days down the river, we pulled in to a sand bar on the edge of the forest to make camp for the night. Just before dark I saw some villagers running along a trail past our campsite. I asked them why they were in such a hurry and they said that there was a man-eating tiger in the area and they needed to get to their village before dark. They also said that I should not camp in the area; we would be welcome at their village if we wanted to come.

I noted what they had said and told my men and my client. But I was not too worried about the big cat, even if it was a man-eater, because of what I knew of its habits, the principal one of which, in this case, would be its reluctance to come into a campsite where there was a fire and human activity. To a tiger, a campsite was a form of village and if we kept a small fire going through the night it would recognize this as indicating that there were people there. A vital element of a tiger's hunting technique is surprise and its ability to use this in an attack, either on an animal, or on a man, is greatly reduced when there is more than one animal in the immediate vicinity, or more than one man. This is something that it recognizes and that contributes to its reluctance to enter a village*.

**The only time I have ever heard of a tiger coming into a village was in the case of the man-eater of Thak (one of Corbett's last hunts) which, while Corbett was after it, actually came into Thak village and stalked the streets at night, looking for victims. But this, I believe, was because the villagers of Thak, to a man, had fled, and the village was empty and deserted.*

We spent two nights camping in the area and even though Ennis, on his second safari with me, was nervous, I assured him that there was nothing to worry about as long as we stayed within the perimeter of the camp. But I also made sure that any chores that might take the men out of the immediate area of the camp site, such as the need for water, were completed while it was still light. And so we were not bothered by the man-eater, even though it might actually have been hunting in the vicinity of our camp.

CHAPTER TWO

An elderly Nepalese gentleman, Mr. Nara Bahadur Bisht, of Mahendranagar, West Nepal, was a young boy in Rupal while the man-eater was operating there. Until he died, recently, at the age of 99, he told me that even today, after all these years, he could still sense the fear that the dreaded cat instilled in the village people of the Dandeldura district. It was he who told me the story of what happened when the count of hill people killed and eaten reached two hundred, and the villagers, in desperation, banded together to face the challenge of the man-eater and take action.

The ruler of Nepal at the time the Rupal man-eater was operating was Chandra Shum Sher Jung Bahadur Shah. He seems to have been regarded as a reasonably good ruler. But his interest in the actual well-being of his people appears to have been somewhat limited, something clearly illustrated by the method he used to accept petitions for redress of grievances, or appeals. He lived in Katmandu and once a week would come out of his palace on a huge black horse and, accompanied by a dozen or so of his retainers, probably all of them immediate family, would gallop around the Tundi Khel, a big, flat, grass covered park, in the center of the city. There, anyone who wished to present a petition had to write their message on a piece of paper and affix to it a one thousand rupee royal stamp, a huge sum of money in those days.

At a signal from one of his retainers the person wishing to address him was allowed to run after his galloping horse, holding up the paper. If the ruler were in a mood to do so and if the runner were fleet enough to catch up with his powerful stallion, he would reach down and take the paper. Those appealing, probably because some of whom might have been old, were allowed to employ professional runners to chase the monarch but as his horse was obviously the best his stables could produce, either way not many appeals got through. So it was when the people of Dandeldura appealed for help from the depredations of the Rupal man-eater. I do not know how their petition was presented to the monarch in Katmandu but it was very possibly done, or at least attempted, in the customary way, during the monarch's weekly gallop on the Tundi Khel. Whatever way it was attempted, the galloping monarch turned a deaf ear.

In addition to two hundred people killed and eaten, a large number of villagers had also been attacked and injured by the man-eater, some of them being horribly mutilated, with bites to their faces and heads that left them permanently disfigured, and bodily tear wounds from the beast's claws that took months to heal if, through resultant septicemia, the victim did not die, as usually happened.

Although attacks on humans by normal, healthy tigers are rare, in remote areas, where there are no medical facilities, a person attacked by a normal tiger stands an equal chance of being killed as in an attack by a man-eater. Because a normal, healthy tiger will be in full possession of all of its physical capabilities and, being provoked -which is what will generate the attack in the first place-will use them with effect. This means claws as well as teeth and, oddly, it is the claws rather than the teeth that may bring death to a victim, subsequent to an attack. For the claws of the big cats are hollow as a result of which they often contain decayed animal tissue from a previous animal kill. In an attack where the claws are used this bacteria ridden matter may be forced deep into wounds. The result is often septicemia, which, without medical attention, is nearly always fatal. Thus an attack by a normal tiger may often have results as fatal as in an attack by a man-eater. The difference will be that the victims of the normal tiger attack, if the result is septicemia, will succumb to blood poisoning over the course of few days. In a man-eater attack, if the victim cannot get away, death is usually a lot quicker.

With tigers, any kind of bodily injury, no matter how small, may detract from the capabilities that it needs to attack, pull down, and kill its natural prey. Whether it is a deer, or a wild boar, every single part of tiger's killing mechanism is needed to quickly and successfully affect a kill. Broken canine teeth, broken dew claws, injures to the muscles of the shoulders or forearms, all detract from the speed and efficiency of the perfectly timed and synchronized attack that a tiger makes on its prey. Failure to instantly lock onto the head of the chosen animal and pull it down may give the animal time to escape. Failure to twist the neck back and get the canines into the prey's throat may allow the animal split second relief, something that it will seize upon, instantly, for fight or flight. (With big animals, like buffalo, or a big wild boar, there may be a fight reaction. But with most animals that are the tiger's prey, the immediate response to a bungled attack is flight.)

Across the years, people who have survived the attacks of man-eating tigers have done so mainly because the cats in question were injured animals. There have not been many survivors. But Corbett talks about some he encountered and I too have met men and women who have managed to get away from man-eaters, in both India and Nepal. The mutilated victims of the Rupal man-eater, the few who survived an attack by it, were probably in the forefront of the movement when at last, in desperation, the villagers of Dandeldura district banded together to do something about their plight.

CHAPTER THREE

A meeting was held in Rupal to discuss the problem of the tigress. Suggestions were tossed back and forth and eventually it was decided that if enough men could be mustered, it might be possible to drive the animal out of the district. If a large number of men made the attempt, not only would their numbers guarantee them safety from an attack, but the impetus of the demonstration might well persuade the cat, once driven out, not to come back.

Next came the question of which direction they should try to drive the tigress, and where it might go. It was decided that it might not be fair to impose it on their neighbors to the north, in Baitadi. Or to people to the east, the good citizens of Dandeldura town. Or to the south, where lived the Taru people in today's White Grass Plains. The answer, therefore, was India, to the west, where the rolling hills of Kumaon contained forest and brush that would provide good habitat for the cat.

The west was also a good idea because getting the big cat to go in that direction would mean, after it left the district and crossed it into Kumaon, having the physical barrier of the Sarda River between them and the animal. Tigers are good swimmers and crossing the Sarda would impose no difficulty on the cat, should it want to come back. But tigers will not swim big, cold rivers like the Sarda unless driven by the need for food and as there were plenty of people in Kumaon, and thus plenty of food, there should be no reason for it to want to come back. So a massive beat was agreed upon, with every villager within twenty miles being on his honor to attend.

And the signal for the beat would be the next human kill, a timing for which there was a very good reason.

When a tiger kills it does so from hunger and so it will usually eat immediately from the kill, whether this is a wild boar, or a deer, or a human being. Then, its belly full, it will find cover and lie down and sleep. If it has not eaten the entire kill, and if it has not been seriously disturbed while eating, it will lie up near the kill. It will do this in anticipation of a second or even a third meal and also to keep scavengers away from its food.

The villagers of Dandeldura knew that the Rupal tiger had never been hunted. (Indeed, with the fear its depredations had engendered there was no one who would even think of going after it.) And so they guessed that it would follow the normal pattern of most tigers and, after a kill, and after it had eaten, would lie up near the remains of its victim. And so they waited for the next kill, which took place a few days later. When this happened they quickly determined, from scavenger activity–most probably, in their hill country, crows and ravens-that the tiger was lying up in a thick patch of bamboo just west of Rupal village and so when they assembled for the great beat, they made this the focal point of the drive.

The men for the beat gathered from fifty villages. They came in answer to men calling out from village to village, ridge to ridge, with a 'cooee'* system that was and still is a common method of communication in the Nepal hills.

The men formed their beating line, two and three deep, in the shape of a huge U. The base of the U was to the east, towards the

**The 'cooee' system of communication is best described as long distance verbal interaction between people and consists of men and women using the human voice, often over considerable distances, to communicate. I have seen this carried out many times in the Himalaya and it is amazingly effective. The best time for it seems to be in the early evening and my guess is that the dampening air, with its increasing humidity, serves to carry the human voice more effectively at this time. I have watched and listened to men and women talking to each other across a mile of deep valley, gearing the volume and pitch of their voices to the carrying capability of the density of the air and, amazingly, seeming to barely raise their voices. This was the* method *used to gather what I am told was a thousand men, for the great beat for the Rupal maneater.*

town of Dandeldura and the open side faced the west, the river, and Kumaon. At a signal from one of the village headmen a thousand voices were raised in a great shout and the men of Dandeldura, beating drums and rattling tin cans filled with stones and banging their *kukris*, their great curved fighting knives, on trees and rocks, surged forward together.

The tigress, lying up in the scrub near her kill, heard them coming. When she did, sensing that for the moment discretion might be the better part of valor, she turned and headed for the Sarda. No one saw her cross the river but she must have done so for from that day onward the killings in Nepal ceased and within a few weeks, with confidence restored, roads were reopened for travelers, communication between villages was resumed and in the evenings, returning to their normal lives, men and women sat on the porches of their houses and talked about the things that villagers talk about, including, in their case, no doubt, the hundred and one stories generated by the reign of terror of the man-eater of Rupal.

CHAPTER FOUR

A hundred miles to the west of Dandeldura, over the mighty Sarda river and across the rolling hills of Kumaon, lies the little mountain town of Naini Tal, the one-time British summer capital of the United Provinces of north India. In the days of the Raj, in India, there were, for many provinces, two alternating capitals, one on the plains and one in the hills. This practice was established to allow for the great difference in climate between the seasons. Thus, government seats, during the cold weather, from November to April, were in the plains. For the remainder of the year, during the sweltering monsoon months of the Indian summer, they were in the hills. This even applied to the capital of the vast sub continent itself, which was Delhi. In winter the empire was ruled from this ancient capital of the Mogul Empire in India. But when the *loo,* the hot wind that brought the great dust storms up from the deserts of Rajastan, began to blow, the government moved, lock, stock and barrel, to Simla, one of their hill stations in the Himalayan foothills.

It also applied to what was once the kingdom of Oudh, but which the British renamed the United Provinces. In the U.P. they made their winter capital at Lucknow, in the torrid plains of the Ganges. But for their summer place of rule they chose the cool, clear air of the six thousand-foot ranges of the middle Himalaya, at another hill station, called Naini Tal. Naini Tal, meaning the "baby lake", (*naini,* or *nani,* means baby; *tal,* means lake) where, in 1875, a child was born to a pair of India domiciled parents of Irish descent, Christopher William and Mary Jane Corbett. The child was a son they named Edward James, a boy who in time grew to be the man named Jim Corbett.

Like me, Jim Corbett's family came from the city of Dublin, Ireland*. His grandfather, Joseph Corbett, was born there in 1796. Joseph must have been a bit of an adventurer because he left Ireland at he age of eighteen, with his young wife, Harriet, to find his fortune in India. Arriving in the sub continent he promptly joined the British army. He died there sixteen years later, at the age of thirty-four, in 1830, leaving behind seven children.

One of Joseph Corbett's seven children was Christopher William, who grew up in India and in time married a Mary Ann Morrow, of Landour. Mary Ann died while still quite young and Christopher William subsequently married a Mary Jane Doyle, of Calcutta, a widow with three children from a previous marriage. They moved to Naini Tal in 1862, where Jim Corbett was born to them, thirteen years later, on July 25th, 1875.

Jim Corbett went to school in Naini Tal and when he reached the age of eighteen he applied for and was given a temporary posting with an Indian railway company. When that term of employment came to an end he obtained a permanent position as a shipping inspector at a place called Mokameh Ghat, on the Ganges, twenty-five miles east of Patna and not far south of the Nepal border. He seems to have lived a spartan life during this time and his fine book, My India, talks about this, but in an uncomplaining way. Through these years he also developed a great interest in Indian natural history, reading all that he could find on the subject and

---

**My great grandfather, Joseph Byrne, was born in Dublin, Ireland, in 1825. One of his sons, John Byrne, was born in the same city in 1850. John Byrne had five children, two boys and three girls. One of the boys, Joseph, born in 1897, never married and died childless. The other, Cyril, born in 1898, married Evelyn Winifred Pringuer, of London, in 1918, and had four children, of whom I was one. Like Joseph Corbett I too left Ireland to go to India when I was eighteen. And like him it was to join the British Armed Forces, though in my case the Air Sea Rescue Branch of the Royal Air Force.*

spending a great deal of time at his favorite sporting pastimes, hunting and fishing. Also during this time, probably mainly at the bidding of the government, he turned his attention to what may have been for him, and certainly proved so for some others, including myself, the ultimate sport, that of going after man-eaters tigers and leopards. The first of these was the Rupal man-eater which, after it crossed into India and began killing villagers there, became known as the man-eater of Champawat.

CHAPTER FIVE

Champawat is a small, bustling city set in the hills of Kumaon, about twenty miles west of the Nepal border. It is basically a long, single main street fringed with shops and, throughout the day, thronged with pedestrians, trucks and buses. Thc transportation that now pours through the city is the result of the new system of roads laid out by the government of India throughout the districts of Kumaon and Gharwal. Champawat lies on one of these, the main road from Tanakpur, in the south, to Pithoragarh in the northern hills.

On a small hill, not far from the center of the city, is the *dak* or government bungalow where Corbett spent part of his time when he hunted the man-eater of Champawat. In Corbett's day, and now, access to it is via a winding lane that leads up from the city center. Now the small bungalow, still bearing the architectural dignity of the days in which it was built-the turn of the century when Champawat was a little more than a sprawling village set in a shallow valley between two hills-is buried under a mass of government electronic communications equipment and solidly ringed with a heavy wire fence. Because of this public access is denied.

I was shooting with a friend, Simon Biddulph, up the Jaldaka River in North Bengal, where we were both tea planters, when I first heard of Corbett. The year was 1948. Simon was a fine sportsman a great campfire story teller and he and I were both amateur big game hunters. As such, part of our self imposed apprenticeship in the sport, in addition to spending as much time as we could in the magnificent North Bengal forests—a paradise for the outdoorsman on those days—was to read everything that we could find on the subject. This naturally included Corbett's books, which we literally devoured, reading them over and over again and discussing them in intense detail at home in our tin roofed bungalows, at the bar of our planters club and at the campfire when we were hunting.

Corbett, in his great book, Man-eaters Of Kumaon, commences his story of the man-eater of Champawat by telling us that he was shooting at Mailani*, in the UP, with a friend of his, Eddie Knowles, when he first heard of the man-eater of Champawat. The year was 1907. He describes Knowles as a fine sportsman with an inexhaustible fund of *shikar* yarns-campfire stories, no doubt-and in these two openings to the story of the man-eater of Champawat, I think the reader will see a interesting similitude.

******Mailani is in Uttar Pradesh and lies just below the Nepal border, a few miles south of the small city of Palia Kalan, where I used to go to get supplies and gasoline-hand pumped from an ancient Esso cylindrical dispenser with a big glass receptacle on top-when I hunted in west Nepal. Both Mailani and Palia are on the narrow gauge railway line that comes up from Shahjahanpur and runs north, through Sultan, to terminate at Gauri Phanta on the border. It was on this line that the man-eating tiger of the Girwa-Kauriala delta was run over by a train. (See my book, GONE ARE THE DAYS.)*

CHAPTER SIX

Corbett had probably heard of the man-eater of Champawat before 1907. Indeed it is highly likely that every villager in Kumaon knew about the dreaded tigress. However, it was not until Corbett went after it, and later wrote about it, that it became known as the man-eater of Champawat, by which time it had killed, in both Nepal and India, over four hundred people. Whether he knew about it or not, he was officially informed about it for the first time by Berthoud,* the British Deputy Commissioner at Naini Tal at that time.

Berthoud was a friend of Corbett and so when he personally asked him if he would go after the man-eater, Corbett did not hesitate. He just asked Berthoud to let him know when the next killing took place, upon which he would set out. He also requested him to order all other hunters out of the area, for, like me, Corbett had a phobia about being shot, or even shot at, by another hunter.

A week later runners brought a message from a village called Pali, fifteen miles west of Champawat, that a woman had been killed there and Corbett, his gear ready and with six porters standing by to carry it, set out at once.

Corbett took the old trail east out of Naini Tal and on the first day covered seventeen miles, on foot, to a village called Dhari. He

---

**Berthoud, a much loved and admired British civil commissioner, died at an early age and today the only thing by which he is remembered is a stone pillar, buried in weeds, in the old British graveyard at Halduwani, on the edge of the plains, south of Naini Tal.*

was a strong walker and whereas seventeen miles in a day does not seem like a great hike, it is important to keep in mind that all of Kumaon is high hill country. The hills, which would be considered mountains in some countries, are in the four to six thousand foot range and the trails that crisscross them seldom follow their contours, but just go straight up them and straight down, something I know from experience.

Next day he passed through Mornaula and in the evening reached a village called Dabidura. The following day, five days since the woman had been killed, he reached Pali, to find the whole village in a state of absolute terror.

On being informed that the man-eater was still in the vicinity, he made immediate plans to go after it. As soon as he had his men settled in a secure house in the village, he set out alone and then, that night, did what is to me one of the most incredibly foolish and dangerous things that it is possible to do in a man-eater hunt. This was to spend the night out, alone, on the ground, waiting, hopefully, for the big cat to come along and give him a shot. A cat that had to date successfully stalked and killed and eaten over four hundred hill people.

Looking back at what he did, and studying his later writings, it is easy to see that in spite of his hunting background, when it came to man-eaters, Corbett at this time was completely inexperienced and knew next to nothing about the basic tenet of man-eater hunting, which is, simply, that while you are hunting one it is also hunting you.

Alone and on the ground, in daylight, with an adequate weapon-a high-powered rifle-and the skill to use it efficiently, an experienced hunter has some chance against a man-eater. At night, with the natural restriction that the lack of light places on his vision, with a sense of smell that is poorly developed and with hearing that is only half as acute as that of the big cat, a man has little chance of detecting the animal's deadly approach.

Again, as soon as the cat becomes aware of his presence, which, with its superb eyesight and hearing it will quickly do, his chances are further minimized, because the second it detects him it will begin to stalk him. It will pinpoint the slightest sound he may make and with its phenomenal night vision, it will see him long before he will see it. And when it is ready, it will launch an accelerated attack and be on him with its teeth in his throat before he has time to even raise his rifle, let alone get off a shot. To spend the night out, on the ground, in the territory of a man-eating tiger or leopard, is nothing less than a quick and rather nasty way to commit suicide.

In my opinion, Corbett, with a couple of decades of routine big game hunting behind him, but with no knowledge or experience of the psychology of man-eaters, could only have been incredibly overconfident, an immature state of mind that, but for the chances of fate that kept the tiger away from the village that night, would have consigned him to a gruesome death.

Corbett survived the night. But in the morning, probably from hearing the villagers talking about what he did, he admits that staying out for the tigress as he did was a very foolish thing to do. From my readings of his books and from what I personally learned about him from villagers in my research, I do not believe that he ever did anything like this again. "I was young and foolish it those days," Corbett is reputed to have said.

He is lucky to have survived that youthful foolishness.

CHAPTER SEVEN

The woman who had been killed by the tigress had been cutting fresh leaves for fodder from a tree at the edge of a ravine, about half a mile from the village. She was one of a party of about twenty women. The tigress, obviously alerted to their presence by the sound of their voices, stalked them, and when the woman in question had finished cutting her supply of leaves and was climbing down the tree, it came up underneath her and, standing on its hind legs, seized her by the ankle. It pulled her off the tree and then, according to the other women, who watched in horror, grabbed her by the throat, leapt up the side of the ravine with her and disappeared into some dense brush. The women of the party huddled together for a while and then, no doubt screaming in terror, ran back to the village and told their men what had happened.

The men, in the forlorn hope that they might be able to rescue the women taken by the tigress, immediately assembled and, banging drums, and shouting at the tops of their voices, but with only one man armed-with an ancient muzzleloader-ran from the village to the ravine where the woman had been taken.

Were it not for the tragic circumstances of the woman's death, what happened next would have been comical. Arriving at the ravine they stopped and peered in and as they were doing this the tigress, which was lying up in the nearby scrub, no doubt eating its victim, gave vent to series of deep growls. The men instantly turned and, falling over each other in panic, fled back to the village.

Back at their houses they mustered up courage for a second attempt and if their first sortie ended in a macabre form of comedy, their second only added to it. For when they arrived at the ravine for the second time the tiger again growled at them and as soon as it did the man with the muzzle loader fired his gun into the air, a blast of sound that brought the tiger roaring out of cover and this time sending the whole party back at probably twice the speed of their first retreat. Later, when questioned by Corbett, and asked why he had fired his weapon in the air, rather than into the scrub where the tiger was, the man said that he did this so that he would not hit the tiger. It was already very angry at being disturbed at its meal, he said-its terrifying growls supported this-and had he hit it he said it would certainly have come after him and killed him.

Tigers do not normally climb trees and a person in a tree, fifteen feet above the ground, is reasonably safe from a provoked tiger. But they can reach up a long way and a fully grown man-eater, standing on its hind legs, can hook a victim off a tree from probably twelve or thirteen feet up. In the White Grass Plains of Far West Nepal, where I spent most of my professional hunting years, there are, to this day, trees marked by the claws of tigers to heights of twelve feet. These are territorial markings on selected trees that a tiger scratches to mark its range; ten to twelve feet is the average height of the territorial marks of an adult tiger.

But a tiger, without climbing the tree, will go higher if there is a need and I saw an instance of this in the forests of the Bauni river, in the WGP, in the winter of 1998-'99, when a tiger clashed with a leopard.

I was in camp, waiting for clients for a photo safari, when a Game Scout came to tell me that a leopard had been shot by a poacher and was lying in the jungle nearby. I took a Jeep and together we drove to where the leopard's body was lying in the forest, about twenty feet back from the edge of the forest road. The animal, a big dog leopard, was lying on its side, its mouth open, quite dead. Its only visible injury was a single small hole in the roof of its skull, about the size that a bullet from a high-powered rifle would make.

While I was examining the cat another Jeep arrived with the area Game Warden, a pompous little man who liked to order people around in a loud voice. Ignoring me and my companion, he walked into the brush, took one look at the leopard, said, "Yes, shot by a poacher," turned around, walked back to his Jeep and drove away.

Later he sent some men to pick up the leopard's body and later still wrote a report to his seniors at the Department of National Parks and Wildlife to the effect that a leopard had been shot by a poacher and that, acting in his official capacity, he would put into effect measures to ensure that the culprit would be found and arrested.

When he had left I asked the Game Scout to sit and wait for me in the Jeep and then walked back to where the leopard lay and carefully examined the ground sign at the scene of the incident, to see what I could learn from it. In my mind's eye, now, I can see Corbett doing the same thing in the ravine where the woman of Pali was a taken and I am sure that not a scratch on the tree from which the tigress took her, not a broken twig, not a spec of blood, evaded his keen eyes and that when he left the scene of the kill to start his search for the tigress, he had in his mind a complete picture of what had happened, a picture that was the sum total of all that he had read in the sign at the kill site.

In my case, with the killing of the leopard, and emulating Corbett, the story of what happened was not too difficult for me to put together and after I had spent half an hour carefully reading the sign, both in the forest and out on the forest road, I was able to piece together the story of what happened, a story that did not include a poacher.

In the night the leopard had probably been hunting in the *sal* tree forest, looking for deer. At dawn, with the light growing, it had decided to leave the light cover of the forest and find some cover in which to lie up for the day. Unfortunately, as it stepped silently out onto the jungle road, it found itself facing a big tigress, one that lived in the area and that used the soft sandy surface of the road for silent, early morning stalking of its prey.

Tigers and leopards are highly territorial and while they will sometimes suffer a temporary infringement of their territory from another cat of their own species, they will never tolerate it from another species. In this case, the tigress, without hesitation, hurled itself towards the leopard. The leopard, instantly realizing the futility of challenging the larger animal and the danger it was in, turned and fled into the forest. It may have looked back once and seen that the tigress was very close behind, which engendered a decision to try and get off the ground and into the safety of a tree as fast as possible. For while tigers are not tree climbers, leopards are and when faced with a danger like this, Mr. Spots will go up a tree like a squirrel. In this case the leopard made it to a big *sal* tree with a wide, smooth bole, the surface of which told me the story of what happened then. .

The leopard hit the tree running and its first bound took it ten feet up. It then brought up its rear legs, to get its hind claws into the tree and propel its body up another six feet or so, to where it would be safe from its pursuer. But at that moment the tigress closed on it. It hurled itself forward, arching upwards on its hind legs and using its front legs like forearms to seize the tree and gain the last few feet needed to get its teeth into the leopard's rump. This is what it did and together the two big cats came tumbling down from the tree, the claws of the lesser cat making long but futile tears in the bark as it tried to prevent being dragged backwards. Together they crashed to the ground and here, briefly, as tiny blood spots on the leaves of bushes five and six feet up, and broken bush stems and crushed leaves indicated, the leopard fought for its life. The fight ended quickly, with the tiger biting into the leopard's head, sinking a single, huge canine tooth into and through its skull, and killing it instantly. This was the hole in its head that the warden had believed was made by a bullet, fired by a poacher. The real story, clearly told by the sign, was quite different.

When Corbett was satisfied with his examination of the site of the tigress' kill, he set out to try and find where the big cat might be lying up and he spent the whole of the following morning, nervously walking around the village and looking for sign that would tell him this. At midday he returned to the village and had a meal and that night sensibly stayed in the village, in a house provided by the headman. The room he stayed in appears to have been windowless and for ventilation Corbett left the door open. But as a safety precaution he jammed its framework with thorn bushes.

Fear of the man-eater made the villagers of Pali reluctant to go out in the forest with Corbett and it was not until after he had demonstrated his excellent marksmanship that he managed to instill in them the confidence that would allow them to come out of the village and work with him and provide the intelligence he needed to plan his hunt for the man-eater.

He did this by taking the men on a hunt for *Gooral*, the little goat antelope of the Himalaya that is a prized food of the mountain villagers. Using an old Martini Henry he shot the first one at a range of two hundred yards and when the body, rolling down the hill, disturbed two others, he shot both of them while they were on the move. The villagers were delighted with the meat. More to the point, they were very impressed with his shooting abilities and told Corbett that they were now ready to work with him. On hearing this he selected two men and once again set out to try and find the remains of the tigress' kill.

Searching up the ravine from where the woman had been taken out of the tree, he soon found the pitiful remnants of her body. There was almost nothing left, confirming the fallacy, as Corbett stated, that man-eating tigers do not eat the heads and bones of their human victims. They eat everything and on this occasion all that was found, and then taken back to be cremated, were a few splinters of bone and part of the victim's clothing.

That evening Corbett went out of the village again to visit a small cluster of houses on a hill not far away. There he met a woman who not long before had been involved in an experience with the man-eater so terrifying that she had been struck dumb by it and for a year, since it had happened, had not spoken to a anyone, not even her children.

The woman had been out cutting grass with her sister on a hill-side not far from their homes when the man-eater suddenly came charging out of the brush. It went for her sister, seized her and went racing off with her in its mouth. In an act of extraordinary courage the woman ran after the tigress, waving her sickle at it and screaming. The tigress ignored her for about a hundred yards and then dropped its victim and turned and came at her. She instantly fled and did not stop until she reached the village. A rescue party was quickly organized and set out after the tigress. But the big cat had disappeared with its victim and the men returned to the village without seeing it. It was then that they discovered that the surviving sister had been rendered speechless by the incident and that what they initially thought was temporary muteness, due perhaps to hysteria, was permanent.

Corbett spent the next three days looking for sign of the tigress. But it seemed to have disappeared and when hours of patient searching produced no sign of it, no pug marks, no droppings or urinal scratches, he decided to look in another area.

Intelligence provided to him by the authorities in Naini Tal, and confirmed by the villagers at Pali while he was there, indicated a preponderance of kills by the tigress in and around Champawat, to the east. And so, to the dismay of the villagers of Pali, but promising to return if the tigress came back, he loaded up his men and left, hiking the first six miles to a village on a ridge called Dunaghat, where he stopped and cooked a meal and then, in the same day, nine more, to Champawat, which he reached by evening. Here he met the Tahsildar, the local tax collector, to whom he had been given a letter of introduction, in Naini Tal, before he left. The Tahsildar took him to the Champawat *dak* bungalow, which he made his headquarters for the hunt.

CHAPTER EIGHT

Corbett mentions in his writings that there had been no record of man-eaters in Kumaon before this time.* This is not too surprising because tigers are not hill animals and for a tiger to be living in the hills-in the case of the Rupal-Champawat tigress, in the hill country of both Nepal and India-was unusual. Tigers are essentially shy animals and one of their needs is dense cover, both for lying up during the daytime and for hiding their kills. On the whole, the hill country of the middle Himalaya does not lend itself to this type of vegetation.

Corbett stayed only one night in the Champawat *dak* bungalow and then, at the suggestion of the Tahsildar, moved to a smaller bungalow on a hill above the Champa river, four miles northeast of the town in an area where, the Tahsildar told him, many people had been killed by the tigress. As soon as he had settled in there, the Tahsildar left him and returned to Champawat.

On his first day in the new area Corbett spent the morning walking around to familiarize himself with the terrain. In the afternoon the Tahsildar returned from Champawat and he and Corbett were standing outside the little bungalow, talking, when a man came hurrying in from a nearby village, to say that a girl had just been killed by the man-eater. Telling the man to lead the way Corbett immediately set out to investigate the story.

**For a further discussion of this question, see the EPILOGUE, at the end of the book.*

The man took him to a small village set among open fields and as they approached the scene of the latest killing he told Corbett what had happened. A group of village women had been out cutting fodder to feed young animals when the tigress had suddenly appeared and seized one of their party, a young woman.

At the village Corbett spoke to a villager who had been a member of the party and she pointed out a tree, on the edge of a nearby hill, where the girl had been taken. Corbett noted how sparse the vegetation was on the open hillside and wondered to himself how the tigress had been able to get so close to a group of a dozen women without being seen. He mentions again in his writings how new he was to the game of man-eater hunting and his stating this indicates to me how little he knew of the extraordinary ability of a man-eater, when stalking a human being, in the use of cover. But then, I had to learn about it myself when I first started hunting tigers and I had to experience it at first hand to fully understand a tiger's capabilities in this art. One phase of my education in this took place during a photographic safari in the Bauni river forest, in the WGP, with a client, in the winter of 1955.

My client, a young woman named Patricia Kennedy, from New York, wanted to see a tiger and I told her that I knew where one had a lair, up the river, about a mile from our camp. I also told her that because the big cat's lair was on the east bank of the river, close to the water, that it might be possible to stalk it from the west bank side and, using the available cover, get close enough to see it and perhaps photograph it across the little river.

We left camp in the early afternoon, when I knew the tiger would be sleeping, and walked up through the forest on the west side of the river, keeping about three hundred yards back from the bank of the river, to a point opposite where I knew the cat had its lair. Here I asked my client to take off her shoes, which she did and then together, walking slowly, our footsteps silent on the damp loam of the jungle floor, we approached the river. Soon the opposite bank came into view and when it did I cautioned my client to be very quiet, to watch where she was placing her feet and to keep close behind me. We moved forward towards the water's edge and as we did so the tiger' lair, a small patch of thick brown grass, about three feet high, came into view on the far bank.

I guessed that the tiger was lying down in the grass, sleeping, and so I whispered to my client to use her wide-angle binoculars, to see if she could see it, or its outline. It was very quiet, the only sounds being the splashing of a couple of otters about a hundred yards down stream and the chattering a of a group of Rhesus Macaques in the trees off to our right. There was also no movement of any kind and so when a Red Jungle Fowl suddenly appeared on the far bank and started walking towards the tiger's lair, it immediately caught my eye. My client also saw it and, before I could caution her, raised her hand and pointed. Her movement was instantly seen by the sharp-eyed bird and with a shriek it burst into flight and went racing down the river, chattering in alarm.

The chattering woke up the sleeping tiger and I am sure that it instantly pinpointed us. It rose, turned, slipped through the grass and within a second or two was gone, into the forest. My client saw nothing to indicate this. And the only thing that I saw, the *only* movement in that thick brown grass, was one single stem, bending slightly and then straightening up again.

When a Barking Deer called in alarm on the far side of the river, two hundred yards away to our left, I knew that the tiger was gone. But when I told my client that a four hundred pound cat probably measuring seven feet in length had been there, no more than thirty feet from us, and that it had got up, had pinpointed us and then had slipped away without our seeing as much as a whisker of it, I do not think that she believed me. Such is the ability of the big cats to use cover and this, obviously, is what Corbett's tigress did when it stalked the group of village women and then, having decided on a victim, gone in and seized her in a smooth, silent rush that took all of them, including the unfortunate victim, completely by surprise.

At the village Corbett told the people to stay inside and keep quiet and then, leaving the little hamlet and walking out to the hill, he quickly found where the girl had been killed. There was a pool of blood where she had been taken and nearby, a pathetic sight, a necklace of blue beads that she had been wearing.

The pug marks of the tigress led off up to the brow of the hill and the sign was not difficult to follow. It had carried the girl by the middle of her body and her feet, trailing down, left a series of scrape marks on one side of the line of the tigress' pugs while on the other side were strands of her long black hair, snagged on bushes and accompanied by gouts of blood.

Corbett had reached the top of the hill when he heard someone approaching and he looked around to find a villager coming up behind him. The man, from the village that Corbett had just left, was armed with a converted .450 rifle that did not have a safety catch and Corbett, who obviously had the same phobias that I did as a professional hunter about people walking behind with loaded weapons, quickly got rid of the man by making him sit on the top a big rock and ordering him to stay there. He then went on alone after the man-eater.

The spoor of the tigress indicated that after crossing the hill, it had gone down the other side. The hill was steep and covered with bracken and patches of mountain bamboo. At the bottom of the hill the cat had dropped into a deep, narrow, dry *nullah.* Corbett entered this and followed it for about a quarter of a mile. At a point where another ravine came in from the left, Corbett came across a small pool where the sign told him that the tigress had lain down to eat on its victim. The sign further indicated that on his approach the tigress had got up and left. On the sand at the edge of the pool lay part of the victim's leg, severed below the knee. Corbett, finding the sight of the severed limb distressing, halted to examine it. When he did this he allowed it to occupy his attention to where, for a moment or two, he seemed to have almost forgotten the imminent danger of the man-eater. This was a mistake that very nearly cost him his life.

CHAPTER NINE

While Corbett had been following the tigress, the animal had stopped from time to time to eat. it Tigers normally kill only when they are hungry and as the tigress had just killed, it obviously needed to eat. This it had been doing at the pool when it detected Corbett's approach and now, still hungry, and agitated that it had been disturbed while eating, something that constitutes one of the areas of provocation in tigers, it decided to double back and deal with the cause of the disturbance.

It did this with all of the guile and skill at its command and when it saw Corbett at the pool, it began to stalk him, not down the *nullah*, but through the cover along the top of its fifteen-foot bank. Reaching the edge of the brush covered bank and seeing him at the pool, directly below, it lay down and gathered itself for the short, fast charge that would carry it over the side of the *nullah* and down on top of him. Had it done this, Corbett, absorbed in the tragedy of the killing and morbidly fascinated by the pathetic sight of the girl's severed leg, with his rifle held horizontally across his body in a position from which he would never have been able to raise it in time to shoot, would not have stood a chance.

Corbett was kneeling on the sand beside the severed leg when something, perhaps a sixth sense, perhaps a subtle change in the patterns of sound in the *nullah*, told him that he was in danger. Glancing around he quickly saw that the most obvious source of any threat was the nearest cover, up on top of the bank above him. Now, though he had allowed his attention to be foolishly diverted by the sight of the remains of the young woman, his reaction to his sense of danger was made without hesitation.

Knowing, probably from experience, the difficulty of shooting accurately with a heavy rife from a kneeling or squatting position, he did not attempt to bring the rifle to his shoulder. Instead he stayed in the same kneeling position and, swinging the rifle to his front, slammed its butt into the ground. Quickly placing two fingers on the rifle's triggers, he raised his head to look at the top of the bank. The tigress, close, ready to launch its charge, saw what he had done and instantly interpreted it as threatening. It swung around and, unheard and unseen, slipped away. The only sign of its departure was a few little stones and some dirt that slid down the bank and dropped into the pool. Later Corbett said that his newness to man-eater hunting was what made him act as foolishly as he did. He was lucky. Another two or three seconds of inattention could well have been fatal for him.

Leaving the pool Corbett tracked the tigress for several more hours. But her spoor took him into a wilderness of rocks and broken ground, dangerous stuff for stalking a man-eater, and with the sun edging towards the western horizon, discretion suggested that he give up for the day. Before he did, however, he climbed to a high ridge above the village to look at the country around him. From there, studying the lay of the land, he noticed that its configuration loaned itself to the possibility of a beat.

In front of him was the valley of the Champa River, running roughly east west. The river coursed between high, steep banks covered with short, thin grass and scattered with tall pines the needles of which lay thick on the ground. Here and there, on the slopes leading down to the river and in its bed, were plies of big, gray rocks. Immediately below him the river entered a deep gorge and here, hemmed in by high rock walls, it turned and ran north. The western wall of the gorge was steep but not too steep for men or animals to use. The eastern wall was a sheer precipice, rising five hundred feet from the rushing waters of the river.

Corbett studied the layout of the area for a while and thought that if he could get sufficient men for a beat, and if they could get the tigress moving from wherever it was lying up, its natural line of movement from beaters might possibly be through the gorge below him. This in mind he left and, accompanied by the man with the gun who had followed him when he first set out, walked back to the village.

At the village he met the Tahsildar and asked him about getting men for a beat. He explained that beaters would not be asked to physically go in on the tigress, to try and drive it out of cover, but could instead stay back and endeavor to do this with a demonstration, one that would include a lot of noise. The Tahsildar, at first dubious of the idea of a beat, brightened up when Corbett explained his plan; he promised to see what he could do. Corbett proposed the beat be carried out next day, while the tigress was still in the area and hopefully lying up with its belly full. The plan understood, the Tahsildar again left for Champawat and Corbett returned to his little bungalow above the river.

Next day Corbett was up early and with the sun still low on the eastern horizon met the Tahsildar on the rim of the steep hill which formed the north bank of the river. At first he was dismayed to find only two or three men with the Tahsildar. But soon others began to arrive so that by midday, when they were ready to begin the beat, and when the tigress would hopefully be sleeping soundly, two hundred and ninety-eight men had assembled on top of the hill.

Gathering them around him, Corbett gave them instructions. They were not to leave the top of the hill under any circumstances. They were to stay there and they were to keep together and when Corbett gave them a signal, which he would do from a position on the opposite hill, a place that he carefully pointed out to them, they were to fire their guns, shout and throw rocks down the hill into the brush where the tigress was, hopefully, lying up.

This done Corbett set out for the opposite hill, on the south side of the river. The Tahsildar went with him, explaining that while the presence of tigress presented considerable danger, it was nothing compared to the hazards of being among two hundred and ninety-eight men armed with muzzle loaders and assorted home made guns, when they began to fire them.

Corbett and the Tahsildar went east along the ridge where the men were now assembled in a long line and after dropping down into the gorge, and crossing the Champa, they climbed up the opposite side. When they reached the top of the hill they doubled back and went west, upstream, to a point opposite where the men were waiting on the north bank. Here they left the ridge and started down towards the river. But after a while the slope proved too steep for the Tahsildar and so Corbett left him behind and went on. As he did so the beaters, without waiting for his signal to start the demonstration–something for which, I know from experience, village beaters are notorious-opened fire and with a series of wild yells started hurling rocks and stones down in the gorge.

Corbett, taken by surprise, ran the last three hundred yards down the steep hillside which, covered with pine needles as it was—and as it still is today—was slippery enough to tax the agility of a mountain goat. His route took him down along the edge of a deep ravine that entered the gorge just where it turned north and seeing a patch of thick green grass at the ravine's entrance, high enough to partially cover him, he sat down in this to wait for the tigress. As he did so the cacophony of sound from the hill opposite increased and when the booming of guns and the shouts of the men and the beating of drums was at its highest, the tigress suddenly appeared to Corbett's right front, bounding down the hillside in front of him, about three hundred yards away.

Corbett raised his rifle and started to take aim. But at that moment the Tahsildar, who had also seen the tigress from his position on the hill behind and above Corbett, fired both barrels of his shotgun at the big cat. He missed, or was too far away to hit the animal. But the shot alarmed the cat and it whipped around and went racing back the way it had come. Corbett, without much hope of hitting it, took a long shot at the tigress that missed.

Immediately after Corbett fired, the tigress disappeared and, worried at the thought that it might have gone up the hill to charge the line of men, he was delighted when the animal suddenly broke cover to his left front and, leaping across the boulders that filled the bed of the mountain river, came straight towards him. He swung the heavy rifle up and fired again and this time, proving his prowess as a first class shot—for he was using a rifle that had been sighted in at sea level and, at this altitude, and with the very heavy round that it fired, probably required to be aimed above his target—his bullet went home.

His shot, hitting the animal in the after part of its body, brought the big cat to a halt. It turned towards Corbett, pinpointing him immediately in the short green grass. Head lowered, snarling, it stood for a second or two and this gave Corbett the opportunity for a carefully placed second shot at the point of the animal's shoulder. The distance was thirty yards and without hesitation he took aim and fired again.

Corbett's second bullet went home but to Corbett's dismay the big cat ignored its impact and just stood there, glaring at him, teeth bared and ears laid back. And Corbett now had a problem which was that, never expecting to be able to get more than a couple of shots at the big cat, he had brought only three rounds of ammunition with him. Another mistake which, like his attention lapse at the pool in the *nullah*, now placed him in a very precarious position.

For a few seconds things hung in the balance. On one side was the young hunter, crouched down, facing a man-eater that had killed and eaten over four hundred people and that was wounded and enraged, facing it with an empty rifle. On the other, a big cat, hurt, angry and trying to make up its mind to charge what it must have known was obviously the cause of its pain. Then, possibly because of the shock of its wounds, possibly because it reasoned that with all the humans in the area and the tremendous racket they were still making that getting into cover might be more important than staying in the open to challenge its tormentors, the big cat slowly turned and moved away.

Corbett now remembered that the Tahsildar was still up behind him somewhere and that he had a shotgun. He shouted at the man and when he did not get a coherent reply turned and ran up the hill to find him.

After his shots at the tigress, the Tahsildar had reloaded his weapon and when Corbett grabbed the gun out of his hands, the man let him have it readily. Corbett turned and with the shotgun at the ready, ran down the hill towards where he had last seen the tigress.

The big cat, after its confrontation with Corbett, turned and crossed the stream again and went up the opposite hill. It moved slowly for about three hundred feet and then turned left, westward, and made for a big, flat-surfaced boulder that protruded from the side of the hill like a giant wedge. Here, no doubt frantic with the pain of its wounds, it attacked and vented its anger on a small bush, tearing it to pieces with savage growls and snarls. Then it climbed up onto the big rock and, turning, stood at bay.

Corbett, racing down the south hill with the Tahsildar's shotgun, saw the tigress standing on the rock. He did not hesitate. Leaping from boulder to boulder to cross the stream, he ran towards where the animal was waiting. Courageously, for he was armed only with an old fashioned and untried shotgun, he approached to within twenty feet of the tigress and fired a shot at her.

The Tahsildar's ancient weapon seems to have lobbed its solid lead round out at a very low velocity for, as Corbett found out later, it hit the tigress in the foot and lodged between her toes. But the big rounds from Corbett's rifle, probably six hundred grain slugs, which is what a .500 DBH will throw, had done their damage when they smashed into the animal and now she was fast succumbing to the shock of her wounds. As Corbett watched, the big cat laid its head down on the edge of the rock slab that it had chosen for its last stand, and died. And with her death the reign of terror of the Rupal Champawat man-eater, or the man-eater of Champawat, which is what Corbett named it after the place where he put it down, came to an end.

Corbett wrote the story of the hunt for the man-eater of Champawat thirty-two years later, in 1939, and his memory of the hunt and its details is remarkable. He remembers how slippery the slope of the south hill was when he ran down it with the Tahsildar's shotgun. This was due to the thick *Carpet* of pine needles from the Chir pines that grew on the slope at that time and that still grow there today. Although I personally possess the agility of someone who has spent a lot of time scrambling in the Himalaya, I found it difficult, climbing up and down both the north and south hills of the Champawat ravine, to keep my footing when just walking, let along running.

Corbett recalls the fact that he only stayed in the dak bungalow in Champawat for a day or so before moving to the second bungalow that stood and still stands on the top of the ridge from which the south slope descends to the river. He recalls the dense patch of green grass that grew at the mouth of the ravine, where he lay in wait for the tigress and got his first shots at her when the beat started. The ravine still has a stand of luxuriant green grass in it, just where Corbett said it was, where it meets the Champa river. And no doubt the big boulders that he went bounding over when he crossed the river to confront the tigress were the same then as they are today, big gray stepping stones that can still be used, as I used them, to get across the small but sometimes turbulent stream.

And finally the big slab of rock on which *the* tigress stood at bay, and then died, still protrudes from the side of the hill where Corbett said it did. In the evening, with the sun reddening the pine covered slopes and the only sound the splashing of the waters of the Champa, one can still see the Rupal Champawat man-eater standing there, her teeth bared, roaring her defiance at a fearless young man, challenging her, on foot and face to face, with an ancient shotgun.

BOOK TWO

THE MUKTESAR MAN-EATER.
1910.

CHAPTER ONE

If you go trekking out of the hill station of Naini Tal, in India's northern state of Uttar Pradesh, and you head north, you will soon find yourself climbing a steep, 8000 foot ridge. The ridge runs east-west and on its western end is a veterinary institution called the Muktesar Veterinary Research Institute.

In the year 1910 a tigress started killing and eating people in the vicinity of this establishment and when the killings began to seriously disrupt the work of the institute staff, its director, the veterinary officer in charge, sent an urgent request to Naini Tal asking that Jim Corbett be sent to hunt the man-eater and put an end to its depredations.

Corbett, alerted by the authorities—most probably by the office of the British deputy Commissioner in Naini Tal—immediately agreed to go after the tiger. Arming himself with a double-barreled .500 rifle that used a modified cordite powder and accompanied by a servant and two porters, he set out at once, on foot, for Muktesar. He traveled by way of Ramgarh, ten miles from Naini Tal, and there spent the night in the Ramgarh *dak* bungalow. Next morning, instructing his men to follow him to Muktesar, he loaded his rifle and in the dark, long before sunrise, set out alone for Muktesar, reaching the junction of the Almora road and the Muktesar road as the dawn light glowed in the hills to the east.

CHAPTER TWO

The history of the Muktesar man-eater, and what turned it into a killer cat, is in many ways similar to that of other man-eaters. As has been touched on in the INTRODUCTION, big cats, both tigers and leopards, become man-eaters and turn to killing human beings when something happens to prevent them killing their natural prey. The normal prey of tigers and leopards is deer and wild boar though with both cats, if they are hungry enough, food will be anything they can catch and kill.

Attacking and pulling down a deer, or a wild boar, particularly the latter, requires that the cat in question be in full possession of all of its physical capabilities. When something happens that infringes on these capabilities, such as gunshot wounds, or injuries obtained in a fight with another animal, or, in some cases, something as simple as injuries sustained in tackling a porcupine, the quills of which may become lodged in the muscles of the cat, weakening them, then the big cat may lose the physical ability vitally necessary to killing another animal. When this happens it will begin to go hungry and for an animal whose whole life centers on food, this quickly produces psychological changes that alter its normal attitude towards man. As its hunger increases, so its wariness—the natural respect that it has for a big brained creature that, it senses, has capabilities superior to its own—decreases, and when this happens, spurred on by the powerful physical and mental effects of the first stages of starvation, it turns to killing human beings.

Oddly, the principal cause of many of Corbett's tigers becoming man-eaters was not, as might be expected, severe injuries, or gunshot wounds, but encounters with porcupines, skirmishes that sometimes left six to ten inch quills embedded in the muscle and tissue of their legs, paws and shoulders, with subsequent physical deterioration. So it was with the Muktesar man-eater which, in an careless encounter with a porcupine, lost an eye and had some fifty quills driven into its right foreleg.

With the Muktesar tigress, some of the quills doubled back into what must have been very painful injuries and these became aggravated when she tried to pull them out with her teeth. One day, soon after the encounter with the porcupine,* and while the big cat was lying up in a patch of grass, probably trying to remove the quills, a village woman stumbled across it by accident. The woman was cutting grass and, it seems, had slowly worked her way up to where the cat was lying, unaware that it was there. When she got too close for its liking, the tigress, instead of moving away, attacked, killing the woman with a single crushing blow to the skull.

A few days after this a woodcutter decided to chop firewood from a dead log, in the forest near where the woman had been killed. Unfortunately for him the tigress was lying behind the log that he chose and again, very possibly because of the aggravation of its injuries, the tigress, instead of leaving, as a tiger will normally do, attacked the man and killed him.

The man's body fell across the tree and Corbett, investigating the story of the incident, believed that the tigress may have tasted the man's blood when she killed him. She may also have been hungry. Whatever the reason, the big cat suddenly perceived the man's body as a source of food and, before she left, ate part of his back. As

**People who live in places where there are porcupines, both in the US and other countries, will know of the propensity of dogs to chase and attack these well armed little animals and the painful results that ensue for their pets. They will also know that the average dog never seems to learn for the encounter and will do it again at the first opportunity. Tigers appear to possess the same psychology and repeatedly attack porcupines with results that may sometimes lead to their becoming man-eaters.*

there was no record of her killing and eating anyone before this time, this woodcutter appears to have been her first victim. She subsequently began killing people on a regular basis and when Corbett set out to hunt her, she had killed and eaten twenty-four human beings.

CHAPTER THREE

Arriving at Muktesar, in Corbett's time a small hill town with a post office and a bazaar, Corbett found his way to the *dak* bungalow, where he had breakfast. After breakfast he left word for his men to say that he had gone out to gather information about the man-eater and leaving the bungalow walked out to the southern side of the hill on which Muktesar lies. Stopping to admire the view of the hills, falling away into the valley of the Kundal River, he was soon joined by several shopkeepers, headed by the local postmaster. He talked with them for a while and then set off down what was called the Dhari road,* to visit an apple orchard owned by a friend.

Proceeding down the hill he soon found himself following a little girl leading a bullock and after chatting with her for a while she told him that a bullock had been killed by a tiger the previous day. Corbett got her to show him where the animal had been taken and after escorting the little girl to her home, went off to look for the kill.

Searching, he soon found a drag mark and following this quickly came to the kill, a small white bullock. Believing that the animal

---

******Visiting the area, I was unable to find anywhere called Dhari. But due north of Mukteswar is a village called Darinola and Corbett may have been using an abbreviation of the name, calling it Dhari, something that commonly happens in north India. In his writings he indicates that the apple orchard of his friend, Badri Shah, was in a fold of the hill to the left of his viewpoint of the valley below Muktesar, and so I believe that it was in this direction that he started his search for signs of the man-eater. This assumption fits, geographically, with further descriptions of the area where the hunt was conducted and where the tigress was eventually shot.*

had very possibly been killed by the man-eater, he resolved to sit up for it and after mentally selecting a small tree, about fifteen feet away from the kill, he left the area to make a quick visit to his friend Badri Shah.

At Badri Shah's house he had a meal and then, accompanied by his friend and two men, returned to the scene of the kill. There he climbed into the little tree he had selected and settled himself in the middle of a big rose bush that enveloped it. After the men had passed up his rifle and told him that they would come back for him next morning, they left him. When they did he settled down to wait for the man-eater, hoping that it would come and give him a shot. The time was four p.m.

About an hour after the men left, a Barking Deer started to call from a ravine about two hundred yards below Corbett's tree and when Corbett heard it he guessed that the tiger was on the move. Listening to the little deer's calls, he was able to pinpoint the approach of the tigress and when the calls died away he guessed, correctly, that she had come up to within sight of the kill and was now lying down and, from a concealed position, was watching it and at the same time carefully inspecting the area before emerging to feed. Corbett had been told that several other hunters had tried for the tigress before he came to Muktesar and he presumed that contact with man, or possibly even being shot at, had made it extremely cautious and now accounted for it present behavior.

Soon it grew dark and when the light was completely gone Corbett suddenly heard the soft footsteps of the tigress approaching the tree in which he was sitting. Reaching the tree the big cat lay down beneath it and as it did so the sky darkened and thick black clouds put an end to the last of the light, including the starlight on which Corbett had depended to see the cat.

Himalayan starlight, spreading its light down through the cold, clear air of the mountains, can be quite bright and I have personally used it many times to walk long distances on mountain trails, carrying a flashlight only as a backup. Corbett also used it in his hunting and in this case had hoped to be able to see the cat by it. But now the light was completed gone and so when the cat, slowly and very cautiously, came out to eat at the kill, he did something that in hunting only rank amateurs will do, something that has caused many a fatal accident, something that is called the "sound shot."

A sound shot consists, simply, of shooting where sounds indicate the target may be. In normal hunting it is considered very foolhardy and is something that should never be done, especially when there is the possibility of other people in the immediate area. But in Corbett's case it was quite justified, for three reasons.

The first was that because of the total darkness caused by the thick cloud cover, this was his only way of being able to pinpoint the big cat and get a shot at it. The second was that he knew, because of the presence of the man-eater, that there would be no other people moving around at this time of night in the vicinity. And the last was that while his shot might not be fatal, and might only wound the man-eater, this would not make it any more dangerous that it presently was.

When the tigress started to eat Corbett waited for a little while. Then he slowly raised the .500 and aimed it at where the sounds were coming from. From the position of the bullock he guessed that the tigress would be broadside onto him and after taking aim a couple of times at where he guessed the animal's head and shoulders should be, he carefully pressed the trigger.

Corbett's shot missed and in a flash the tigress was gone. He waited for a while, listening for any sounds that might indicate that the cat had been wounded and then lowered his rifle. As he did so the tigress growled from the top of a nearby bank, indicating that she had not gone very far and also that she had detected the movement he made when he lowered his rifle. The growls, and the fact that she was still close by, also told him that she was unwounded.

When the tigress continued to growl, Corbett, fairly confident that it would not come up the tree after him, for tigers almost never climb trees, sat quietly and smoked several cigarettes while he waited for her to emerge from her concealment and make another approach to the kill. He was doing this when it started to rain quite heavily and when the rain continued he knew that that the cat would leave. Tigers do not care for heavy, cold rain and the man-eater, being no exception, would have made for cover as soon as it started. This is what it did.

Corbett, having hoped to get a shot at the tigress fairly soon after starting his sit, had not expected to stay out all night and had on only light clothing, probably a khaki shirt and shorts. Soon he was soaked and when a cold wind arose he was quickly chilled to the bone and probably in danger of hypothermia. The obvious thing to do would have been to get down from the tree and head for Badri Shah's house. But with a man-eater in the vicinity, even though it had gone to take cover from the rain, this would have been courting a nasty end. In the dark the big cat would have had all of the advantages and in any case, with the starlight gone, Corbett would probably have had a problem following the winding hill trail back to Badri Shah's house.

And so he waited until morning, wet and cold, and when Badri Shah and his men came to pick him up, they had to help him down out of the tree and then massage his legs to get the circulation going again. A pot of hot tea brought by the men helped and after checking the kill to see where his sound shot of the night before had gone—it missed the tiger by six inches—the group set off down the hill.

One man went ahead and Corbett followed with Badri Shah. Coming down the hill, Corbett's keen eyes quickly picked up spoor of the tigress following the man who had gone ahead of them, down the hill. Although he does not say so, this meant that when the men were helping him down from the tree, and massaging his legs, the tigress was lying up nearby, probably watching them. It was also an indication of how clever, and how dangerous, she was. Fortunately for the man who went ahead, she did not close on him and attack him and when Corbett and Badri Shah got to the latter's home, they found him there, safe.

CHAPTER FOUR

Thinking about the lay of the land where the tiger was living, looking at the deep ravines and the heavy brush that made stalking the cat both difficult and dangerous, Corbett wondered if they might not be able to drive her out in the open, with a beat. He talked with Badri Shah about this and when the orchardist agreed to get a beating party together, he sat down with him and made a plan.

At midday, Badri Shah, working with one of his overseers, a man named Govind, managed to round up thirty men for a beat. A deep ravine with dense brush, below where Corbett had spent the night, was selected as a likely place for the tigress to be lying up and soon after midday the beat got under way.

The plan was for the thirty-man party to divide into two separate groups and to beat the ravine, not by going into it-which would have been much too dangerous for them-but by walking along its upper edges, shouting and throwing stones into it. This is a method of beating that will sometimes get a big cat up and moving and it is one that I have used myself many times when the brush has been too thick for beaters.

Soon after the beaters set off to take up their positions along the edges of the ravine, Corbett walked back up the hill towards the kill site. He picked up the tigress' spoor again, fairly quickly, but then lost it in the dense brush. While he was trying to find it he came across the remains of a cow. The carcass was about a week old and bite marks in the throat showed that it had been killed by a tiger, in this case, Corbett guessed, most probably the man-eater. Most of the carcass had been eaten and Corbett, perhaps thinking that he might attract the tigress by moving her kill, something that will sometimes provoke a big cat and bring it out in protest, dragged the carcass to the edge of a small cliff and heaved it over. While he was doing this he heard a shot being fired, the agreed signal between he and Badri Shah, and his man Govind, to start the beat.

Beating for tiger with native villagers can be very effective when the beat goes well and the big cat is moved slowly but surely in the direction of the waiting guns. But when the brush is very thick and villagers have to make detours to get through it and as a result get scattered, or if, again because of the density of the brush, they start to get nervous and bunch up, then Murphy's Law intervenes and whatever can go wrong will go wrong, with results that will vary from the exasperating to the hilarious.

Whatever happened in Corbett's beat for the man-eater is not clear. In any case, when the shouts of the beaters indicated that they had become scattered and disoriented, he called off the drive and as soon as the men gathered he gave them all cigarettes and sat down with them and the overseer, Govind, to talk. When he did this something happened that to me, as someone who has studied Corbett's great hunts, was nothing less than an incredible streak of luck.

CHAPTER FIVE

With the beaters sitting around him, Corbett was sitting facing Govind, and talking with him, when suddenly he saw a look of surprise come over the man's face. He swung around and to his astonishment saw what had caused it...the sight of the tigress walking towards them across an open field, about a quarter of a mile away.

Corbett and the men were in the open and now the men, no doubt cautioned by him in a series of quick whispers, all stayed very still and very quiet. For although the tigress had apparently not seen them yet, any movement on their part, any noise, would have instantly attracted its attention.

Corbett waited until the tigress passed through a patch of cover, one that obscured its view of them and then, telling the men to stay where they were and keep very quiet, turned and ran in the direction of the approaching cat. Using cover as it was available, he moved forward until he was close to where the tigress had just disappeared in a patch of brush. This took him to where the old kill was lying, the carcass that he had flung over the small cliff earlier in the day and he was carefully making his way forward towards where it was lying when suddenly he heard the unmistakable sounds of the tigress chewing on it. She had found the old kill and had decided to eat from it.

Moving into a position from where he hoped to see the animal when she stopped eating and started to move on, Corbett took up a position on the hillside on a narrow trail above a small stream. There was a drop of about thirty feet to the stream bed at the base of the hill below him and the bed itself was clear of brush. If, as he surmised, the tigress, after eating, would head for the stream to drink, his position was one that would give him a clear shot at her when she did.

Suddenly the sounds of the tigress eating on the carcass ceased, and there was silence. Then Corbett saw the animal going up the hill above him and although there were a number of small saplings between him and the cat, any one of which might deflect the course of his bullet, he took a chance and fired at her.

His bullet struck a sapling close to the tigress' head and splinters from the smashed tree may have hit her in the face. She immediately spun around and either by chance, or with deadly intention, came straight at him. Standing his ground, rifle to his shoulder, he did what was absolutely the right thing to do when a charging tigress comes straight at you...he waited until she was too close to miss. When she was six feet away he pulled the trigger, putting the big slug into the lower part of her neck, at the shoulder.

The impetus of the big cat's charge carried it past Corbett, close to his left shoulder. Mortally wounded, it probably crashed onto the path behind him and a little to his left. Then the impetus of its charge and the weight of its big body carried it on, down the bank and into a pool in the stream directly below where he stood. There, its blood slowly reddening the water, the Mukteswar man-eater died.

Corbett was soon joined by the beaters and together they carried the tigress up to Badri Shah's orchard, where Corbett skinned it. While doing this he found fifty plus porcupine quills, from one to nine inches in length, embedded in the cat's right foreleg and in the pad of its foot.

Corbett had two of his men carry the tigress' pelt up to Muktesar, where it was exhibited outside the post office for all to see. He stayed there with it, no doubt talking to the people who came to view it and at midnight went to the *dak* bungalow, where he slept for four hours. At four a.m. he was up and away, back on the trail to Naini Tal and by midday next day was home.*

**What I find continuously impressive in Corbett's stories, and this against the experience of my own background as a professional hunter, is his incredible stamina and physical capability, of which we see some sterling examples in the hunt for the Muktesar man-eater. Again and again in his hunts we see him going without food for days at a time and then undertaking long, strenuous hikes in hill country, hikes that would, in my opinion, tax even the strength of a native hillman. He also seemed to be able to just about ignore the need for sleep; e.g., setting out on a twelve hour hike from Muktesar, back to Naini Tal, after three days of strenuous hunting and only four hours rest at the dak bungalow.*

I also find that I have to admire the humility with which he records his death-defying encounter with the Muktesar cat. It would have been very easy for him to say, for instance, in his account of the hunt, how the tigress charged him with the singular intention of attacking and killing him. Instead, without hesitation, he allows for the fact that his shot at the tigress, splintering a sapling in her face, may simply have confused her and that when she came at him she was in panic and just trying to get away. In support of this humble alternative is the fact that the trail that she used, on which Corbett stood, was possibly the only one running right across the face of the hill, as it was when I as there and so this is what she naturally chose for her flight.

at midnight went to the dak bungalow, where he slept for four hours. At four a.m. he was up and away, back on the trail to Naini Tal and by midday next day was in ...

[illegible]

BOOK THREE

THE PANAR MAN-EATER.
1910.

CHAPTER ONE

I think it appropriate to begin the story of the man-eating leopard of the Panar valley with a quote from a book, published in the 1930s, called JUNGLE TRAILS IN NORTH INDIA, by Sir Martin Hewitt, a British sportsman hunter from the days of the Raj. The quote reads:

A *man-eating leopard is much worse than a man-eating tiger, for it combines the most amazing boldness with the greatest cunning, and a truly wonderful aptitude for concealment. It has been known to enter a house and take a person out of it, after lying up in grass, less than a foot high, with people continually passing within a few feet. One infested a district near Almora for a long time, and though its list of victims was very large, no one could bag it for* years... *There was a large reward offered for its destruction, and the scourge was disposed of eventually by a sportsman from Naini Tal.*

It is not certain, but the 'sportsman from Naini Tal' may well have been Corbett, at that time—the thirties—not as well known as he was to become in later years.

When Corbett was hunting the Rupal-Champawat tigress he heard about a man-eating leopard that was terrorizing the villagers of the Panar River valley, in the district of Almora, east of Naini Tal. Three years later, in 1910, when the deaths attributed to this single animal had mounted to over four hundred, he was approached by the authorities to go after it. He was just about to do so when

Berthoud, the Deputy Commissioner at Naini Tal, urgently requested him to answer the appeal of the director of the Muktesar Veterinary Institute and go after the man-eater that was terrorizing the people there. Granting Berthoud his request, Corbett went firstly to Muktesar and when he had dealt with the tigress there he immediately made plans to go to the Panar River valley to hunt the leopard that subsequently became known as the Panar Man-eater.*

Leaving Naini Tal in late April, 1910, Corbett set out on foot for the Panar area with three porters and a servant. He took the Dabidura road, east, via the village of Lamgara, and after an all day march through the hot hills of the early summer, camped for a night in the forest with his men. Next day he marched on, stopping at Lamgara for a meal and arriving at the Dol *dak* bungalow, on the edge of the man-eater's territory, by evening.

He spent the night at the bungalow and next morning, telling is men to wait for him there, set out of foot to gather information about the man-eater from local villagers. He spent the whole day doing this and as the sun was setting, came to an isolated farm house. On the dirt road leading to it he found the pug marks of an adult, male leopard and at the house he met a young man, a farmer, who had a terrifying tale to tell.

The night before, the young man said, while he and his wife were sleeping, with the door of their one room house open for coolness, a leopard had come in out of the darkness and, climbing silently on to the porch and slipping in through the open door, had seized his wife by the throat and started to drag her out of the house. She just had time to grab hold of her husband's arm and awaken

**Contrary to what many people believe about Corbett, to the effect that he spent his time hunting man-eaters, in actual fact he was a working man earning his living on a full time basis and contributing to the support of his mother's large family. As a result, he only went after his man-eaters as and when work allowed and this is probably the main reason for the three year gap between the hunt for the man-eater of Champawat, in 1907, and the hunts for the Muktesar tigress and the Panar leopard, in 1910. In some cases he even had to take a break in the middle of a hunt to attend to his work, which he did in both the Muktesar and the Panar hunts.*

him and he, using the frame of the door for purchase, managed to break the leopard's hold and drag his wife back inside and close the door. The leopard promptly attacked the door while the young couple cowered inside in terror. With dawn streaking the eastern sky the cat, unable to break down the door, disappeared into the brush. But in the meantime the young woman's dreadful sufferings, which included deep claw wounds, had rendered her unconscious in addition to which septicemia, probably from decayed animal tissue in the hollow claws of the leopard, had quickly started to set in.

At first Corbett thought of going for help for the woman. But an examination of her injuries quickly convinced him that she had little chance of recovery and so he elected to stay and make an attempt to come to grips with her attacker. Reluctant to spend the night in the house with the dying woman, he had her husband help him to shift some firewood under the front porch of the house to make a hide where he could conceal himself. As the sun set, he crawled into this and sat down to wait.

Soon after Corbett took up his position the sun sank behind the western hills and darkness quickly closed in on the little house. The moon, two nights short of full, would not rise for about an hour and this short but dangerous period of darkness worried Corbett because he felt that the big cat, deprived of its meal of the night before, might well be lying up in the nearby brush waiting for another chance at the people in the house.

Then, out of the blackness, from half a mile away, a jackal called in alarm and Corbett's superb knowledge of jungle lore instantly told him that he was safe for the moment. Because jackals will call in alarm at the sight of a leopard or a tiger and, like some other animals, such as the Langur, will continue the call only as long as the big cat is in sight. The continuous calling of the jackal, obviously alarmed at the sight of the leopard, from a considerable distance away, told Corbett that the leopard might be on the move but that it was not close. In addition, he knew that leopards approach a kill site very slowly, very cautiously, and that, judging from the distance indicated by the jackal, there was a good chance the moon would be up from behind the hills before the leopard arrived. This is what happened and Corbett breathed a sigh of relief when, a little later, the three-quarter moon climbed out of the hills to the east and bathed the little house and its front yard in thin, silvery light.

As the moon rose the jackal stopped calling and then there was silence, the deep silence of the mountain night, when people sleep and wild, nocturnal animals move about soundlessly. Towards dawn the moon sank behind the hills and for another short period Corbett waited in darkness, wondering if the leopard was close by, watching, waiting with the extraordinary patience of which these clever cats are capable when they are hunting.* Then a yellow band of light silhouetted the eastern hills, heralding the dawn, and soon afterwards the sun rose, bringing with it a measure of safety for him from the killer cat.

Soon after dawn, Corbett, who had eaten nothing but a few wild raspberries since the day before, bade the young man goodbye and set out for the Dol *dak* bungalow. On the way he met a road overseer on a pony who agreed to carry a message to Stiffe, the British Deputy Commissioner of Almora, requesting aid for the victim of the man-eater. Stiffe responded at once but, as Corbett found out later, the young woman died before anything could be done. In 1910,long before antibiotics were even thought of, septicemia followed by blood poisoning and death was inevitably the fate of someone clawed and bitten in an attack by a big cat.

***Readers might wonder why Corbett did not have a flashlight with him, as a safeguard against the darkness, when he elected to spend the night out like this. The answer is that in 1910 the flashlight, as we know it, had not yet been invented.**

CHAPTER TWO

Soon after the incident of the attack that took the life of the young farmer's wife, Corbett left the area and returned home to Naini Tal. From there it is presumed that he went back to Mokameh Ghat, a Ganges river, ferry boat crossing point, east of the city of Patna, where he worked for the railways because in his writings he mentions, with pride, that it was in this year, 1910, that he and his work gangs set up an all-time record by manually handling and transshipping, across the great river, five thousand, five hundred tons of goods in a single day. He stayed away until September, when he returned to Naini Tal and then, in that month, with the monsoon rain thundering out of the leaden summer skies, set out again on the trail of the Panar man-eater.

The Panar River has its sources in small streams in the hills east of Dol, hills in which scattered villages bear names like Sangrouli, Sunari, Deoli, Tandra and Taraini. Soon, fed by tributary rivers, it forms a single course and widens and deepens to run eastward, down the beautiful Panar River valley. Hill people, well aware of the vagaries of mountain rivers and how they can rise ten or more feet in a monsoon night, will not live in the beds of these mountain rivers, even though the land there is flat and fertile. So there are no villages or indeed any human habitation within the Panar river flats. But on either side, in the rolling country that rises in terraced steps from the river, hundreds of small farms dot the green and brown hillsides, single unit dwellings of simple men and women who live by wresting a living from the soil.

Here and there, usually sitting squarely on the ridge tops, are tiny villages, tight knit groups of gray, stone walled, slate-roofed houses surrounded by terraced fields. Between the villages every inch of cultivatable land is used for crops and as such provides little or no cover, or habitat, for wildlife. But the broad sweeps of the hills themselves are laced with deep ravines cut into them, through the centuries, by monsoon runoff. The sides of these deep *nullah*s are usually very steep, too steep for cultivation and so they are covered with brush that thickens as it descends into their depths. These brush-choked *nullah*s make perfect habitat for leopard and it was in one of these that Panar man-eater had its lair, emerging only at night to hunt and kill its victims.

For his second attempt to come to grips with the Panar leopard, Corbett headed due east out of Naini Tal, towards the small hill town of Pithoragarh. He left Naini Tal at four in the morning of September 10th with four porters and a servant and it is a measure of the man, and of the loyalty and hardiness of his Koumani porters, that he covered the twenty-eight miles to Almora, in heavy monsoon rain, in a single day. He had planned to spend the night in Almora with his friend Stiffe, the Deputy Commissioner. But by the time he arrived there he was completely soaked and not having any dry clothes to wear, and probably embarrassed at the thought of turning up wet and bedraggled at Stiffe's house, he spent the night instead at the Almora *dak* bungalow. Next day he continued on down the Pithoragarh road until he reached the village of Panwa Naula. He spent a second night at another *dak* bungalow.

Leaving Panwa Naula next morning he and his men headed east for about a mile. Then they left the Pithoragarh road and, turning right, south, dropped off into a series of small, shallow valleys and sharp ridged hills that fell away to the Panar river. He spent four days in these hills with his men, going from village to village in the Salan and Rangon districts-hard hiking in this steep, narrow trailed hill country-searching for news of the man-eater.

On the evening of the fourth day he arrived at a village called Chakati and here the headman told him that a person had just been killed by a leopard at Sanouli, a village on the south side of the Panar River. He spent the night at Chakati and next day, after a long hike on winding trails through the broken hill country that borders the north side of the Panar River valley, came to the river.

The river was in flood and, as there was no bridge, had to be forded. This was done with some difficulty and it took several hours for Corbett to get all of his men, plus two others he had picked up as temporary guides, across the torrent. Once across, probably with the day growing late, and knowing how that it might be difficult to find a campsite in the cultivated land above the river, he spent the night on the south bank of the river.

Next day he set out to find the village of Sanouli, the place of the man-eater's latest victim. Although his description of the route that he took indicates that he should have been able to reach it from his river bank camp in one day, he found himself spending yet another night on the trail, this time in a wide, open valley which was probably the bed of one of the tributary streams of the Panar. There he and his men spent the night on the cold wet ground that is common to river flats and the following day, stopping only to buy two goats, to be used as bait for the man-eater, they reached Sanouli.

Sanouli in Corbett's time was a small village perched on the side of a big sweeping hill, high above the Panar River. It is much the same today, a little village, with gray stone houses falling in tiers down to terraced fields. The hill on which the village is situated forms an amphitheater and on its upper rim are two more small villages. Within the amphitheater, below these villages, was, in Corbett's time, and still is, a patch of dense brush about twenty acres in extent. The Sanouli villagers told Corbett that the man-eater used this as a lair from time to time and that in their opinion, having just killed and carried away one of the village women, was living in it right now.

CHAPTER THREE

The men of Sanouli told Corbett that in March and April four people had been killed by the man-eater in the immediate area of their village. The first three had been taken from the other villages on the rim of the hill and the fourth had been taken from Sanouli itself.

All the victims had been killed at night and because the man-eater had established a reign of terror in the area, one that would have kept everyone inside after dark, this meant that the victims were actually taken from their houses. Corbett would have realized this and no doubt he must have envisioned the spotted killer dragging its victims away, men and women screaming in horror at the prospect of being eaten, struggling, calling for help in vain. For unlike a man-eating tiger, which usually kills its victims quickly with a single, powerful bite, man-killer leopards will usually be more intent on getting away from the scene of the attack-especially when other people are present-as quickly as possible. As a result, the victim will often be alive and aware of what is going to happen to them while they are being dragged out of their houses and into the brush, a prospect the thought of which sends a chill into the bravest of us.

All of the Sanouli area victims, Corbett was told, had been taken into the aforementioned twenty-acre patch of brush to be eaten and the villagers, who had no guns and whose courage melted at the thought of going into the leopard's territory, had not gone near it.

In the evening of his first day at Sanouli Corbett took one of his goats and tied it out at the edge of the brush patch. He tied the second one close to an open-sided platform* in the village where he planned to sleep and, after a meal, settled down for the night.

The use of goats is a traditional method of hunting leopard in Asia. Leopard, which hunt with their eyes and ears, will pick up the sound of a goat's bleating from a considerable distance, pinpoint it and then home in on it. Using two goats at a time is better than one because whereas one may bleat for a while and then lie down and go to sleep, two will often call to each other, back and forth, for hours.

The following morning Corbett found the goat that he had tied near his porch alive and unharmed. But going down to the brush patch he found the other one missing, with ground sign, including a broken tethering rope, that indicated that it had been taken by a leopard. Looking at the patch of brush where the bait had been taken he guessed that the leopard was lying up inside it and that the animal was very probably the man-eater.

He thought about going into the brush patch to stalk it. But stalking a big cat requires noiseless movement and as the density of the patch clearly precluded this, he decided against it.

******One wonders about Corbett sleeping on an open-sided platform in an area where there was deadly man-eater operating, a cat that did not hesitate to come into villages at night and that had actually taken hundreds of people from their houses. There were essentially three reasons why he did this. Firstly, Corbett, (like myself, I have to admit,) simply did not like sleeping under a roof and, whenever he could, man-eaters regardless, preferred to sleep in the open. He did this at Kala Agar in the heart of the killing fields of the Chowgarh tigress, (See BOOK FIVE) sleeping in his tent behind the dak bungalow there, in a little stonewalled compound from where, two days before his arrival, the tigress had taken a woman. Secondly, he avoided, when circumstances allowed, and as I have always done, sleeping in village houses. There were and are a number of simple reasons for this preference and these are what might be called the other living things that one will encounter in an Indian village house. These include fleas, lice, Indian bed bugs, scorpions, centipedes, rats, mice, dogs, cats and, in addition to chickens, ducks, goats, sheep and other animals brought in at night for protection against predators, innumerable people and children who cough and spit and chatter and sing and talk in their sleep and get up at all hours to answer calls of nature. Thirdly, he depended on the fact of his being a very light sleeper and being able to awaken quickly at the slightest unusual noise, or smell, or change, however subtle, in the general pattern of the night sounds, quickly enough to be able to seize his rifle-always loaded and close to hand during the hours of darkness-and take action as the situation demanded.*

Returning to the village he consulted the men there about the terrain and about the ground cover in surrounding areas and was disappointed to find that the next nearest cover, outside of the brush patch, was more than two miles away. Had it been closer he might have attempted a beat to drive the cat out of the patch and give him a chance of a shot. But while big cats can be driven out of cover by well organized beaters, this is only possible when there is other cover within a short distance, that the cat can head for and get into quickly. Big cats and indeed, most other big forest animals, will not allow themselves to be driven out of cover unless there is existing and equally dense cover close by into which they can retreat. They will know the additional cover is there, because all wild animals know their own territories very well. If it is not there they will also know this and, when driven, rather than face open terrain, will turn and double back and sometimes even charge and attack whatever it is they think is trying to force them into the open. So it would be with the man-eater at Sanouli; with the next nearest cover to its home brush patch two miles away, beating it presented too dangerous a prospect for beaters.

Corbett, not wanting to subject the villagers to the possibility of an attack by the man-eater, decided that a beat would be too dangerous. A normal leopard, he reasoned, driven against its will towards open terrain, would be hazardous enough. But a man-eater, in this case one with over four hundred victims to its credit, would fearlessly hurl itself at the beaters and indeed, instead of going through their ranks with the simple intention of getting away, as a normal cat might do, would probably attack them with savage intent.

In the afternoon Corbett went down to the brush patch again and sat for a while listening to the calls of the various birds that made it their habitat, in particular those of Scimitar Babblers, Bul Buls and Drongoes, birds that will call in alarm at the sight of a cat, thereby signaling its movements. When, after he had been there a while, he heard some of them starting to call in alarm he quickly interpreted what they had to tell him—which was that they had encountered the leopard in the brush—and then used the information to help him pinpoint the position of the cat.

He then began to stalk the animal and, as the brush was too dense for him to enter it quietly, he did this from around the outside of the patch, using what might be called a provocative approach. Knowing that the birds would also call in alarm when they saw him, and thus alert the leopard to his presence, he guessed that the cat would quickly become aware of his movements at the edge of the brush and possibly attempt to stalk him, in which case it might show itself and give him the opportunity of a shot.

Anyone who has ever hunted big cats, and indeed even people who have done any kind of in-depth reading on them, will instantly recognize the extent of Corbett's courage in what he was now doing... which was to stalk, on foot, a killer cat that was both close by and very possibly aware of his presence. They will know that a leopard, a very clever feline, can use cover like few other animals and that the Panar man-eater, with intimate knowledge of every inch of its own ground firmly fixed in its brain, would probably have been able to stalk to within a few yards of Corbett, and even begin a lightening fast charge, before he was aware of it. They will also see in what he did an example of his complete confidence in his own ability with hunting weapons, a skill that he believed would enable him to draw down on the animal if it did charge, align the sights of his weapon on it and get in a killing shot before it closed on him.

The cat may well have stalked Corbett from inside the brush patch, paralleling his movements, step for step. But, wise to the ways of humans, the remains of four hundred of them having passed through its belly, it may also have recognized something unusual in the sight of a man, alone, moving slowly, watchfully, in a place where no man had ventured alone for years. Something that rang warning bells deep in the recesses of its feline mind, something that advised discretion. And so, with the cautiousness that is the trademark of all wild cats, it refused to be enticed out of the cover of the brush and stayed hidden, deep inside it. As the sun sank behind the darkening hills and the shadows lengthened, Corbett abandoned his dangerous game of cat and mouse and returned to the village.

That evening Corbett went down with an attack of malaria* and for twenty-four hours lay semi-conscious on his sleeping platform in the village. It is presumed that the villagers recognized his symptoms and, realizing how vulnerable his fever made him to the possibility of attack by the man-eater, kept watch over him. Whatever they and his men did to protect him, he survived the night and by the following evening his fever had dissipated and he was ready to resume the hunt.

On the night that Corbett was down with fever the men of Sanouli took Corbett's second goat, the one that he had set out near where he slept in the village, and tied it out where the first had been killed, at the edge of the brush patch. Next morning, going in a group to check on it, they found it untouched. When Corbett heard this he was pleased because this meant that the cat would probably not have eaten since it killed his first goat two days ago and would now be hungry again, hungry enough to be baited with his remaining goat.

Like Corbett, I too contracted malaria in years gone by. I had eight bouts spread across five years when I lived and worked as a tea planter in India. I believe that what I had was called Benign Tertian malaria. It was not recurrent malaria because after I left north Bengal, where I contracted it, it never reoccurred. But Corbett's malaria, which dogged him all his life, must have been the recurrent form.

CHAPTER FOUR

Immediately below the village of Sanouli, falling down the swell of the hill in giant, six-foot high steps, was a series of terraced fields. At the edge of one of these, half way down the hill and about three hundred yards from the nearest village house, was a lone oak tree. The tree grew at the edge of one of the terraces and leaned out from it over the field immediately below it. The shallow angle of its growth made climbing it a simple task of walking up its bole and when Corbett, scouting for a place to sit up for the leopard, found the tree and noticed that one of its main branches grew horizontally from its trunk about fifteen feet about the ground, he decided to use it as a *machan,* for a night sit for the man-eater.

Corbett, though his general experience with man-eaters at this time was limited to just two other big killer cats—at Champawat and Muktesar—knew enough about the tree climbing ability of leopards to realize that the tree he was going to sit in, with its leaning bole, offered no protection at all from a determined cat coming up it to attack him. And whereas a normal leopard will seldom climb up a tree to get at a man in a *machan*, even if wounded, a man-eater was different; to a man-eater a man in a tree represented food and once it detected him the Panar man-eater, with years of experience in the killing of humans behind it, would not hesitate to try and get at him. As a result he took unusual precautions and in the light of what happened, later that night, it is fortunate that he did.

Two fields below where the oak tree stood was—and still is today—a stand of Blackthorn bushes. Corbett sent his men down to the stand to cut long branches of the thorny bushes and after he had taken his seat in the tree, his back to its bole and towards the village, his legs stretched out along the big horizontal branch, he had the men tie the bushes securely to the trunk of the tree, with the thorny ends of the stems facing downwards and the cut ends close to him, on either side of his body. These latter ends he gathered around him, tucking them under his arms. With nothing else to hold on to in the tree, they provided him with a certain measure of stability, something to which, he stated later, he felt he owed his life.

While his men were tying the bait goat to a stake in front of and below the tree, he buttoned his jacket up in the front to protect his throat and pulled his hat well down on his head, to protect the back of his neck. He was doing this and his men, having tied the goat, were sitting smoking and waiting for his order to leave, when suddenly a Scimitar Babbler gave a piercing alarm whistle from the Blackthorn stand at the base of the hill, a call that was immediately echoed by the warning whistles of a group of White Capped Laughing Thrushes. Corbett knew that these calls very probably indicated the approach of the leopard.

Looking over the ground where all of this took place, even though when I was there it was many years later, I could see that from the brush patch, where the leopard had its lair, it would probably have heard the men cutting the Blackthorn bushes at the base of the hill below the village. And my guess is that even though the light had hardly begun to fade, hunger, combined with an unusual boldness, one engendered by its experience with people, persuaded it to leave the cover of the patch and come out to investigate the possibility of a human meal. It managed to do this, unseen and undetected, until the Scimitar Babblers spotted it and gave their warning calls.

When it found itself detected by the birds, rather than emerge into the open fields, the cat probably lay down in the Blackthorn stand to wait for darkness. From there it would have been able to see the men working in and around the oak tree and from the low angle of sight that it would have had, from the base of the hill, it may also have seen Corbett making his preparations to sit in the tree itself.

All of this may have presented to its agile mind an ideal scenario for a quick attack and a kill. However, though hunger may have been pressuring it, its innate cautiousness, plus the fact that there were five or six men in the work group around the little oak tree, dissuading it from doing anything. The Panar man-eater liked its victims to be alone and if there was more than one it preferred the cover of darkness for an assault. So it lay and watched and, with the deadly patience of its kind, waited for the darkness that would allow it to emerge and hunt for its human meal.

CHAPTER FIVE

On hearing the warning calls of the birds Corbett signaled his men to return to the village. They left quickly, talking loudly to each other as part of the common ruse applied in tiger and leopard hunting to persuade a waiting cat, lying up within earshot, that everyone has gone and that it is now safe for it to emerge from cover. It is one that will even work with a watching cat as long as it has not seen anyone actually getting into a *machan* and staying behind. For cats cannot count and when a number of men arrive at a hunting site and then leave less one, or even two, it cannot tell the difference.

All was quiet for half an hour after the men left. Corbett, skilled in the art of spending hours, sitting or standing, without moving a muscle, crouched silently in his tree and the leopard, patient, though its stomach growled for food, lay in the Blackthorn buses and waited for the sun to go down. Soon the shadows began to lengthen and the day quickly came to an end.

When it was almost dark the cat made its move. Slipping out of the Blackthorn patch, belly to the ground, its long tail no doubt twitching in anticipation of an attack and a kill, it used the cover of the six foot high terraces that ringed the hill to make an unseen approach towards Corbett's tree. It was probably well on its way, slipping along the base of each terrace in turn and then sliding over the top into the field above, when it was spotted by two Drongos. They instantly called out in alarm.

Drongos are insect eaters and to enable them to find and catch their miniscule prey, nature has endowed them with incredibly acute eyesight. They will hunt though the evening hours and into the very last of the light, at which time they can still see and catch insects too small to be visible to the human eye. Now two of them had spotted the leopard.

When the Drongoes called, the goat, which had been facing uphill in the direction of the village, suddenly turned around and faced in the opposite direction, towards the Blackthorn stand. When Corbett saw this he knew that the leopard was on its way and because it was extremely doubtful that there would be another leopard operating in the same vicinity, Mr. Spots being as territorial in his nature as the tiger, he knew without a doubt that it was the Panar man-eater. When he heard the Drongos making mock attacks on something moving below the terraces, swooping up and down and chattering their alarm calls, he guessed that he would not have long to wait before the cat appeared.

While there was still enough light to see, Corbett kept his eyes on the goat and by following the movements of its head, was able to some extent to guess at the direction of the leopard's approach. Then the light faded and darkness closed in and after that he had to depend on his ears and hope that if the leopard came he would hear something that would warn him of its approach.

Corbett had armed himself with a double-barreled .12 gauge shotgun loaded with what he said were slugs.* However, he may

---

** By slugs, Corbett meant pellets, which is what L.G. projectiles are. Nowadays, and especially in the US, these are called buckshot and come in various sizes. For what Corbett was now faced with, he could not have chosen a better weapon or a better load than a .12 gauge with L.G. Fired at close range, the big, fifty-grain pellets pack a killing force and fired at a longer range, even with the spread a shotgun will give them, each pellet has nearly the impact of a .22 rifle bullet. When I first started to hunt in north Bengal, as an amateur, this is what I used for medium sized big game, like wild boar and deer. I soon switched to a rifle. But in my early hunting days, using a twelve gauge with L.G., I found that even a big boar will go down and deer, if hit in any vital part of the body, such as the neck, were killed instantly. With professional hunters, in Africa, a .12 gauge with L.G., is the weapon of choice for following up on a wounded leopard.*

have used the term loosely, because what he had in the gun were not slugs, which, for a .12 gauge are either single, spherical shaped or cylindrical shaped lead projectiles, but L.G. loads and we know this because later, explaining further about his ammunition, he said that his cartridges contained eight-slug loads, which is the number of projectiles that an L.G. contains.

Now, no doubt cradling the shotgun between his knees, thumb on the safety catch, Corbett waited for the leopard. For a while the night was silent and there was no sign of movement on the part of the cat, no sounds at all, and he was beginning to wonder what the leopard's strategy was when he suddenly felt a gentle tug on the stems of the Blackthorn bushes tucked under his arms. He knew instantly that it was the leopard and that the animal had silently climbed part way up the bole of the tree behind him and was now trying to pull the thorn branches out of the way to get at him.

Corbett's quandary, now, was created by the fact that the cat had come up the tree from his rear and that because of the precariousness of his perch—he was using the Blackthorn stems to help keep his balance—he was unable to turn around and bring the shotgun to bear on the animal. So he stayed where he was, still and silent, waiting to see what the cat would do next.

The cat's next move was startling. The gentle pulling that had alerted Corbett to the fact that it was in the tree behind him now suddenly changed to violent tugs and these were accompanied by deep, angry growling on the part of the determined and fearless animal. Corbett, unable to see anything in the total darkness of the night and unable to move to bring his gun to bear on the leopard, was helpless. But he found some satisfaction in the growling for while the animal was doing this, expressing its anger, Corbett at least knew where it was. Previous to this, silent and invisible in the blackness of the night, it could have been anywhere and he was well aware that, perched as he was no more than fifteen feet above the ground, the leopard, if it felt it could do it from an unseen position, could reach his perch in a single bound.

Suddenly the leopard changed its tactics. It dropped from the tree behind him and made a rush at the goat and attacked it. The night was too dark for Corbett to see the cat as it passed beneath him but a thin starlight, just beginning to grow, enabled him to see the blurred outline of the white goat. When the sounds of the big cat's attack on the animal suggested to Corbett that it had been killed, and that there was a good chance that the cat was now standing over it, preparatory to carrying it off, he took aim at the general area centered on the vague white shape of the goat's body and pulled one trigger of his gun. The boom of the gun, heard by a hundred anxious villagers, was followed by a heavy grunt from the leopard and Corbett saw the white flash of its belly as it flipped over backwards. It was up in a flash, however, and, whirling, raced away, leaving the goat behind. He heard it go over the lip of the six-foot terrace that dropped from the field below his tree to the one below it. Then there was silence.

CHAPTER SIX

Corbett waited about ten minutes and then he heard his men calling out to him, to ask if it was safe for them to come down and get him. He felt that it was, as long as they stayed away from the lower field, where the leopard had gone, and so he called back, telling them to light pine torches—resin impregnated, green pine splinters—and come down to the tree.

His men soon arrived, accompanied by about twenty villagers bearing blazing pine torches and as they streamed down from the village Corbett shouted to them to stay on the village side of his tree, the upper side, and not to venture into the lower field.

Arriving at the tree they started to remove the Blackthorn branches to let Corbett down, only to find that the leopard's powerful tugging had locked the knots of the ropes that held them together. They had to be cut-reluctantly, for no villager will ever cut a valuable rope for the sake of a knot that can be undone by hand-and then Corbett was helped down from the tree. At once the men gathered around to ask him what had happened.

Corbett told them that he had hit the leopard and that it had dropped into the lower field and was probably wounded. He added that the prudent thing to do now was to wait until the morning light, and then go and look for it. But at this the villagers expressed disappointment and, with simple village logic told Corbett that if he had hit the animal with a bullet from a gun as powerful as his, it would surely now be dead. They asked Corbett to at least go to the edge of the next field and see if there was blood from a wound and

Corbett, knowing how they felt about this animal that had terrorized them for so long, though against his better judgement, agreed to do so.

The light from the pine torches lit up the field around the oak tree where the men were excitedly gathered. But the next field down, six feet below the level of the one they were standing in, was in darkness. So Corbett, believing that the cat might well be lying just under the lip of the next terrace, and aware of the great dangers involved in approaching a wounded leopard in the dark, gave the men very precise and explicit instructions. They were to stay behind him. They were to walk in line behind him, in single file. They were to hold their pine torches high over their heads and, no matter what happened, even if the leopard were to charge them, they were not to run away and leave him. Because if they did, he would be left in the dark, unable to see and, as a result, at the mercy of the leopard.

To all of these instructions the men agreed and when he was sure that they understood what they had to do, especially his order about not running away and leaving him in the dark, he took his place at the head of the line and, with the men silent and expectant behind him, their torches sending waves of flickering yellow light across the field, slowly and cautiously began to move forward.

Within a few yards they came to the dead goat and silently filed past it. Another few yards brought them close to the edge of the next field. Another few feet and they were almost at the lip of the terrace when, suddenly, to the horror of all, the leopard sprang up out of the darkness in front of them and with a series of deep, terrifying grunts, stood in full view. When it did Corbett's companions, their courage turned to water by the sight of the dreaded man-eater, to a man turned and ran for their lives, dropping their torches, shouting in terror and falling over one another in their haste to get away.

Fortunately for Corbett, some of the pine torches stayed lit when they were flung to the ground and this gave him just enough light to aim and fire a charge of pellets into the leopard's chest. He probably gave it both barrels; he does not say. But this is what is demanded in a confrontation with a wounded leopard in the dark of night at a distance of a few feet and so this is probably what he did. In any case the cat went down and stayed down and as far as Corbett was concerned, that was all that mattered.

At the sound of his shot the villagers halted in their headlong flight and turned back and Corbett, to ease the embarrassment they must have felt at the way they had behaved, just asked them quietly to find a bamboo pole and some rope, to carry the leopard back to the village. His main interest at that moment was a hot cup of his beloved tea, for the cold night air had brought on what he thought was another attack of his recurrent malaria and suddenly all that he wanted was to get back to his folding cot in the village, drink his tea, curl up in his blankets, and sleep.

So ended the bloody career of the dreaded man-eating leopard of Panar and the reign of terror that it established in the Panar River valley, one that lasted for ten years and brought an end, in the most horrible way, to the lives of over four hundred innocent people. The big cat that did this was given its name—the Panar man-eater—by the British authorities governing the area, long before Corbett hunted it. If it had not been so named Corbett might well have called it the Sanouli man-eater, after the village of Sanouli, where he hunted it and outwitted it, and, in a few desperate hours in the dark of night, defeated its attempts to add him to his list of victims.

The dak bungalow at Champawat where Corbett stayed for a few days while hunting the man-eater of Champawat.

The Champa river, at Champawat.

The hillside where Corbett shot the man-eater of Champawat and, center, the big black boulder where the tigress stood at bay and made her last stand.

The author sits in the precise place from where Corbett took his first shots at the Champawat man-eater.

The bungalow above the Champa river gorge where Corbett stayed for the final days of his hunt for the Champawat man-eater

The custodian of the gorge bungalow on the Champa river.

Champawat. A big village in Corbett's time; today it is a bustling city.

Chandra Shum Sher, ruler of Nepal, 1911, (with King George of England) whose refusal to help the people of Rupal, in Nepal's Dandeldura district, galvanized them into action...a massive beat with which they drove the Rupal man-eater into the Champawat area in Kumaon.

Hill country in the Dandeldura district of Far West Nepal, where the Rupal man-eater had its habitat.

Sanouli village in Tali Salan district (previously Rangun Patti) in Kumaon, where Corbett hunted the Panar man-eating leopard.

Window of a house at Sanouli. The Panar man-eater broke into several houses in Sanouli to get at its victims.

The Panar river, shallow in the winter months, may rise 15 feet in the monsoon, as is indicated by the high water mark.

An elderly lady of Sanouli who, born about 1910, knew about the Panar man-eater. She was the only one in the village who did so.

Sanouli villager, Karok Singh, who helped the author in his research at Sanouli and offered the use of his house.

Bahadur Singh Negi, headman of Sanouli, who welcomed the author with a gift of milk and then assisted in the research.

The author's Forty Pound tent and campsite on the bank of the Panar river.

The author sits in the tree from which Corbett shot the Panar maneater. Corbett: "...an old oak tree. On the underside of the trunk and about fifteen feet from the ground there was a branch...this branch, which was about a foot thick, offered a very uncomfortable and very unsafe seat..."

The author's porters, who came bundling into his tent when two leopards began calling, close by, in the night, in the Panar river valley.

Nanital, Corbett's summer home in Kumaon.

St. John's In The Wilderness chapel which was used by the Corbett family.

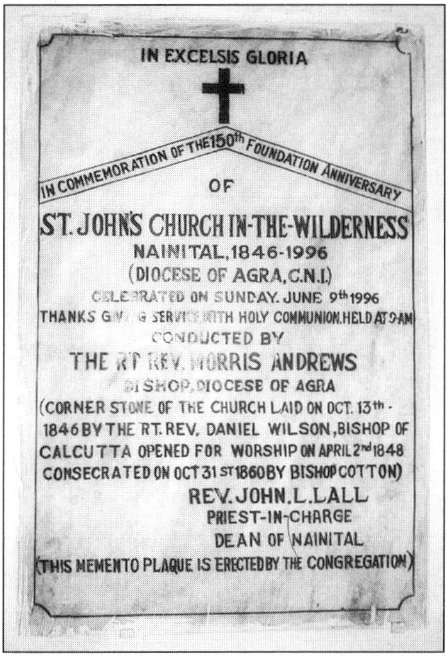

A plaque to commemorate the foundation of St. John's In The Wilderness

Corbett's metal boat, from which he fished on the lake at Nanital, lying outside his house in Nanital in 1990.

The author hunting tiger in the Nepal Terai in the fifties. The rifle is his .375 Holland and Holland.

Panwanoula dak bungalow where Corbett spent a night on the way to the Panar valley. Local petty official objecting angrily to author taking pictures of "thee prohibited government building."

Terai jungle morning.

Bees in a simul (silk cotton) tree in the Nepal Terai. Each comb contains multitudes of the little insects; they can be very dangerous if disturbed.

House at Dunaghat where Corbett camped while on his way from Pali to Champawat during the Champawat man-eater hunt.

The trail down from the Muktesar dak bungalow to where Corbett hunted the Muktesar man-eater. Note dense brush on either side.

Bahadur Singh, present day custodian of the Muktesar dak bungalow, whose grandfather helped carry the Muktesar tiger up from the Bulmaria stream, where it was shot, and skin it.

The Muktesar dak bungalow in 1990. A fine old British bulding in an excellent state of preservation.

BOOK FOUR

THE MAN-EATER OF TALLA DES.
1929

CHAPTER ONE

The year 1929 saw a number of man-eating tigers operating in two areas of Kumaon. There were five in all. Two of these was the Chowgarh tigress* and her big, pale colored cub, hunting and killing villagers in the Kala Agar region. The remaining three, another tigress with two big cubs, lived in the Talla Des district, just west of the Sarda river and not far from the Nepal border.

The Deputy Commissioner of Naini Tal in 1929 was Hamish (Ham) Vivian, a friend of Corbett and when Corbett was approached by him to look into the matter of the Chowgarh tigress, he immediately agreed to go after the man-eater. However, for reasons not recorded, the killings of the Chowgarh tigress and her cub seemed to ease off for a while and because of this Corbett decided to first tackle the problem of the Talla Des man-eater. And so he told Vivian that he would firstly go after the big cat that was the immediate problem of his counterpart in Almora, Bill Baynes, and then go after the Chowgarh tigers. This decision started him on the trail of the Talla Des man-eater.

**In regard to this lull in the killing cycle of the Chowgarh tigers see BOOK FIVE which contains a discussion of the hypothesis that the big, pale-colored cub of the Chowgarh man-eater took part in the killing of humans with its mother. The indications were that, although young, it was a powerful and active cat. If this was the case, then it may have been able to hunt and kill deer and other game and thus provide for itself and its mother. This would account for the break in the human killing cycle at Kala Agar, one that persuaded Corbett to postpone a hunt there until he had dealt with the Talla Des man-eater.*

Corbett set out for the Talla Des district on April 4th. He was not well. He had been with a shooting party at a place called Bindhukhera, twenty-five miles from his winter home at Kaladungi and towards the end of the shoot, while riding in a *howdah* on the back of a hunting elephant, one of the party, whom he does not name, accidentally fired his or her rifle close to his left ear, shattering his eardrum.

Initial treatment by a doctor at Kaladungi determined that the eardrum had burst and this was later confirmed by the Civil Surgeon at Naini Tal, a Colonel Barber. What both doctors probably suspected, but perhaps did not tell Corbett, was that the principal danger with the injury was the possibility of infection. Sure enough, the injury did become infected and an abscess formed, something that in those days, long before antibiotics, was something that was crudely treated with hot poultices and steaming potions.

Corbett stayed at home for a while and there is no doubt that his family, in this case his two sisters, must have looked after him. Then, either because he was embarrassed by his infliction and the attention it demanded, or perhaps because he was tough enough to be able to ignore it, he decided to leave and go off on his own into his beloved forests.

He may have needed an excuse to explain his desire to get away. If he did, he had one in the next man-eater on his list, the big cat that lived in Bill Baines' administrative area, the Talla Des hills. Whatever the reason, his attitude is a superb example of what American's like to call true grit, in that, sick, with an abscess in his ear that must have been very painful, and unable to hear properly, he nevertheless decided, not just to go off and suffer out his misery alone but also to use the time usefully, as he had done for so much of his life, in the service of others, in this case the hill people whom he loved. And, as though fate was watching him and wanted to give a spur to his intentions, on the day he left Naini Tal, the Talla Des man-eater killed what was believed to be its one hundred and fiftieth victim, a boy, near the village of Talla Kote, in the Talla Des district.

Leaving home, Corbett took six men with him and together they walked from Naini Tal down to the railhead at Kathgodam, on the edge of the Indian plains. From there they planned to go by train to Tanakpur, a big sprawling Indian town on the Sarda River, directly opposite the town of Bramadeo Mundi in Nepal. From Tanakpur they would go north, on foot, to the Talla Des district.

Tanakpur is where, in the fifties and sixties, I used to pick up my safari supplies; gasoline, kerosene, rice, sugar, tea, vegetables, fruit, rope for *machan* building, camp tools and that kind of thing. In those days it was, and indeed still is, a typical, small Indian city, with mean houses leaning into narrow alleyways that lead to fetid pools, winding, constricted streets littered with trash and animal dung and teeming with people, wandering cows and pariah dogs, and lined with dilapidated tin roofed shacks serving as shops. In other words, as Indian cities go, just another Indian city, with nothing remarkable about and little to separate it from thousand of similar sprawling centers of human habitation in the torrid sub continent. However, in the realms of the jungle lore of far west Nepal, and from the days of the Raj, it happens to be associated with an extraordinary wildlife legend and for this its name is remembered, at least among hunters and naturalists. It is a legend that tells of an epic fight between two tigers and an elephant.

The story goes that the British Deputy Commissioner of that time, a time many years before Corbett's day, was awakened in the night by his servants telling him that there was a great fight going on in a dry part of the Sarda riverbed below the town. Apparently two hungry tigers had attacked an elephant and were endeavoring to kill it and eat it. It is not certain how much of the fight the Deputy Commissioner was able to see in the dark of the night. But next morning, from the sign on the ground, it was apparent to him that what took place was in effect a savage battle between the big cats and the lone pachyderm. The tigers succeeded in killing the elephant and after eating their fill, crossed the river and went back into the jungles of Nepal.

In Corbett's day there was no direct railway line from Kathgodam to Tanakpur and so, to get to his destination, he was forced to take an all-night, round-about route, with midnight changes at the old British cantonment of Bareilly and the town of Pilibhit. He might have stopped at either place, particularly Bareilly, a fairly substantial city. But I can understand why he would not have stayed at Pilibhit, a sleazy, flyblown little town with little to justify its existence, a place of which I myself have anything but pleasant memories.

Some years ago I took the same route from Kathgodam, hoping to get to Tanakpur next day. But the Kathgodam train was delayed as a result of which I missed my Pilibhit to Bareilly connection and was told by the Pilibhit stationmaster that the next train would be at nine the following morning.

I had three men with me and at first we considered just camping on the station platform for the night. But some festival was taking place down the line and the station was packed with hundreds of people waiting to catch the next day's train. An alternative was to head out into the country and find a field and put up a quick fly camp. But it was raining heavily and so when the station master suggested that we go to a hotel in the city, we took his advice and went trudging off through the dark, muddy streets to an establishment called the Ashoka, a big, old, converted private house with the rooms set around an odorous and filthy courtyard. I paid the reception desk clerk, a surly *babu*, for two rooms, one for the men and one for myself, and collecting room keys we hiked up to the third floor.

The rooms were filthy, with the carcasses of long dead cockroaches littering the floors and they smelled strongly of human urine. They also seethed with mosquitoes. But each had a light-a single bulb hanging on a piece of wire-a ceiling fan and a bed and though the mattress was lumpy and the threadbare sheet that covered it was stained with the leavings of previous guests and gray with age, that did not matter. We were happy to be out of the rain and all we wanted to do was sleep.

Telling the men I would see them in the morning I locked the door of my room, turned the fan full on and, stripping off to shorts and an undershirt, for it was hot, switched off the light and lay down on the bed to sleep.

I think it was about half an hour later. I may have dozed but suddenly I found myself being bitten on the sides of my arms and the soles of my feet. The bites were familiar; typical, stinging mosquito bites. But above me the fan whirled at speed and in all of my experience in mosquito country I have always found that the down draft of a fan will defeat the attacks of most of the insidious little pests. So I was very surprised to find that I was getting bitten. Because, though the Indian mosquito is tenacious and determined when it smells human blood, its wing structure is not designed to allow it to fly well in fast moving air or to home in on chosen targets with any degree of accuracy.

I surmised therefore that I was wrong about the source of the bites and that they must be coming from bedbugs, something common to Indian small town hotels. So I swung out of the bed and turned on the light, to see an extraordinary sight.

The bed sheet was ringed, all around where I had been lying, with hundreds and hundreds of mosquitoes. They were crawling across the sheet like a black, invading army, battling the downdraft of the fan and slowly advancing towards where I had just been lying. Looking down I saw that the wooden legs of the bed were also covered with the creatures, all slowly crawling upwards and then I realized what their tactics were.

Unable to land on their target of choice because of the fan's downdraft, the cunning little winged terrorists had devised a clever alternative. At first they circled around and let the fan draft push them down to the floor. There they landed and, turning towards the bed, worked their way, on foot to the nearest leg. Reaching it, they simply climbed it, moving steadily upwards until they got to the edge of the bed and the sheet, which was tucked into and under the lumpy mattress. When they reached the sheet they met the full force of the fan and from there on it was a desperate struggle to prevent being blown away. It was incredible to see them, digging in their tiny legs, gripping the sheet, being lashed from side to side by the fan's downdraft, falling, getting back up, being blown away, returning again, to fight their way, slowly, inch by inch, towards their chosen target. Me.

About this time I heard my men muttering from the other room and I guessed that they were encountering the same attack. But there was nothing we could do about it. For myself, I took off the filthy sheet and wrapped it around me and tucked it under my feet and turned off the light. From time to time I rolled back and forth on the bed, in the darkness, as I discovered next morning, crushing to death hundreds of the insidious little attackers.

And so we spent a miserable night in the urine stinking inn and left next morning, covered with mosquito bites, any one of which could have been from a malaria bearing mosquito. Corbett does not recount staying the night at Pilibhit. I think I know why.

CHAPTER TWO

Corbett, who did not miss his connection at Pilibhit, arrived at Tanakpur at noon the day after leaving Naini Tal. He went to the Tanakpur *dak* bungalow where his men cooked a meal and after they had eaten, set off on a trail up the Sarda river, intending to cover the twenty-four miles to a guest bungalow, at Kaladunga, some time that night.

Nowadays there is a motor road running north out of Tanakpur. In Corbett's day there was only a trail and this ran from the edge of the city to the foot of a high hill called Punagiri. There it divided, one arm going up the hill to the Punagiri temples and then circling back down to Kaladunga. The other went directly up the west side of the river to Kaladunga.*

The river trail that Corbett took and that I hiked on when I did my research on the Chuka and Thak man-eaters, (see BOOKS EIGHT and NINE) follows the alignment of an old tramway line put in by a British government timber contractor, Mr. J. P. Collier. The contract, between the British and the Maharaja of Nepal of that time, called for one million cubic feet of *sal* lumber to be cut and hauled out of Nepal and into India; to do this Collier built a tramline that ran for four miles up the west side of the Sarda. Where the line ended he laid steel cables across the river, set at an angle to deflect and gather in the floating logs which were dropped in from

---

**Kaladunga, on the Sarda river, north of Tanakpur, is often confused with Kaladungi, Corbett's winter home, due south of Naini Tal.*

the other side. At the point where the logs were put in, on the Nepal side, he continued the tramline into Nepal, running it all the way, west to east, through the present day White Grass Plains Wildlife reserve, my old hunting grounds of the fifties and sixties, to the Taru village of Hirapur, where it came to an end.

When the contract was completed the line was abandoned. The steel rails were collected and probably taken back into India and reused elsewhere and the line was closed. The little steam engines which hauled the logs on flat cars from Hirapur* were also all taken away with the exception of one which can still be seen sitting at the west end of the Sarda canal dam-the Boom-at Banbasa.

The little embankment along which the railway ran, from eight to ten feet in height, can still be found in the forests and grassland of the White Grass Plains and the Taru people, if asked about it, will tell you that it is from *collia sahib*'s railway. A better memento to Collier, however, is probably the beautiful bungalow he designed and built at Kaladunga, and in which he and his wife based during the work. It still stands, high above the Sarda and from its front porch there is a lovely view, eastward, into the valley of the Rangun river, in Nepal. (For further information on Collier's bungalow at Kaladunga see the book's EPILOGUE.)

Corbett and his men walked sixteen miles up the Sarda river gorge on the first day out of Tanakpur. With the day coming to an end, he made camp under a rock shelf—a sensible thing to do in any gorge where steep sides present the danger of falling rocks—and there he and his men spent the night.

**Mr. Nar Bahadur Bisht, one of the original landlords of Hirapur, the man who told me about the Rupal man-eater (see BOOK ONE) knew Collier and remembered he and his wife coming into Hirapur in a special railway carriage that Collier must have used as a mobile office and living quarters. He recalls Collier's English wife as a tall lady wearing long white dresses and high laced boots. Before he passed away, recently, he told me an amusing anecdote about Collier. Someone in his family asked the Britisher if he could bring them a .12 gauge shotgun and it seems that there may have been some confusion as to whether Collier thought the request was for a .12 gauge shotgun or twelve shotguns. So he brought them twelve shotguns, one of which is still in the possession of the Bisht family in Mahendranagar.*

Next day he started early, passing through Kaladunga and the riverside village of Chuka, his goal for the end of the day being the crest of a high ridge on the other side of which lay the Talla Des District. A little north of Sem he left the main Sarda river trail and cut northwest, up the valley of the Surya Khola, to its upper end, from where the trail climbed very steeply to a small, unnamed hamlet. When he reached there, although the hamlet was a thousand feet below the crest of the ridge, he and his men, tired after the long climb up the very steep trail in the hot April sun, stopped and spent the night. After a meal he got his men bedded down in one of the village houses while he spent the night in the open, his camp bed set up beside a little spring that provided water for the two families whose members comprised the hamlet. For company he had an oil lamp and his rifle, in this case a Rigby Mauser .275 which I believe he purchased from the famous old British gun shop of Mantons, in Calcutta.

Corbett could have heard about the man-eater's latest kill when he was in Tanakpur. Bill Baynes may have wired him; there was a telegraph line connecting Tanakpur with Naini Tal at that time. In any case, he now formulated a hunting plan based around this kill and decided that his first step would be to find out where the boy had been taken and start from there. He would do this because the man-eater, if undisturbed, would probably lie up near the kill after eating from it, something that would contribute to his hunting plan in that it would reduce the area he would have to search. It would also give him a chance of pinning down the big cat's hunting routes which, her killing pattern indicated, she had been using for many years.*

**Tigers do not migrate and if left undisturbed and with the basic necessities of survival, which are food, water, cover and space, will stay in the same area for years on end. When I hunted in the White Grass Plains in the fifties and sixties, I knew of a tigress that had a lair in a patch of elephant grass in a place called Sundarijhal, close to the Bauni river. We did not hunt her, my trophy collecting clients preferring males to females. The bones of domestic buffalo, wild boar and swamp deer, littering her lair, indicated that she carried many of her kills back to it to eat them. She lived there, undisturbed, for at least ten years, during which time she produced at least two sets of cubs.*

Next morning Corbett was up early and after a wash at the spring, and something to eat, he cleaned and oiled his rifle and set off, telling his men to follow him. Because of the presence of the man-eater, communication between villages had virtually ceased and so the people of the hamlet where he spent the night did not know of the latest kill, or where it had taken place. So, taking a chance, he started his search by climbing up to the saddle immediately above the hamlet. Crossing the saddle he found a forest road. The road ran east west and knowing that to the east it could only go as far as the Sarda, he left a stick sign on it to inform his men which way he had gone and started in that direction. He intended, if he found nothing of interest to the east, to go at least to the end of the road, which he probably guessed would be high above the Sarda, rather than down at the river itself, and then cut back and go westward.

He walked east on the ridge road for an hour and came to a village named Tamali. Here the villagers told him that the man-eater had been operating in the immediate vicinity for from eight to ten years and the last person killed had been a woman, taken in a field below the village, on the 20th of the previous month. They implored Corbett to stay with them, to protect them from the man-eater and had the woman's death been more recent, suggesting the possibility of the man-eater lying up near the village, he might have done so. But the killing of the boy, wherever it was, was still only a few days old and knowing that concentrating on this would give him a better chance of closing with the big cat, he left them and started back, west, on the forest road. When he reached the point where he had first come onto the road, after crossing the saddle, he removed the stick sign he had left for his men and replaced it with another one, informing them that he had now gone west.

CHAPTER THREE

Corbett walked west for four miles, to where the forest road turned north and made its way across the upper part of the watershed of one of the tributaries of the Lohaghat river. There he came to another village, which he called Talla Kote, where he was told by the headman that two days previously, on April 5th, a woman had been killed and taken away by the man-eater. He was also told that the villagers, acting on the orders of Baynes, the Deputy Commissioner of their district, had not disturbed the woman's body, but had left it for the *shikari sahib* whom, they had been informed, was coming to hunt the dreaded man-eater.

While Corbett was making his way to Talla Kote, a group of some thirty men had gone out from the village to look for the body of the woman, the man-eater's latest victim. With them was a young man of about seventeen, whose name was Dungar Singh; the victim was his mother. Soon after Corbett arrived at the village they returned, to tell him that all they had been able to find of the woman's remains were her teeth. However, knowing through Baynes' orders that Corbett was coming, they had built a *machan* at the place where the big cat had eaten the woman. When they said this, young Dungar Singh stepped forward and told Corbett that he would lead him there.

Corbett, admiring the young man's courage, agreed to let him be his guide and a little later they left the village together and, accompanied by a group of men and women, made their way to a narrow saddle below the village, one that marked the upper end of two long, deep valleys. The one on the western side fell away to the Ladhya river and the one to the east dropped down towards the Sarda.*

At the saddle the party halted and turning to the left, eastward, Corbett's young guide, Dungar Singh, pointed out a place about a thousand feet below them where his mother, cutting grass for live-stock in the company of some other women, had been killed by the man-eater. He then pointed out a tree under which the scouting party of men had found her only remains, her teeth, when they went to look for her. And he told Corbett something interesting, something that people who live in forested hill country notice and recognize, which was that when they were on their way down to search for his mother both a Langur monkey and a Ghoral-the little goat antelope of the hills-had called in alarm.

Corbett, with his mastery of jungle lore, would have quickly analyzed the calling of the two animals. A Ghoral may call in alarm on seeing a person approaching but a Langur will not. As both will call on seeing a big cat, either a tiger or a leopard, Corbett immediately surmised that the two animals, and certainly the Langur, had seen the tigress on the move; he also would have guessed that the party of men, coming down the hill, were what had disturbed it. This meant that the big cat, its belly still full, was probably lying up in the vicinity of the kill.

Corbett immediately decided to go down the hill to where the woman had been killed. When he advised Dungar Singh of his intentions the young man immediately volunteered to come with him. Telling Corbett to follow him, he led the way back up towards the village and from there to a goat track that led down into the valley.

**In his writings Corbett sometimes calls this beautiful western river the Sarda, other times the Kali, or again the Mahakali. In actual fact all three names are used. Kali seems to be the name more commonly used in Nepal while Sarda is the name more frequently heard among the hill people of Kumaon.*

Corbett started down the goat track with Dungar Singh and had gone a short distance when he heard two men following him. Looking around he saw that one of them was carrying a shotgun. He was not very happy about having them accompany him, especially as one of them was wearing heavy and noisy boots. But he allowed them to come and the four of them had walked about four hundred yards down into the valley when suddenly Dungar Singh whirled around and looked back up towards the saddle they had just left.

On the saddle a group of men were standing and gesticulating and as soon as young Singh saw them he motioned Corbett and the others to wait and keep very quiet. Then, cupping his hand to his ear, he listened carefully to what one of the men, apparently his brother, had to say. When he had finished listening he turned to Corbett and no doubt in what was great excitement told him that his bother said that there was something red lying in the sun in an abandoned field below them.

To Corbett 'something red' meant the possibility of a tiger, for in bright sunlight the black bars of a tigers stripes tend to visually fade and the predominant color that strikes the eye is the deep, orange-red of its coat. Corbett must have felt a surge of excitement at the possibility of the man-eater being close and no doubt his immediate reaction was to move quickly down towards where the villagers had seen the red object, and investigate it. However, assessing the situation with the calmness that has his trademark, his first thoughts were for the safety of the two men who had followed him and, no doubt, where their shotgun was concerned, his own safety. So the first thing he did was to relieve them of the shotgun and take them to a nearby tree; he ordered them to climb into it and to stay there until he came to get them. They did so, willingly, and Corbett, no doubt with smile, noticed that with the discovery the reddish object lying in the field below, and the possibility of it being the tigress, their eagerness to come with him suddenly seemed to have evaporated.

CHAPTER FOUR

The goat track that Corbett and the men had followed down from the village led to a terraced field. When Dungar Singh told Corbett that from its lower end they should be able to see down into the abandoned field where his bother had said the red object was, Corbett, telling the boy to stay close, started down the inner side of the field, keeping close to its terraced upper wall. When he and the guide got to the end of the field, they went down on their hands and knees and crawled to its lip, on which there was short growth of grass. Peering through the grass they looked down, to see two tigers lying on a patch of grass in the bright sunlight, about a hundred and twenty yards away.

People who have read of Corbett's exploits talk about his luck. He did have extraordinary luck at times, there is no doubt about that and this appears to be one of those times. But whereas some people deserve luck and others don't, Corbett certainly did. For luck in reality is the sum total of many things coming together in the right place and at the right time, things to which it is actually possible to contribute. And with Corbett those contributing factors included his immense knowledge of the wildlife of the hills and forests where he lived and hunted, and his superb and unequaled ability to interpret the jungle lore-the sounds, the smells, the ground sign-of their habitat. Now, all this had come together to give him, on the very first day of his hunt, a chance of coming to grips with a clever and elusive man-eater that had terrorized the hill people of the Talla Des district for eight years.

The two tigers that Corbett and young Singh saw below them, both of them sleeping in the sun, lay about ten feet apart. The one nearest had its back towards them and the other had is stomach facing them. Corbett decided to shoot them both,* taking two shots as fast as he could and hoping that the smack of a bullet going into one, rather than the crack of the rifle, would give him his second shot before the other animal was up and away.

Corbett decided his first shot would be at the cat furthest away from him and aligning the sights of his .275 on the heart area of its rib cage, he carefully squeezed the trigger. The cat he fired at, mortally hit, did not move but the other one was up in flash and in a single bound left the field and jumped up on to a five foot bank, where it stood, broadside on, looking back at its companion. This, of course, was a bad mistake on its part and Corbett did not hesitate to take advantage of it. He slammed another round into the firing chamber of the .275 and fired again and was delighted to see the second animal flip over backwards and fall into a depression behind the bank.

At the same time, keeping his eyes on both the dead tiger and the place where the second tiger had disappeared, he saw a movement in the weeds at the edge of the field. Not waiting to see what it was, but suspecting that it might be a third tiger, he thumbed the sights of the .275 up to two hundred yards and waited for the ani-

---

**As an experienced hunter, Corbett would obviously have been concerned about taking two shots at two tigers lying so close together. What would have worried him would have been the effect of the sound of his bullet, hitting one, on its companion, and how quickly that companion would be aroused to where, with the speed that only a big cat can generate, it would be up and away before he could get a shot at it. He was probably not too worried about the second cat's reaction to the crack of his rifle and how this might alert it to his presence, because he was a hundred a twenty yards away from and above the animals and tigers, like other animals, seem to be unable to pinpoint gunshot sound. I have noticed this in my own shooting and I think that it may have to do with the shattering blast of sound that a modern big game rifle produces when it fires, as well as the echoes it sets up, especially in hill country, sounds that are totally foreign to the hearing of wild animals. A big cat, tiger or leopard, that can pinpoint with great accuracy anything from the rustle of a leaf to the sound of a deer calling from a quarter of a mile away, does not seem to have the same ability with the sound of a rifle.*

mal to break cover. It soon did, going fast across the face of the hill and when he saw that it was indeed a third tiger, he waited until he had a clear, broadside shot at it and then gave it his third bullet. At the shot, one that under the circumstances—at a moving target at a distance of close to two hundred yards—proved Corbett to be a first class marksman, the tiger's legs collapsed underneath it and it slid to a halt. Then gravity, combined with the angle of the hill where it fell, started it sliding downwards and it did this until brought to rest by a small oak tree at the edge of a rock cliff. There its body lodged, jammed against the tree, one half of it hanging on one side of the tree, the remainder on the other.

Corbett watched the cat for a while, finger on the trigger of his rifle, ready for a third shot. When it did not move, but remained draped across the little tree, he relaxed, satisfied that the animal was dead and what mainly contributed to his thinking in this direction was very probably the way the cat's legs collapsed underneath, suddenly, completely, when it went down. Because of this he may be excused to some extent by what he did now which was to ignore the unwritten law of shooting large dangerous game,* especially big cats, which says, simply, that unless you are absolutely certain that it is dead, you shoot it again, and again, until you are.

**In big game hunting there is a procedure called W. A. A. P. The initials stand for Wounded Animals Approach Procedure. In my book, GONE ARE THE DAYS, the procedure is thoroughly explained and the explanation is accompanied by examples of the fatalities that can occur when it is ignored. The most important part of the rulings of WAAP is the admonition about shooting large wild animals, especially big cats, which emphatically demands that they always be shot a second time. All cats are hard to kill and even when shot through the head, or the heart, with a heavy rifle, can still sometimes summon up an adrenaline rush that will arouse them out of near death comas and bring them down on the hunter in a fury of rage and destruction. Corbett should have known better than to do what he did with the third tiger of his otherwise incredible day's shooting, which was, after it went down, just to sit and watch it and congratulate himself on his success. He was to regret his mistake, one that in the ensuing days very nearly cost him his life.*

CHAPTER FIVE

Three shots, three tigers down for the count. Corbett could not believe his luck. In addition, he was quite certain that at least one of the cats he had shot was the Talla Des man-eater, because there were not a lot of tigers in the hills in those days and here were three operating in an area where there had been a large number of human kills across many years. He quickly guessed that one of the animals was a tigress and the other two her cubs, because tigers are solitary animals, living alone for the most part and usually only coming together only to mate. A tiger living with more than one other tiger will nearly always be a female with cubs.

Now, exhilarated by his success, he called the two men who had followed him from the village down from the tree and, lighting a cigarette, turned to talk to them and to Dungar Singh. As he did, the big cat hanging across the oak sapling slowly began to move. Corbett later surmised that blood may have drained into its head and shoulders and tipped the balance that held it draped across the little tree. Whatever it was, the animal suddenly slid off the tree and down a grassy incline and over the edge of the cliff. As it did, Corbett, quite certain that the cat was dead, threw up his rifle and in a moment of elation fired a quick shot at it as it fell through the air. He missed, and the big cat dropped into space. He and the men heard a thud as it hit the hillside below the cliff and then there was silence.

Corbett may not have known that he missed that last shot. But he did not seem to care because he was confidant that the big cat was dead. So now he finished his cigarette and started down the hill to check on the other two tigers, especially the one that had fallen into the depression behind the bank, the only one that until then had not been visible.

He was halfway down the hill when suddenly Dungar Singh called out in alarm from behind him. Swinging around he raised his rifle, half expecting another tiger. Seeing him to do this the young man, pointing up the hillside, shouted out to him that there was indeed another tiger in addition to which it was the one which had fallen over the little cliff.

Hardly believing what he was seeing, Corbett looked up the hill. On it, at a distance of about four hundred yards and going diagonally across it, was the tigress. She was moving very slowly and looking at her Corbett saw a big patch of blood on her shoulder where his shot, the one that had dropped her like a stone, had hit her. Running to a small sapling Corbett flipped up the three hundred yard leaf on the sights of the .275, grabbed the sapling with his left hand and then, laying the rifle across his lower left arm, waited until the tigress stopped to rest. When she did he took a very careful shot and when he saw a little puff of dust go up from behind the animal, and watched it lurch forward and continue on across the hill, he concluded that he had missed.

Another shot was now the obvious thing. But he had only brought five rounds with him that day and this last shot left him with no ammunition. Now, in what must have been exasperation with his impetuousness at having taken that flying shot at the big cat when it was dropping off the cliff, Corbett watched the man-eater slowly walk away, to disappear within a few minutes over the top of the hill.

CHAPTER SIX

Next morning Corbett skinned the cubs of the tigress. When they were skinned out he opened up the bodies to see what was in their stomachs and in doing so found out why only the teeth of the man-eater's last victim had been found, and nothing else. The tigress and her cubs had consumed all of the body and then the cubs had torn the woman's blood soaked clothing into strips and eaten that too.*

In the afternoon he went out again to look for the tigress. When the animal had disappeared, after his last shot, he noticed that she was heading in the direction of a patch of scrub and he spent some time searching this in an unsuccessful attempt to find her. In the evening he returned to his camp.

Next day he took his own men to the area and, assisted by some of the villagers, tried to beat her out. To make it safe for the men, he had them just throw rocks into the scrub from the comparative safety of a nearby hill and not enter it. But this proved unsuccessful; if the tigress was in the scrub she refused to be beaten out and so Corbett sent the men home.

He spent the next three days searching for sign of the tigress and an account of that search, with much of the wisdom of Corbett's

---

******The cubs of a tigress that killed our camp cook in the White Grass Plains, in December, 1999, did the same thing, eating most of his clothing. The few small pieces of his shirt and trousers that I later found at the place where they ate him were perforated with dozens of little holes, teeth marks of the cubs. For the full story of this, see, in BOOK TEN, Mangal, A Jungle Tragedy.*

knowledge of jungle lore woven into it, is well worth reading in his own story of the hunt. During this time, however, his ear began to seriously bother him. The abscess which had developed inside it began to fester and swell and soon it reached proportions where he seems to have been in constant pain. The ear and the whole side of his head became massively swollen to the point where his right eye was almost completely closed, restricting his vision. He could not eat and was existing on milky tea, and little else.

One evening, it might have been around April 10th, three days after he had shot the man-eater's cubs, the pressure inside his head reached such proportions that he felt as though it was going to burst. His fear, of course, was that the abscess would burst inwards, into his brain. When the intense pain reached a point where he felt this was imminent, he called for his men and told them that he was going to go out into the forest and stay there and wait for whatever was going to happen. He drank a cup of tea and said that if he was not back by the following evening they were to pack up his things and go back to Naini Tal. Saying this he picked up his rifle and walked out of the camp into the darkness, leaving his men, most of them believed that they might never see him again, standing staring after him.

There was a moon, nearly full, and this provided a small measure of safety. For Corbett, like any good hunter, could shoot in moonlight as well as in daylight. But he must have been desperate with pain to go out at night like this in an area where he knew a hungry man-eater was lying up. Hungry, because now, with the last human kill having taken place before Corbett arrived in the area, she would not have eaten for at least five days.

Not long after he left camp Corbett picked up fresh pug marks of the tigress. He followed these for a while and then, coming to a big tree that had a family of Langurs sleeping in the upper branches, sat down to rest, knowing that the big gray monkeys would warn him if the cat came around. Sure enough, he had only been there a while when one of the long tailed simians called out in alarm. Corbett was instantly alert, or as alert as he could be with his head pounding and with shooting pains darting through it.

Soon, as the Langur had predicted, the tigress came into view and for a moment or two he considered taking a shot at it. But the cat was too far away, a hundred yards or more, and in his very shaky and unstable condition he considered this a little too far. As he watched, the cat lay down in the moonlight to rest. She lay still for half an hour and then got up and started to walk away. When she did Corbett also got up and started to follow her, hoping to get close enough for shot. To do this he moved forward every time the cat disappeared from view and then froze when she, and he, were visible to each other. Suddenly the cat dropped into a shallow ravine. When she did this Corbett ran forward silently, bent over to keep his profile low. This should have brought him to within shooting distance of the big cat. Instead, it aggravated the pressure of the abscess in his ear and suddenly he was overcome with nausea and dizziness. Looking around he saw two oak saplings in front of him, growing close together, with intermingled branches. Propping his rifle against one of them he climbed into them to a height of about ten feet and settled himself into the mass of branches. Folding his arms in front of him and resting them on his knees, he bent his head forward to rest on them. As he did so the abscess burst, sending a stream of pus and bloody water out through his nose and ear. But thankfully not, as he had feared, into his brain.

CHAPTER SEVEN

Corbett called this period of his illness his 'bad time'. In actual fact it was much more than that; it was an extremely dangerous time for him. Medically he should have been in a hospital. Instead, sick and in constant pain, he was out in remote, high hill country far from any possibility of medical care and, in addition, unbelievably, spending his time hunting a man-eater! Why he did this we will never truly know, although we can surmise that, sick as he was, he just did not want to be a burden on his family and that if his illness was going to kill him, which it certainly would have if the abscess had burst into his brain, he wanted to be allowed the quiet dignity of dying alone, deep in the forest that he loved and far away from grieving friends and relatives.

Corbett stayed in his little natural *machan* in the oak saplings through the night. Next morning, exhausted, but feeling a hundred per cent better, he returned to his camp. There he found that his faithful Gharwal men, ignoring the safety of a house provided for them by the headman of the village, had sat up, outside, all through the hours of darkness, waiting for him.

As soon as he had had some tea, water for which his men had kept on the boil for him all night, Corbett went and laid down in his tent. He slept for hours, until he was awakened by the voices of the villagers talking with his men. He heard someone say something about goats being killed and getting up, called to find out what was happening. He was quickly told that while he had been sleeping the tigress had attacked and killed six goats not far from the village.* Seeing Dungar Singh among the group he asked him if he knew where this had happened and when the young man answered in the affirmative, he picked up his rifle and told him to lead the way to the place of the killing.

Corbett had shot the big cubs of the man-eater, and wounded their mother in the valley that dropped from the saddle beyond the village, eastward, down towards the Sarda river. The goats, he was told, had been killed in the opposite valley, the one that fell away to the west, towards the Ladhya river. Dungar Singh now led him into this valley, down a winding goat track, across a stream and to a flat, open area intersected by a small rock ridge. Beyond the ridge was a hollow and in it were three dead goats. Dungar Sign told him that the tigress had attacked and killed six in all but that the goat herders, running for their lives when she appeared, had managed to pick up three of the dead animals and carry them back with them to the village.

Corbett, accompanied by his brave young guide, stopped to survey the scene and as they were standing there they both heard a *Kaleege* pheasant calling. The *Kaleege* is the common Silver Pheasant of the hill country and, like others of its family, will call in alarm at the sight of a cat. Hearing the pheasant calling, Corbett immediately guessed that it had seen the tigress and after getting young Singh to point out exactly where the calls were coming from—for the hearing in his left ear was not yet back to normal and one needs two ears to be able to accurately pinpoint sound—he told the young man to leave him and go straight back to the village.

Later Corbett found out that the man-eater did something very unusual on this night, something that tigers almost never do. She circled the village and then actually went into it, hunting through the darkness for a human victim. My guess is that as it was now five days, possibly six, since she had last eaten, that it was severe hunger that made her do this. I can only surmise that Corbett's courageous men, sitting outside all night, must have kept a big fire going and stayed together and stayed close to it. Otherwise she might have got one of them. 'Almost never' is wording worth keeping in mind in regard to the behavior of tigers. They do have regular and known patterns of behavior, this we know. But they can also at times be very unpredictable and the action of the Talla Des man-eater, in actually going into a village, is an example of this.

As soon as his guide was gone Corbett looked around for a tree into which to climb and wait for the tigress. He had no doubt that she was coming back. She was hungry, of that he was certain. Killing domestic animals like this, in the middle of the day-an unusual action for a tiger-confirmed this. Again, the only reason she had left after killing the goats was probably the shouts of the herders and they had now departed the scene, leaving it quiet and undisturbed, something she would note.

Looking around for a tree to climb Corbett was unable to find anything suitable. There were some fine, big trees close by. But they were pines, with smooth boles devoid of any lower branches and thus next to impossible to climb. The alternative was to find some brush and there was some in the area of sufficient density to offer him some concealment. But it was now mid afternoon and Corbett was thinking ahead, to the coming of night. On the ground, in daylight, well armed with a rifle with which he could hit just about anything he aimed at, he would have been comparatively safe. But as soon as night fell, if he had not disposed of the tigress by then, being on the ground would be very dangerous.

Looking around Corbett noticed two rocks, a big one and a small one, that formed part of the rock ridge running across the flat area above where the goats lay. Inspecting them quickly he found that if he sat on the smaller one, the larger concealed most of his upper body. Moving quickly to them he sat down to wait for the tigress to appear.

He had been in position just a few minutes when two Himalayan Blue magpies appeared. They quickly spotted the dead goats and after carefully inspecting the surrounding area, came in to feed. They were joined soon afterwards by a King vulture, which came down and landed in a nearby tree.

Corbett describes the King vulture as usually being one of the first of the various species of hill vultures to find a kill. The reason for this, he states, is the bird's small size in comparison to the larger size of the other species. This necessitates it being first at a kill; if it is not, it will quickly be shouldered aside by other, larger birds and, in a world where eating is survival, left to go hungry.

What he does not mention about the little bird is the delightful legend that surrounds it. The Taru people of the Terai call the King vulture the Raj Gid, "*raj*" meaning king and "*gid*" meaning vulture. If you ask them why it is so named they will tell you that it is indeed a king in its own right because if it is late coming to a kill, the other scavengers, even the jackals, though they have arrived before it, will all sit back and wait for his majesty to eat first. An amusing little belief. But in reality, a myth.

Corbett was especially glad to see the magpies on the kill. Sharp eyed, very alert birds, they would be on the lookout for the tigress and might well see it approaching before he did. Sure enough, after eating on one of the goats for about half an hour the magpies, to the accompaniment of new alarm calls from a *Kaleege* pheasant, suddenly left the kills and flew away. As they did, the weather changed, with heavy cloud rolling down across the hills and reducing the light.

Within minutes of the weather change Corbett spotted the tigress slowly approaching through the pines along the top of a twenty foot high bank. When she came into line with where he was sitting, hunched down behind the rock and with only his head and shoulders visible to her, the big cat lay down. She was sixty yards away.

When she lay down the cat presented a fair shot for Corbett. But a full view of her was blocked by a big pine that obscured much of her body and rather than take a shot at her head, a small target in the poor light at sixty yards, Corbett waited for her to get up and move away from the tree. She did this within a few minutes, rising and standing to look down at the dead goats, broadside on, and thus presenting him with the target that he wanted. He did not wait, and getting his sights aligned on her heart area as quickly as he could, squeezed the trigger.

At the sound of the shot the cat leapt forward, racing past the goats and within seconds had disappeared from view. Corbett, seeing a puff of dust rise from the ground behind her—the impact of his bullet into the dirt—and thinking that he had missed her, was devastated. But he quickly recovered and, angry at himself for having missed what should have been a perfect shot, jumped to his feet and went racing after her.

Corbett ran for several minutes in the direction that the tigress had gone. Then he heard a Ghoral call in alarm and stopped to try and pinpoint it, to determine if it had seen the tigress and, if so, where she might be. As he was doing this he heard men shouting and looking back up towards the saddle below the village, saw a group of men standing and waving their arms and pointing. They were pointing ahead of him and he quickly realized that from their elevated position on the saddle, not only could they see down into the brush ahead of him but that they had seen the tigress. He did not hesitate, but ran forward again, following a small footpath. As he did he came across fresh blood sign, blood from the tigress, on the ground.

Now that he had a blood trail to follow he slowed down and within another two hundred yards came to where the footpath entered a flat area covered with short, dense brush. Here, he guessed, the tigress would lie up. For, while he still thought that had missed her with his shot of a few minutes ago, he knew she was carrying the wound of at least one of his shots of the previous day and because of this would not be inclined to travel very far. He also knew that now, because of the men shouting and visible on the top of the hill, and the shot that had just been fired at her, that she would be very aware that she was being challenged. She would be alarmed, possibly enraged and, if so, ready to wreck vengeance on anyone that came near her, something that made her one of the most dangerous animals on the face of the earth.

In his hunting, like me, Corbett had known rifle cartridges to misfire. Now, realizing that he was closing in on the big cat, and knowing that when he got close enough she was almost certainly going to charge him, he stopped to check the bullets in his rifle. Sliding back the bolt of the .275 he carefully examined the rounds to make sure they were from a fresh batch that he had recently purchased at Mantons, the gun dealers in Calcutta. Then, sliding one into the firing chamber, he thumbed the safety catch to Fire and commenced stalking the tigress.

The little trail that Corbett had been following led straight into the brush. The brush, which Corbett called bracken, was waist high and arched over the trail. Guessing that if the big cat was lying in this cover that she would be listening for him coming, he now commenced a very slow approach towards the edge of the brush. He did this to minimize any unavoidable sounds he might make, hoping to get close enough for a shot at her before she detected him. At the same time, although he knew that the tigress might be lying up on either side of the trail he was following, to the right, or the left, he sensibly kept his eyes straight ahead, relying on his peripheral vision to detect her.

He was within three yards of the edge of the bracken and, in my opinion, dreading having to go into its dense and dangerous cover, when he saw a movement ahead, about a yard to the right of the trail. It was the tigress and the movement he saw was probably caused by her gathering her back legs underneath her, preparatory to launching an onslaught. Corbett probably had no more than half a second to get a bullet into her and whipping the .275 to his shoulder he snapped the sights onto her body and fired. He immediately followed his shot with a second one. Both rounds went home, the first ripping down through the big cat's body and the second snapping her neck.

Corbett's Gharwalis carried the tigress up to the saddle and soon after this Corbett skinned the animal. When he did, he was quickly able to determine which of his six shots had hit her, and which had missed. He found that his first shot, a soft nosed round with what was called a split nickel case, taken when she racing across the hillside, had smashed into the ball and socket joint of her right shoulder. The impact of the bullet had knocked her out, her legs had crumpled and she had collapsed, to slide to the little oak tree and end up draped across it.* But when she slid off the tree, to fall over the cliff, the impact of hitting the ground at the base of the cliff seems to have jolted her back to consciousness and she had recovered. His second shot, a snap shot fired in the enthusiasm of the moment, while the cat was falling from the cliff, missed her. His third shot, the long one when she was going up the hill and was probably four hundred yards away, had missed. His fourth, fired at her at a distance of sixty yards when she stepped out from behind the pine tree, had hit her but, not impacting on any bones, had passed right through her. His fifth and sixth shots killed her.

While he was skinning the tigress Corbett found many porcupine quills embedded in the muscle and tissue of the big cat's right shoulder and right foreleg. The damage that these inflicted on the muscular system of her leg, severely reducing her ability to catch and kill other animals, was almost certainly what turned her into a man-eater.

Three days after shooting the man-eater Corbett was back in Naini Tal and a little later was present at a special ceremony in Almora, when the Deputy Commissioner, Baynes, personally commended young Dungar Singh for his courage in accompanying Corbett in the hunt for the man-eater, and for helping him to bring an end to its depredations.

**A soft nosed, nickel encased round is a lead projectile enclosed in a metal-in this case nickel-jacket. The purpose of the nickel coating is to project the soft lead body of the projectile as it passes through the barrel of the rifle. The projectile, the bullet, is designed to mushroom on impact with a hard object, causing maximum damage to whatever it hits. The mushroom effect also creates a shock wave that is often extremely detrimental to the nervous system of the target animal. The shock wave created by the impact of Corbett's .275 round, when it mushroomed on impact with the heavy bone of the tigress' shoulder, is what rendered her temporarily unconscious.*

BOOK FIVE

THE CHOWGARH MAN-EATERS
1929.

CHAPTER ONE

In my book, GONE ARE THE DAYS, I recount the story of a very unusual incident where a tiger, after being wounded, climbed a tree to attack an English lady hunter. Tigers do not normally climb trees and so the story of this incident—and what happened when the lady stuck the barrel of her rifle down the tiger's throat and had it misfire, and how she fell out of the tree, *with the tiger,* and survived by something a little short of a miracle—was circulated among British hunters in India for years. The incident, noteworthy enough to be commemorated by British authorities with a stone pillar and a plaque, occurred at a place called Jaulasal, in the southern forests of Kumaon, no more than twenty miles from own shooting grounds in far west Nepal, and the date was December 31st, 1925.

Ten days previously, on December the 15th, a tigress killed a Bhutia man near Lohali, also in Kumaon and not far north of Jaulasal. The two incidents are not connected, other than by their closeness in time. But the date on which the Bhutia was killed is significant because this is the first recorded victim of the big man-eating cats that in time became known as the Chowgarh tigers, and from then until March 21st 1930, between them killed and ate sixty-four human beings.

Bhutia, sometimes spelled Bootia, is the common name given to hillmen of the northern reaches of the inner Himalaya of India and Nepal. The Bhutia people are basically agriculturists. But many of them trade back and forth across the mountains, exchanging yak wool and semi precious stones for tea and sugar and salt and their travelling carries them from the plains of India to the far reaches of Tibet. For their long journeys they ride ponies or walk and much of their merchandize is carried on the backs of sheep and goats. When they are on the road they are always accompanied by large mastiffs which they keep chained at night, to guard their domestic animals against predators.

In the winter of 1925 one such man took up temporary residence in the hill forests of Kumaon, near a village called Lohali. One day his goats wandered into the crops of the villagers of Lohali and when they went to see him, to complain, they found him missing. A search was organized. The man's big dog was found, chained to a post near the hut, dead. And under a tree near his camp the searchers found the all that was left of the Bhutia, his skull and a few splinters of bone. He was subsequently believed to be the first victim of the Chowgarh man-eaters.

Corbett first heard about the Chowgarh tigers at a district conference in Naini Tal in February 1929. Britishers Bill Baines and Ham Vivian were Deputy Commissioners of Almora District and Naini Tal District at this time and both had approached Corbett about man-eaters that were operating in their respective administrative areas. In order of importance, which meant relative to the number of persons the cats in question had killed and eaten, these were, one, the Chowgarh man-eaters of Naini Tal District, two, the Mohan man-eater of Almora District, three, the Kanda man-eater of Gharwal District and four, the Talla Des man-eater, of Naini Tal District.

Ham Vivian and his wife Nora were close friends of Corbett and when Vivian approached him on the subject of the Chowgarh tigers, Corbett agreed to go immediately. He already knew about the tigers and the reign of terror that they had imposed on the area where they operated. In fact his knowledge of their depredations is made clear by the fact that he kept a chart of their killings in his house for two years, before, at the request of Vivian, he went to hunt them.

Vivian's request* to Corbett in regard to the Chowgarh tigers was made in April, 1929 but when Corbett discovered that the tigers had been less active during the preceding winter, the winter of 1928 and '29, he decided to try for the Talla Des man-eater first. This is what he did. The hunt for the Talla Des man-eater, as already described, took only nine days, April 4th to April 13th and immediately on his return Corbett set out on the trail of the Chowgarh tigers.

When he went after the Chowgarh man-eaters he had four other man-eater hunts behind him, at Champawat, Talla Des, Panar and Rudraprayag and these were spread across the space of 18 years, 1907 to 1925. However, although he did not hunt other man-eaters during this period, he obviously kept up his hunting and his studies of natural history because when he went after the Chowgarh man-eaters his account of the methods he used show a considerable improvement in his hunting skills from earlier days when, as he put it, he was young and inexperienced. Nevertheless, in spite of this, in spite of his experience and his hard-earned expertise, one of the Chowgarh man-eaters almost got him. Indeed it ambushed him from behind a rock and managed, with incredible stealth and ingenuity, to get within a few feet—actually eight feet—and a few seconds of putting a permanent end to his hunting career. This is the story of that hunt.

South east of Naini Tal in the district of Kumaon lies a forty-mile long ridge that is known as the Kala Agar ridge. In Corbett's day the ridge, which in places rises to a height of eight thousand feet, was heavily timbered with dense forests of oak and rhododendron. Today there is more cultivation and more villages but the ridge, which runs roughly east to west, still has some fine stretches of forest along its rim and the views to both the north and south, with rolling hills stretching away to the horizon in both directions, are

---

**Contrary to the impression that people may gain from Corbett's writings, he seldom went after a man-eater until he was officially requested to do so.*

quite beautiful. In the general area of this ridge, for five years, the Chowgarh man-eaters, a tigress and her fully grown cub, had established a reign of terror and when Corbett went to hunt the two big cats they had, to that time, killed and eaten forty-nine human beings.

In Corbett's day a dirt road used by villagers ran along the north face of the ridge. Not far from the western end of the ridge the road formed a small loop in which lay the Kala Agar *dak* bungalow. Corbett decided to make the bungalow his base for the hunt and he arrived there one warm evening in April, to be told that the last victim of the man-eaters was a young man of twenty-two who had been killed while out tending cattle. Corbett also learned that the tigers, or at least one of the pair—for at this time it was not known to the villagers that there were two, operating together—had last been seen ten days before, towards the eastern end of the ridge, where they had killed a man and a woman.

Ignoring the recent killing of the young man as well as the killing of the man and his wife, because all three were more the a week old and the bodies had been removed, Corbett, working from a government map that pinpointed the killings across the whole area of the forty mile ridge, noted that the tigers seemed to have concentrated a considerable amount of their hunting in and around a village called Dalkania, ten miles east of Kala Agar. He spent one night at the Kala Agar *dak* bungalow and next morning, after breakfast, set off on foot with his men for Dalkania.

His route lay east along the ridge road for eight miles and then, from an intersection, down a trail for two miles, to Dalkania. With his men following him, he walked slowly, examining the surface of the road for sign of the tigers and it was early afternoon when they reached the intersection. There they met a group of villagers from Dalkania who had been informed of their pending arrival by men and women calling from ridge to ridge and, via the 'cooee' method, passing the word along.

The men he met told him that a party of women had been attacked by a tiger that morning, near a village ten miles north of Dalkania; the big cat, it appeared, had been unable to make a kill. When Corbett asked how to get to this village he was told that there was a trail; the men indicated that they would take him there if he wished. But he was also informed that the trail ran through dense forest and when he heard this he decided to decline their offer of guiding him there. Dense forest meant that he would have to give his full attention to the possibility of the presence of the man-eater and the dangers of an ambush by the big cat. With villagers, and his men, trailing along behind him, and the need to keep a protective eye on them, he would not be able to do this. So he told them they should all go to Dalkania and wait for him there. Before they left, however, he had his cook prepare a good meal—probably, as an impromptu meal on the trail, rice and curried vegetables—and after eating this he set off.

CHAPTER TWO

In tracing the course of Corbett's actions after this, from the moment he set off to investigate the killing of which the villagers had informed him, it will be of interest to the reader to take note of and keep in mind the timing of the sequence of events that followed. To do this, we shall call the day that he set out and on which, at three in the afternoon, he had his roadside meal, Day One. Because, although he makes light of it in his writings, the hardship that he imposed upon himself over the next few days would surely have deterred many a lesser man and certainly not a few of the amateur hunters I have met in my time.

Seeing his men off for Dalkania, Corbett shouldered his rifle and set out on his ten-mile hike. The distance involved should have taken him about two and half hours to cover if the trail had run through open country. But its course lay through deep ravines smothered in dense brush and filled with tumbles of huge boulders, behind any of which the man-eaters could have been lurking. And, just like when one is doing the first and exploratory run of an unknown river, where around every corner may lie unexpected hazards that make it vital to stop and scout, so it was with Corbett.

Every boulder had to be carefully scrutinized; every patch of dense brush that encroached on the trail had to be scouted and examined. Tigers kill by stalking their prey and then taking it down with a swift charge. But they will also ambush prey if they detect it coming towards them and Corbett knew that the Chowgarh tigress was capable of this. So it was that he was still short of the village that was his destination when the shadows began to lengthen, and whereas he would normally have found a dry place in the forest and curled up on a bed of leaves and slept comfortably, as I have done many times, in man-eater country this would be asking for trouble. So he chose a tree with a big fork in it at a safe height above the ground and climbed into it. He tied his rifle to a branch and then curled up in the fork and slept the night. He had no food with him.

In the morning, Day Two, he came down from the tree and went on, arriving at a tiny village a couple of hours after sunrise. Here he met a group of terrified men and women and from them obtained the first news that the tigress might have a companion. The villagers told him that a tiger had attacked a party of women the previous morning. Disconcerted by the screams and shouts of the women and thwarted in its attempt to take one of them, it had retreated into the forest where, just before it disappeared, a second tiger was seen to join it. The two cats, both probably hungry, had then gone down into a valley below the village from where they had called at intervals all through the hours of darkness. The wretched villagers, huddled behind the barricaded doors of their flimsy huts, had spent a sleepless night.

With the hospitality for which the hill people of India and Nepal are noted, something that I have personally encountered many times when hiking in the hills of both countries during my research for this book, the villagers now offered to cook a meal for Corbett. But knowing that in a small village like this their resources would be meager, he refused and instead, there being no tea in the village, accepted a drink of milk sweetened with *jaggery*, a coarse, dark brown sugar made from the sap of, among other trees, the date palm. The villagers then asked him if he would mount guard while they finished the cutting of their wheat, which the big cat had interrupted. This he did and when their harvesting was safely completed, he set off down the valley where the tigers were believed to have gone.

CHAPTER THREE

On entering the valley Corbett quickly saw that it was going to be very difficult to pick up sign of the tigers and track them. The valley was twenty miles long and much of it was covered with dense forest. There were no forest roads, the dusty surfaces of which could have provided him with sign of the tiger's movements. There were probably many game trails but their surfaces would have been covered with leaves and debris to an extent that would hide animal sign and make tracking slow and difficult.

By evening Corbett had reached the upper end of the valley and once again, with the shades of night laying their dark mantles across the forest, he found himself far from any village. So for a second time, again without food, he climbed into a tree and spent the night.

The tigers called on and off through the night and once he heard someone fire a muzzleloader. But otherwise the night was uneventful.

Next morning, Day Three, still with nothing to eat, he continued his search and he kept going until early afternoon at which point he turned his steps back towards Dalkania, to rejoin his men, rest and, hopefully, get a meal.

He was on the way there when he heard a cooee from some men who were grazing cattle in the forest and homing in on the sound he learned that one of their animals, a white cow, had been missing since midday. They told him that they believed a tiger might have taken it.

The cow had last been seen in a nearby *nullah* and thanking them for the information, Corbett made his way towards it, to investigate the incident. He soon found signs of where the cow had been killed and also drag marks indicating that two tigers, after killing it, had taken it down the hillside and into another ravine. Knowing that the big cats would be watchful about anyone following the drag they had made, and that they would probably take their kill into the thickest cover available, he made a mental note of a dense stand of brush deep in the ravine. Then, making a detour, he began a careful stalk.

Making his approach into the ravine Corbett soon found himself in thick brush that reached to his waist and because of the unavoidable noise he made, when forcing his way through this, he had to move very slowly. So it was some time before he arrived at the bottom of the ravine. When he did he was greeted by a deep growl, one that told him that he had made contact with the tigers.

That they had not seen him, or heard his approach, was made clear by more subdued growls which Corbett identified as the satisfied sounds that tigers will sometimes make when eating; these indicated that the tigers were on the kill and devouring it. This was quickly confirmed by what Corbett saw a few moments later, a bovine leg suddenly rising out of the brush ahead of him, shaking from side to side.

Watching, waiting, trying to see the tigers for a shot, Corbett suddenly noticed a big rock about twenty yards away, to his left front. Believing that its elevation might give him a vantage point from which to see the tigers, he made a silent approach to it. Then, head down and keeping out of sight of where the tigers were, he very carefully and very slowly climbed to the top of it.

At the top, when he had regained his breath, he made sure his rifle was loaded and ready and then slowly raised his head over the rim of the rock and looked towards where the kill was. He immediately saw two tigers. One was tearing into the hindquarters of the cow, the bodily area of a kill where tigers always start to eat. The other was lying a short distance away, licking its paws.

Both tigers appeared to be about the same size. But one was lighter in color than the other and believing that the paler one was the tigress and the older animal—for tigers coats fade with age—Corbett took aim and fired at it. To the crack of his rifle the pale colored tiger reared up and fell over backwards. But before he could reload and fire again the second cat whipped around and dashed up the ravine and disappeared.

The tiger that he had put down remained still and after throwing some pebbles at it to make sure that it was dead, Corbett, rifle at the ready, made a careful approach. The animal, he was pleased to find, was indeed dead. But upon examining it he was disappointed to see that it was a young animal that he had shot, one that he guessed must be the tigress' cub. The tigress had escaped. Escaped to continue her depredations for another twelve months and, in this period, and before Corbett caught up with her again, to kill and eat another fifteen men and women.

CHAPTER FOUR

Corbett is to be excused for shooting the wrong animal. He made his choice based on the coloration of the animal's pelt and in this case it just happened that the cub had unusually light colored hair. Thc pelts of tigers fade with age and many of the older tigers that were taken during my professional hunting days were pale in color, compared to younger animals. An example of this, from the great days of tiger hunting in India before the turn of the century and in a time, I might mention, when there were thousands of tigers in southeast Asia, is a huge tiger shot in 1849 by a British hunter, a Mr. C. Shillingford. The tiger was described as "very old, with short hair and light in color."*

Corbett skinned out the big pale haired cub and as he did so the day came to a close. He could have made his way back to where the cattle graziers were camped and stayed the night with them. He could also have had a meal with them, something that would have been glad to provide him. But on the off chance that the tigress could still be around and that she might return to the dead cow for another meal, he decided to stay where he was. He chose a tree close to the kill, climbed into it and settled down to spend the night, again without any food.

**Shillingford's cat was a big one. At twelve foot four inches it was close to the all time record, which was a tiger shot by a Mrs. Laurie Johnson, believed to be the wife of a tea planter, in the Dooars district of north Bengal, at the turn of the century. Mrs. Johnson's tiger measured twelve foot six inches and is the largest ever recorded. The Dooars district of north Bengal is where I did my first big game hunting in the forties and where I served the self-imposed, five year, hunting apprenticeship that preceded my professional career in Nepal.*

The tigress did not return, although she called several times during the night. In the morning, the morning of Day Four, cold, stiff and hungry, he came down from the tree. Now, with the exception of the milk and *jaggery* drink he had had the day before, Day Three, and the roadside lunch on Day One, he was into his fourth day without anything to eat. Tired, fatigued by the lack of food, he decided to give up for the moment and turned his steps towards Dalkania. Wrapping the big cub's pelt in his coat he set off for the little hamlet where the villagers, convinced that he had fallen foul of the tigress, were just about to send a runner to Naini Tal to report to the authorities that he was missing.

At Dalkania, his men, who had been anxiously awaiting his return, quickly set about preparing a meal for him. They had pitched his forty-pound tent in a small field near the village and after a bath and an ample meal he climbed into his cot, pulled his blankets over himself and slept for twelve hours. A well deserved sleep considering the fact that that he been in the field, hunting the Chowgarh man-eater and her cub, most of the time without any food, for more than seventy-two hours.*

**In his writings, from time to time, Corbett modestly states that he kept himself very fit and that twenty-five miles a day, or more, in hill country, was nothing to him. What he does not state is that he was also incredibly tough. Anyone who does not think this should try hiking Kumaon's 8000 to 14,000 foot hills for three and a half days on a single meal of rice and lentils and a bowl of milk and sugar, and top it off by sleeping for three nights perched in the forks of jungle trees.*

CHAPTER FIVE

At Dalkania, Corbett now decided to try another approach to get at the man-eater and he did this by staking out three *pudas*, young bait buffaloes, in the hope that the tigress would kill one and enable him to pinpoint her movements. The *pudas* were tied out at night on various cattle trails in the forest near Dalkania. They were brought back in to be fed and watered each day and this was continued for eleven days.

On the eleventh day a cow was killed by a big cat. Investigation by Corbett quickly determined, however, that it had been killed by a leopard and at request of the villagers, he set out to hunt it. He was in the forest, stalking the leopard when a man came after him to tell him that a girl had just been killed by the man-eater. He immediately returned to the village to find a young woman injured, not killed, by what the villagers told him was the tigress.

The big cat had apparently stalked a group of women over comparatively open ground and had managed to close on its victim before they saw it. But screams and shouts of alarm had driven it away and the young girl, knocked down and left for dead in the ensuing panic, had managed to find her way back to the village.

Her injuries were severe but not life threatening and after Corbett had patched her up with his meager medical supplies—in this case, it seems, all he had was a single bottle of iodine—he left to see if he could track the tigress. With him he took a goat, for bait. A tiger will not normally bother with something as small as a goat, preferring larger animals as prey and for food. But in this case the man-eater's attack on the group of women meant that the big cat was hungry, as a result of which it might just go for the first thing it saw that meant food.

Backtracking the blood trail left by the injured girl, Corbett soon found where she had been attacked. Here he tied the goat and, climbing into a small oak tree, spent the night waiting for the tigress to return. It did not do so and in the morning he returned to the village.

For two days there was no news of the tigress. Then came word that it had killed again, this time near a village called Lohali, five miles south of Dalkania.

Corbett set out immediately, accompanied by the villagers who had brought him news of the new kill. On the way he passed the ruins of the long since abandoned hut of the Bhutia who had been the Chowgarh man-eater's first victim, four years previously.

When he was within three miles of Lohali the villagers left him to go home and then, with a strange feeling that the tigress was close, and that it may have detected him, he started to search for sign of the big cat. He soon found this in the form of pug marks in the soft mud of a little spring and after examining them and making sure that they were the pugs of the man-eater, he went on into the village of Lohali.

There he found a situation which confirmed a suspicion he had had for some time, which was that the big cub had probably been doing most of the killing in which it and the mother had been involved and that the tigress, incapacitated by the injuries that had turned it into a man-eater, had come to depend on it for this. What first started Corbett thinking in this direction was the escape of the young girl who had just been attacked by the tigress, something that seldom happens in a man-eater attack. Now, in Lohali, he found further confirmation of his suspicions in the form of yet another woman who had managed to get away from the tigress. The only difference here was that this woman's injures were more severe, for the tigress had bitten her savagely, and fatally.

Once again Corbett played doctor to an injured village woman and after he had done his best for her, he left the village and looked for a place to spend the night. Near the village he found a big *peepul* tree and after a wash to get the blood of his dying patient off his hands, he settled down on the ground with his back to the tree to spend the night.

Although he does not say so, it is presumed that there was a full moon and that with its light he hoped to be able to see and shoot the tigress if and when she came by. He did say that spending the night in the open was preferable to staying in one of the small, stuffy houses of the little village and I concur with him, knowing from experience that a night under the stars is always preferable to the confines of a noisy Indian village house with people coughing and children crying and dogs barking endlessly through the night. But in this case there was a man-eater around and so I can only presume there was a full moon and that soon after he took up his vigil it rose out of the eastern sky to fill the scrub and the village road with enough light for him to spot the man-eater, especially if it detected him and started to stalk him.

His night's vigil was uneventful and in the morning, with the wailing of the village women telling him that the tigress' latest victim had died, he returned to Dalkania.

Next day, after a short hunt with the villagers, during which he shot them a couple of Himalayan Gooral for meat, and a Himalayan Black bear that got in the way when they tried to retrieve some of their meat and which Corbett, out of ammunition after the hunt, had to dispatch with an axe, he decided to return to Naini Tal.

Before doing so however, he made a quick visit to the woman whose sister had been taken by the tigress a year previously and who had been struck dumb by the incident. He took with him the skin of the big cub and, arriving at the woman's house, laid it on a small stone wall that enclosed the house compound. Then he called out to her to come and see her enemy, the beast that had nearly killed her and, in the process, caused her to lose her voice. He was as amazed as were her children, to whom she had not said a word for a year, when she suddenly began to speak again.

CHAPTER SIX

Corbett left the Kala Agar ridge via the road to Haira Khan, from where he planned to walk on down to Ranibagh, a town on the Halduwani to Naini Tal road from where he thought he could get a car back to Naini Tal. Making an early start he set out from Dalkania ahead of his men and started up towards the Kala Agar ridge road, above the village, his intention being to climb to the top of the ridge and then use its long, descending spine to make his way down to Ranibagh. But within an hour the fates decided that he and the tigress should again meet and not long after leaving the village he once more found himself in the presence of the man-eater.

The route he took to gain the top of the ridge above Dalkania took him through a glade that had a small pool and as he walked into the glade he saw from the ground sign that the tigress had been there, drinking, bare minutes before he arrived. Although she had not been heard of for a week, Corbett was very conscious of her being in the vicinity and had been walking very quietly and taking many precautions. Because of this the tigress probably did not hear him coming. But by chance she must have looked up and seen him as he came up the trail from the village; she was gone when he entered the glade.

Corbett knew that when the tigress saw him approaching she would have taken note of the fact that he was alone and he guessed that because of this, although she had immediately slipped away into cover, she night well try to attack him. Acting on this presumption he immediately put into action a plan that he hoped would persuade the cat that he was unaware of her presence and, as such, offered her a chance of a human meal. Now, together, he and the tigress entered into a deadly game of cat and mouse.

The first thing he did was to stop at the pool and pretend to drink. Then he gathered some sticks and made a small fire, as a villager will sometimes do to keep warm or, if the weather is hot, to deter biting insects, when he stops to rest on the trail. Then, his rifle ready and with a finger on the trigger, he lay down and pretended to sleep. He stayed like this for some time, both eyes open, alert to every sound. But he saw and heard nothing of the tigress and he guessed that when she heard his men coming up from Dalkania, as they soon did, she would silently slipped away.

After he had told his men what happened, and they had rested for a while, they set out together for the twenty-mile march to Haira Khan. About two miles down the ridge they came across a man, a buffalo grazier, sitting on the side of the trail tending his animals and they stopped to ask him where they could find water with which to cook a meal. While his men were cooking Corbett talked with the buffalo herder who told him that the tigress had not been heard of for two weeks and that in his opinion it was now probably living in another district. But Corbett, knowing that the man-eater was still in the vicinity, told the man to be on the watch for the big cat and after he and his men had eaten and he had given the man a cigarette, they left. Sadly, but true to Corbett's warning, they were probably no more than a couple of hundred yards away when the tigress, which must have been lying nearby watching them eat, came out of the brush and sprang onto the grazier.

Initially, the man was very lucky. Just as the tigress attacked he leaned forward to light the cigarette that Corbett had given him and the lunge that the tigress made at his throat and head missed. Instead the cat got him by the right shoulder and it was in the process of biting into his throat when an additional stroke of luck further prolonged his life. This arrived in the form of his buffaloes which, seeing the tiger attacking their herder, promptly attacked the tiger themselves, driving the big cat off and temporarily saving the man's life.

The domestic village buffalo is not normally an aggressive animal. It is generally frightened by both tigers and leopards and a single animal will usually bolt at the sight or even the smell of a big cat. But in a group—and on this occasion there were ten animals in the herd—they can be provoked and when this happens they may even take on a fully-grown tiger.*

The Chowgarh tigress, not a fit animal, did not hesitate when the herder's buffaloes attacked. She turned tail and fled and the herder, badly injured, climbed onto the back of one of his animals and rode it back to his village. There, his friends, hoping in spite of the severity of his injuries to save his life, put him on a stretcher and carried him thirty miles on a bamboo stretcher to a hospital in Halduwani. Unfortunately he died there, soon after arrival.

Corbett, hearing of what happened, wondered how close the tigress had come to getting him, or one of his men, when they stopped to talk to the grazier on the road and I feel that it may have worried him. For he was tired after a month of hard hunting, and of being hunted in turn by the Chowgarh man-eater. Now, with nerves wearing thin, he took his men and turned west down the Kala Agar ridge towards Haira Khan. A few days later he was home in Naini Tal and he stayed there until February of the following year. In that month, with the hills deep in the grip of winter, and the great mountains to the north buried in their frozen, white mantles, he returned again to the Kala Agar ridge to hunt the tigress. While he was away the deadly man-eater had claimed more victims and many other villagers had been attacked and wounded.

**Years ago, near a little town called Bilauri, in southwest Nepal, a tiger charged into a herd of domestic buffalo and tried to take a calf. The herd, males and females, enraged at what the big cat tried to do, promptly attacked it. The tiger stood his ground for a while, attacking in turn and killing two of the huge bovines. Then both sides called it quits, the herd thundering off back to their village, leaving the empty bellied tiger to crawl into cover and lick its bruises. I was on the scene two hours after the incident and with my Holland and Holland .375 put one of the buffaloes, desperately injured but still living, out of its misery.*

CHAPTER SEVEN

When Corbett returned to the Kala Agar ridge in February, 1930, he immediately set about gathering intelligence on the whereabouts of his quarry and in the light of his previous experiences in the area, he decided that the best place to do this would be in general vicinity of Dalkania. So once again he made Dalkania his base.

Corbett spent several weeks in the area during which time, at the request of local villagers, he shot a cattle-killing leopard. He also had an unusual experience with two tigers, both of which, at first, he thought might have been the Chowgarh man-eater.

He had been in the village a few days, talking to its men and women, scouting for the tigress, baiting the area with *puda*s and spending nights in his forty pound tent, when he received news that a bullock had been killed by a tiger in a ravine not far close by. He was quickly guided to the scene of the kill but when he got there he found that vultures had eaten most of the bullock and that little remained other than a few bones.

Leaving at once he hiked with his guides to another village, where the headman provided him with a *puda*. Returning to the scene of the kill, he tied out the *puda* and then, unable to find a tree in which to build a *machan,* climbed up on to a small, nearby rock ledge and sat down to wait. The ledge was very narrow and not at all comfortable to sit on. Under it, the hill shelved inwards, forming a hollow invisible to him from where he sat.

He had been there for a while when the *puda*, which had been lying down, suddenly rose to its feet and then slowly turned towards where Corbett was sitting. This indicated to him that whatever it had sensed was in the hollow underneath him and he was wondering what was going to happen next when suddenly the head of a tiger appeared from out of the hollow, directly below him.

The head remained perfectly still for a moment and although the angle was not good, the cat being almost directly below him, Corbett thought about taking a shot at it. But head shots on tiger are only advisable in an emergency and hunters who know the big cats will usually take this shot only as a last resort.

A tiger's head is of unusual construction. Much of the skull is taken up by the eye sockets while the brain actually lies at the back of the head, in an egg shaped compartment set behind the eyes. I have seen dead tigers with bullet holes in different parts of the skull that left the brain untouched and that may have only temporarily put them down. I have seen lead slugs embedded in the skull bone and once I took a steel jacketed .303 Lee Enfield bullet out of the back of a tiger's head, a round that had hit the animal just under the eye and then, deflected by the bone structure, had traveled under the skin all the way around to the back. Corbett, knowing of the dangers of head shots, decided to wait for the cat to show more of its body and give him a better target. It soon did this, rushing out to hurl itself on the *puda*. It seized the animal by the throat and killed it and then, still holding it by the throat, lay down beside it, giving Corbett a perfect shot at its right side.

The rifle that Corbett had with him was his .275 Rigby. It was a light weapon that Corbett found very convenient to carry when hiking in hilly and brushy country and now, raising it, he took aim at the big cat and squeezed the trigger. To the sound of the rifle's report the tiger leapt up, spun around and took off up the ravine at speed.

Corbett waited a few minutes and I have to say that I am amused when I read, in his writings, that the reaction of the tiger made him think that he had missed it, and shot the buffalo instead. Had he done so, he would not have been the first person to shoot the poor old *puda*. Indeed, not a few of my hunting companions of my Bengal tea planter days were guilty of *puda* trophies!

Now for a while the ravine was silent and Corbett was wondering whether he should go down and look for the tiger that had got away, or wait, when, to his astonishment, a tiger's head appeared below him in exactly the same place as the one at which he had just fired. Waiting until it walked out into the open, which it did after a few moments, Corbett took careful aim at it and again pulled the trigger of the .275. When he did this the animal repeated the action of the first tiger, spinning around and then racing off up the ravine.

Now Corbett did not know what to think. Was the tiger that he had just fired at the same animal that he had tried to shoot just fifteen minutes earlier and that he may have missed? Or was it another tiger? And if so, was either or both of them the man-eater? Which raised an urgent thought in his mind and this was that by waiting as long as he did, and now with the light beginning to fade, he had not allowed himself enough time to get back to a village, either the village where he had bought the *puda*, or Dalkania, before dark. Now, with the possibility of the man-eater being in the area, or a wounded tiger, or even two wounded tigers, he was going to have to stay where he was for the night.

CHAPTER EIGHT

Corbett mentions in his writings that on this occasion he was dressed in light khaki shorts. He also says that a cold wind was blowing. What he does not say is, that as this hunt took place soon after he returned to Dalkania for his second visit, which was in February, it was still deep winter in the hills. As the place where he was hunting now was somewhere not far below the top of the Dalkania ridge, which averages 8000 feet, its altitude must have been close to 6000 feet. This will have meant, even in the warmer air of the forest, night temperatures in the F20s and my guess is that it was with great reluctance that he made the decision to spend the night on the cold stone ledge, dressed as he was in very light clothing. But he did, because the alternative was a long hike back through the forest in the dark, one that would put him at the mercy of the man-eater, were it to detect him.

Cold, stiff and sore, Corbett came down from his stony perch early next morning and made his way back to the village from where he had obtained the *puda*. Then, after a cup of his beloved tea had warmed him, and accompanied by a dozen or so men and women, he returned to the scene of the previous day's shooting.

The villagers who went with him were all very excited at the prospect of seeing a dead tiger. Arriving at the head of the ravine they gathered around Corbett as he pointed out firstly where he had sat and then where he thought the first tiger had gone, after he had shot at it. Almost immediately one of the villagers spotted the carcass of a tiger, lying in the ravine where Corbett was pointing.

Corbett acknowledged the find and then went on to tell the assembled group about how the tiger had appeared a second time from under the overhang and how it had gone bounding up the ravine after he fired at it. Immediately another villager shouted and pointed at a second tiger lying dead no more than a hundred yards from the first. And then Corbett knew that he had shot two tigers, and not one that he had missed with the first shot which had then walked out to give him another try at it.

Corbett is to be excused for what he did. Firstly, he was in an area where a deadly man-eater was operating and so any tiger, unless it were obviously a cub, was fair game, to be shot on sight. Again, because the first tiger disappeared immediately on being shot at, and because the overhang below him prevented him from fully seeing the second tiger, he had no way of knowing that it was not the same cat. I certainly excuse him because very much the same thing happened to me, many years ago, not long after I turned professional.

I was in my safari camp on the Bauni river in the White Grass Plains, waiting for a client, when two Tarus, one of them a very old man, came running out of the jungle to tell me that a tiger had just killed a prized cow near their village, the village of Immelia, and to ask me if I would come and shoot it. This being in the days when there were lots of tiger and where, in the near lawless country of the southwest Nepal jungles there was no such thing as having to go and ask for a license or a permit to shoot one, I immediately said yes. And so we jumped in the Land Rover and took off for he village.

With the old man in the front to guide me, the other in the back and my brand new and as yet unfired Holland and Holland .375 laid across my lap, I drove south and east, as fast as the dirt tracks would allow, to Immelia, a small gathering of houses situated on the edge of a big patch of elephant grass. Arriving there the old man told me to stop and the three of us got out. As soon as we did he pointed to the wall of elephant grass behind the village. "In there, *sahib*," he whispered. "That's where it happened."

On being asked exactly where the dead cow was, the old man pointed again to the elephant grass and told me that it was right at the edge of it, just a little inside it and behind a small rise in the ground.

I loaded the H&H with three, Winchester 300 grain soft-nosed rounds. I thumbed all three into the magazine and then slid the top one into the firing chamber and closed the breech and put on the safety catch. Then, telling the two men to stay where they were and not on any account to try and come after me, I walked down past the little village and out towards where they indicated the tiger had killed the cow.

It was about four in the afternoon. The winter sun was bright and the air was cool. It was very quiet. Behind me, in the village, after I had walked past it, I could hear a few sounds, the murmur of people talking, a buffalo calf calling for its mother, children playing. In front of me was the edge of the grassland, yellowing now at the onset of winter, with the bulk of it stretching away back for about half a mile. It was very thick and dense, typical elephant grass and ideal habitat for tiger. At its near edge, however, it thinned a little and when I got to within about thirty feet of it, walking slowly and scanning every inch of it very carefully, I saw the outline of something white lying just inside the fist yellow stalks. It was the dead cow, lying sideways to me and when I heard crunching sounds and an occasional soft growl coming from behind it, I knew that the tiger was there, eating.

I immediately flipped over the safety catch of the H&H to FIRE and then, very slowly and quietly, moved forward another ten feet, hoping to see the tiger lying behind the cow. But as I did so a Coucal, the common Crow Pheasant of the Terai, a scavenger bird that often hangs around tiger's kills, flapped up out of the edge of the grass in front of me, cackling in alarm. This instantly alerted the big cat to my presence and it responded by surging to its feet from behind the cow with a snarling growl, to stand and glare at me.

I wanted to take a neck shot on the cat. But it was standing straight on to me and so I opted for a chest shot and this is where I aimed and fired. To the roar of the H&H it flipped over backwards, all four feet flashing briefly in the air as it fell behind the carcass of the cow.

I was delighted. My first shot with my brand new Holland and Holland and not only would this give me a nice tiger trophy but I had also dispensed of a cattle killer that was decimating the herds of my Taru friends and they would appreciate it. I stood there, looking around, feeling very smug, and thinking of how proud I was going to be when the Tarus came up and stood around me and congratulated me on my shooting.

Like Corbett, in his time, I am not afraid to say now that I was young and foolish in those days. And indeed I was. For what I should have done, instantly, was reload and stay totally focused on where the cat had gone down and either shoot it again or be prepared for the possibility of it getting up and, wounded and enraged, coming at me. Which is exactly what happened less than three seconds after it flipped over backwards and disappeared behind the cow.

The big cat came over the top of the cow, straight at me, with a roar that shattered the stillness of the afternoon and it was within ten feet of me when with fumbling hands I managed to get a second round into the firing chamber of the H&H and flip the rifle to my shoulder and get a bead on its chest and pull the trigger. It dropped within five feet, head on to me, its eyes full of fire and in a panic I reloaded and fired into it again, another foolish thing to do because, as I had only put three rounds in the rifle, the third shot left me without any more ammunition.

I stood there trembling, watching the big cat die, right in front of me. The sweat trickled down my neck and my whole body was tensed like a steel spring. So I was to be excused for leaping a foot in the air when a hand grabbed me unexpectedly from behind, by the back of my thigh, and a voice, the voice of the old man who had come with me from my camp and who had crept up behind on his hands and knees and who, he told me later, had been there the whole time, me, said, "*Shabash sahib*," meaning, well done.

I forgave the old man for what he did and when he pulled out a packet of bidis, small brown Indian cigarettes, and offered me one, I, who never smoked, accepted it.

We sat for a few minutes looking at the tiger and as we did some other villagers joined us. They quickly gathered around the big cat. One of them, probably the owner of the dead cow, stood looking at it for a few moments and then walked over to look at the cow. Suddenly he stopped, leapt in the air and came flying back, shouting in a panic, "*Sahib, sahib*, there is another tiger."

And so there was, another tiger, fortunately for me quite dead. It was the tiger that I had first seen, that had been alerted by the Coucal to my approach, and that my chest shot had killed instantly. The one at our feet was a second tiger.

I was young and foolish in those days, as Corbett says he was, when he first started to hunt. And looking back at some of the mistakes he made, and some that I made, I feel that it is a wonder that we both lasted as long as we did. But for some reason the fates allowed us to survive our foolishness. Corbett to live his long and extraordinary life and write his magnificent books; I to also live a long and fascinating life and, in these latter years, make my own attempts at recording it in a manner attractive enough for people to enjoy reading about it.

Corbett stayed another week or so at Dalkania, hunting the Chowgarh tigress. But he failed to make contact with the big cat and get a shot at it. So when his work called him away, sometime towards the end of February, he left and returned to Naini Tal.

CHAPTER NINE

In March 1930, Mr. Hamish (Ham) Vivian, British District Commissioner seconded to the Naini Tal district, went on an official tour of his administrative area. He was accompanied by his wife Nora and eventually they found themselves in the Kala Agar region, where they put up at the Kala Agar Forest Bungalow. They arrived at the bungalow with their staff and baggage train in the early afternoon of March 21st and after they had settled in, and their servants had unpacked their baggage, went out on the front porch for tea.

They knew that the Chowgarh man-eater was in the general area of the Kala Agar ridge and no doubt they planned to be cautious in their movements while there. What they did not know was that, not only was the tigress in the area, but she was crouched in the brush, just outside the bungalow compound wall, no more than a hundred yards of where they were sitting. Furthermore she was hungry, and looking for a victim.

The big cat would probably have started its hunt by seeking a victim in the area around the bungalow. But now, possibly attracted by the sounds of the arrival of the Vivian's entourage, its attention centered on the bungalow itself and the people moving around it.

Silently, an inch or two at a time, it crept unseen through the brush to the edge of the bungalow compound. It probably lay there for a while on the outside of the three foot high, stone compound wall and then, to see what was happening on the other side, rose and carefully peered over the wall itself. When it did so it immediately spotted six Koumani women squatting on the little lawn, cutting the grass with sickles.

The big cat did not hesitate. It came over the wall in a single bound and to the horror of the Vivians, sitting no more than twenty feet away, seized one of the woman in its jaws and leapt back over the wall with her.

The Vivians dropped their teacups and shouted for rifles. They were both keen hunters and good shots and if the tiger had remained in view they might have been able to put it down. But by the time they had their rifles loaded and ready, it was too late. The cat, carrying its victim, was gone, into the brush.

Pluckily following the blood trail left by the woman's body, the Vivians soon found her remains and guessing that the cat in question must be the Chowgarh man-eater, immediately sent a runner to the nearest telegraph post, probably at Ramnagar, with a telegram addressed to Corbett in Naini Tal, asking him to come to Kala Agar as quickly as possible.

Corbett received the telegram next day, March 22nd and immediately set out on foot for Kala Agar. The distance from Naini Tal to Kala Agar is about fifty miles and he and his men covered it in two days, arriving for breakfast on the morning of the 24th. He pitched his tent in the little bungalow compound, behind the main building and between it and its separate kitchen area, and at once set about hunting the man-eater.

This was his third visit to the great Kala Agar ridge and his third attempt to come to grips with the Chowgarh tigress. It was to be his last. Indeed it was also very nearly his last hunt, for from the minute he entered the area to hunt the big cat, it almost seems as though it sensed he was there and singled him out as its next victim. Only an extraordinary act of icy cold, controlled courage on his part saved him from its lethal intent and allowed him to continue his unique career as a *shikari* in the deadly game of man-eater hunting.

CHAPTER TEN

While Corbett was on his way from Naini Tal the Vivians tied out a young bait buffalo on the forest road that runs along the ridge behind the bungalow. The tigress came in the night and killed the *puda* and when Corbett heard about this, on his arrival at Kala Agar, he immediately sent for three more *puda*s with which to bait the tigress. Using these, he and the Vivians tried for the tiger for another eight days, during which the District Commissioner and his wife lived in the little bungalow while Corbett, apart no doubt from having meals with them, slept and spent his leisure time in his forty pound tent at the back.

The Vivians left Kala Agar on the 31st of March.* After they left, Corbett, with the field clear of all other hunters, went after the tigress in earnest. He started by baiting the big cat with his *puda*s in the immediate area of the bungalow. The tigress, although it took

---

**In his account of the hunting of the Chowgarh man-eater, written many years after the event, Corbett states that the Vivians left Kala Agar on March 25th. But I think he is mistaken because the Kala Agar Forest Bungalow visitor's book, which I recovered in 1999, shows the departure date of the Vivians, in Ham Vivian's own hand writing, as the 31st. Corbett, according to the Visitors Book, moved into the dak bungalow the day they left, the 31st. He may have considered moving in to it before that and I feel sure that the Vivians, good friends and admirers, would have invited him to do so. But in addition to his love of sleeping in the open, under canvas, there was another factor involved and this was that the little bungalow was very small. Apart from two small bathrooms there were just three rooms. These included two bedrooms and a very small living room with a fireplace. The living room separates the bedrooms and someone occupying the second bedroom, at night, would have been sleeping within fifteen feet of the Vivians. I believe that Corbett was as conscious of the need for privacy of others, especially married couples, as he was for himself.*

none of his baits, stayed in the area. Disregarding the lack of kills, Corbett hunted determinedly for eleven days, setting his baits out at night and checking them first thing every morning.

On the 11th of April he was out with two men, planning to tie up one of his buffaloes on the road just west of the *dak* bungalow when suddenly, with the instinct of a true *shikari*, or because of natural signs, or a combination of both, he felt that the tigress was nearby. He immediately advised the two men of his intuition, telling them to stay with him and keep close. He had them tie the bait buffalo temporarily to a stump and then, telling them to stay immediately behind him, set out to find a vantage point that would enable him to look down into the scrub that bordered the road and perhaps see the tigress.

About three hundred yards from the bungalow, working his way slowly westward on the ridge road, he came to a ravine that dropped off to the right, towards the north. Just beyond this ravine the road entered a thick patch of brush, dense enough to conceal a lurking man-eater and thinking that the big cat might try and ambush him there, he decided to bypass the area by dropping off the road into the ravine, going down the ravine itself and then regaining the road beyond the brush patch.

The ravine, where it dropped away from the road, was about thirty feet wide and quite shallow and, if it is the same today as it was in April 1930, which is probable, it contained light thorn scrub and jumbles of small boulders. Just after he stepped into the ravine Corbett saw a Nightjar, a ground-nesting, insectivorous bird, rise from the scrub in front of him. Looking down he spotted its nest and noticed that it contained two strangely shaped eggs. Corbett collected birds eggs as a hobby and noticing that these two eggs were very oddly shaped, one long, with pointed ends and the other perfectly round, he picked them up to add to his collection. Thinking that they might get crushed if he put them in his pocket, he kept them cupped in his left hand and carried them like this as he went on down the ravine. He carried his rifle, his Westley Richards .275, loaded and with a round in the firing chamber, in his right hand and held at an angle across his chest.

A short way down into the ravine he and his men came to a steep drop of about fifteen feet where a boulder, worn smooth with the rain water of the years, sloped downwards at an angle of about forty-five degrees. Concerned about the eggs he was carrying, and needing a hand to steady himself while sliding down the rock, Corbett handed his rifle to one of his men and, eggs in one hand and using the other to steady himself, dropped down the rock and waited for his men to follow him.*

Corbett did not have to wait long to get his rifle back. He had hardly hit the dirt at the bottom of the rockslide when his two men landed beside him, one of them thrusting the rifle into his hand and whispering that he had just heard a growl from nearby.

Now he stopped for a moment to survey the area immediately in front of him. Starting at the base of the rock down which and he and his men had slid, was a small glade. It sloped gently downwards into a shallow depression, about twenty feet in width. The surface of the depression was sandy, with a few scattered rocks. Corbett described what he saw to the left as a high bank overgrown with a tangle of bushes. At that time the bushes must have been thick enough to conceal what it really was, and still is, which is not an earthen bank, but a solid outcrop of rock rimming all of the lower left side of the depression.

**Corbett's expertise as a hunter is never in doubt with those who understand what hunting large, potentially dangerous animals is all about and particularly when the animals in question are man-eaters. But there are times in his hunting career when he did things which seem to me, as an ex PH, not just unprofessional, but downright foolish; things which might have been forgivable while he still young, but not, in the light of the experience he must have gained in his hunting, especially his man-eater hunting, in his later years. A golden rule of big game hunting, when one is in the field and closing on an animal, and especially a dangerous animal like a man-eater, is never, ever, to allow anything to separate you from your single and only article of protection, your rifle. Handing his rifle to one of his men while he slid down a rock and then waiting for the man to join him, in an area where a deadly cat was moving and, in this case, unknown to him, actually following him and maneuvering to get ahead of him for an ambush, is to me quite incredible.*

On the right of the little glade was something different, a huge slab of rock fifteen or more feet in height and about three to four feet in thickness. Shaped like a giant school slate standing on its side, it leaned into the depression at a slight angle.

Having carefully noted the layout of the area, Corbett started down into the depression, his two men close behind. He moved slowly and very carefully. But, his writing tells us, he does not seem to have believed that his men heard a tiger growl, or, if they did, that it might have been the tigress. Because tigers do not advertise their presence when they are hunting, especially man-eaters, and this known fact may have been what persuaded Corbett that his men were imagining things when they said they heard a tiger growl. He also seems to have forgotten that just a short time before he had sensed that the tigress was in the vicinity. And, so, somewhat incredibly, he still kept the Nightjar's eggs cupped in his left hand and carried his rifle in one hand, his right hand, held across his chest. And he was doing this when he came to the end of the upright rock slab, stopped, and, half turning to his right, found himself looking straight into the face of the Chowgarh tigress.

CHAPTER ELEVEN

Measuring the distance, later, he discovered that the tigress was just eight feet from where he was standing. Right now she was crouched with her back legs tucked under her—the position a tiger adopts preparatory to launching an assault—was looking directly at Corbett and was, no doubt like him, wondering who was going to make the first move.

It is possible that the tigress had been waiting for Corbett and his men in the thick scrub patch that bordered the road when, sensing that possibility, Corbett had taken his men and dropped off into the ravine. If this is the case then what she must have done when she saw them leave the road is cut back through the scrub, fast and silent, in the direction of the bungalow and, after passing the entrance to the ravine, cross the road, drop into the brush that bordered it on its northern side, slip down behind the big rock slab and then take up an ambush position and wait for them to appear.

That the tigress did not go for Corbett the second he came into her view can be attributed to two things. The first was the fact that she was so close—within a single bound of her intended victim—that she may have been convinced that there was little chance that he could get away. (Indeed, Corbett described the expression on her face as almost smiling, and perhaps she was.) The second was what Corbett now did, something that in my opinion was an act of exceptional courage. He did nothing.

Corbett, his brain obviously working in overdrive at the sight of the crouching tigress, her eyes firmly fixed on his, instantly realized that any sudden move on his part would bring her down on top of him. From a distance of eight feet she would need only a single bound to do this, one that would be much too fast to allow him to swing his rife around and get a bullet into her. His immediate problem therefore was to get his rifle into a position for a shot, but to do so, if it were possible, without provoking the big cat into an assault. The only way to do this, he realized, was to do it very, very slowly, with a movement smooth enough to persuade the tigress that he was doing nothing more than perhaps just stretching his arm. And so this is what he did, lowering the rifle away from his chest and then, slowly, an inch at a time, with the big cat's eyes locked on his, bringing it around, one handed, in a long, slow, half circle, until he had the tigress in its sights. Then he squeezed the trigger.

Corbett does not say where he aimed. With his experience it is likely that he did not aim at the head, which, as has been noted, is a very dangerous shot with a tiger. But as the tigress' head was in a raised position, probably about eight inches above the level of the ground, leaving her chest visible, it is most likely that he aimed there and thus managed to get a flat, low-angled shot into her body. I believe this is what he did because later, when skinning the animal, he stated that the bullet impacted her spine and smashed the upper portion of her heart. In any case the shot from the .275, fired at close range, killed her almost instantly and while Corbett watched, her head sank down on her paws and her life came to an end.

Corbett's two men, frozen into veritable statues of stone when they saw him stop at the end of the rock slab and guessed that the tigress must be behind it, now stepped forward and joined him. Corbett waited a while, no doubt to rest his nerves and congratulate himself on a very narrow escape. Then, while his men were collecting the *puda*, he went back and returned the Nightjar's eggs to their nest.

Later he stated that he felt that the eggs may have saved his life. If he had not been carrying them, his left hand would have been free. In this case he would almost certainly have been carrying the rifle in both hands, and would probably have attempted to swing around and draw down on the tigress the instant he saw her. My guess is that he would have got a bullet into her because Corbett was very quick, and a first class shot. But his sudden action would almost certainly have provoked an instantaneous reaction on the part of the tigress, which in this case would have been an attack. And an attack from a big cat, at close range, a cat that is fully prepared, with its back legs tucked under it, tensed, ready to hurl itself forward, would not have been stopped by a .275 bullet. Squarely shot, even in mid air, the cat might have been mortally wounded. But the impetus of its spring, plus the fact that it had Corbett squarely in its path, with its eyes targeted on him, plus the minimal distance involved—eight feet—would have had the cat on top of him, biting, tearing, even in its dying throes. And even a single bite from a big cat can well be fatal, certainly, in the case of a man, if it is in the head and neck area of its victim.

Examining the body of the Chowgarh tigress after she was skinned out, Corbett found that the big cat's claws were split and broken. One of her canines was snapped off and the combination of these two physical defects were, in his opinion, what prevented her from killing other wild animals and turned her into a man-eater. Corbett also mentioned that her incisors were worn down to near stumps and seems to think that this also might have contributed to the cat becoming a man killer. But I do not concur with him on this. A tiger's incisors are mainly used for ripping and tearing meat off a carcass. The killing apparatus of a tiger's mouth is its four huge canines, the teeth it uses, in combination with its claws, especially the massive dew claws, to pull down its prey and then bite into it for the throat hold that allows for strangulation. The incisors play a lesser part in this.

BOOK SIX

THE MOHAN MAN-EATER.

CHAPTER ONE

Corbett had been back in Naini Tal, from Kala Agar, only a short time when Baines, the Deputy Commissioner of Almora, sent him a message. The message was a reminder of a promise that Corbett had made at a district conference about going after another man-eater that was operating in the area of a village called Mohan, not far north from Ramnagar.

The tiger, Baines told him, was becoming a menace and recently, while Corbett was hunting the Chowgarh tigers, had killed three people in one week. Baines promised to write an order closing the area to all other hunters, one of the few stipulations that Corbett required. When this was done Corbett made his preparations for the hunt.

In the Indo Nepal Terai, May is the month that precedes the monsoon and it is the hottest month of the year. At night the temperature seldom sinks below F85 and in the day it can soar to a blistering F115. The air hangs still in the forests and the vegetation, which may not have seen rain for seven months, stands dry and dusty in the burning heat. The hill streams are waterless and the rocks that fill their beds carry the great heat of the sun late into the night. The air is filled with the incessant and strident calls of the Hawk Cuckoo—the screeching little bird that the British used to call the Brain Fever bird—that go on and on, all day, and far into the night.

When I went to India to work for the Dooars Tea Company of North Bengal I arrived in Calcutta in April and so my first month in

Tea, as we used to call it, was in May. I remember the company directors, at the home offices in King William House, Eastcheap, London, being concerned about my going out to India at the hottest time of the year. New employees were normally sent out in November, at the beginning of the cold weather. The purpose of this was to give them time, through the seasonal change, to grow accustomed to the heat as it slowly grew out of the end of winter, through March and April. In the end they sent me out anyway and the reason they broke the normal cold weather rule was that I had already spent four years in Asia in the R.A.F. and therefore, they thought, should have been accustomed to tropic heat. What they did not realize and what, as I was anxious to get back to Asia, I did not tell them, was that most of my service there had been in the islands of the Indian Ocean, where trade winds controlled the equatorial air to maintain even and enjoyable temperatures. Thus I had never really experienced real tropical heat and when I first arrived in North Bengal, I have to say that it took me by surprise.

In Tea we lived in tin-roofed bungalows that were in summer were like ovens. We had fans that worked during the day, and sometimes at night, taking the heat from the ceilings and churning it up and sending it down to the floor; that was the extent of our cooling systems for there was no air conditioning in those days. I think that afternoons were the worst, when the heat was like a furnace. Nights were a little cooler but when the fans, which were run at night on power from batteries, died, as they usually did soon after midnight, one lay on sweat-soaked sheets in a semi comatose stupor. There was no relief from the pitiless heat and if one lay on ones back, it would be to awake in the morning to a little pool of sweat that had collected in the hollow of ones belly button.

May in North India was the month we all dreaded, the month the Brain Fever bird made miserable with its unending screeching, the month when in the old days the British sent their wives and children to the Indian hills, to Darjeeling and Mussoorie and Naini Tal, and also when they moved their capital from the roaring heat of Delhi to the cool mountain air of Simla. This was the month in which Corbett set out to hunt the big cat which, although it was known as the Mohan man-eater, had now made its hunting grounds north of Mohan, around Kartkanoula, a small village set on the side of a big hill.

Corbett's route from Naini Tal was by train via Ramnagar, a bustling Indian town on the edge of the Terai. Arriving there with six men he set off on foot for Kartkanoula. On the first day, possibly because of the late arrival of the train, possibly because of the heat, he made only seven miles, to a village on the Kosi River called Garjia, where he spent the night. There was—and still is—a *dak* bungalow at Garjia.* But Corbett had not had time to get a permit to occupy it and so he slept in the open, somewhere on the west bank of the Kosi River.

The next day, setting out early, he hiked on, another twelve miles, to Mohan, and after a stop there, to cook a meal, made the four thousand-foot climb to Kartkanoula in one long, hot afternoon. At Kartkanoula he found a foresters hut on the top of the hill on which the village lay and when his men arrived he told them to set up quarters in the hut. For himself, he pitched his forty-pound tent between the hut and the road that led to it. This was, and still is, an east-west road that runs all the way along the crest of the ridge. It is a well made road, eight feet in width, and at one time may have been designed as a cart road between the villages scattered along the huge ridge on which Kartkanoula lies.

Settling in on the first day Corbett soon had visitors, men from Kartkanoula and other villages. He was happy to see them because, as in any tiger hunt, village intelligence is vital to whatever hunting plans are going to be made.

**Some of the old British dak bungalows of India, such as the one at Muktesar, (BOOK TWO) have been maintained in good repair by the Indian government. As of recent years the Garjia bungalow seems to have been abandoned and when I visited it in the nineties it was slowly sinking into decay.*

The men that Corbett now met were all locals and sitting down to talk with them he expected the conversation to go immediately to the subject of the man-eater. However, the first thing the men talked about was something different, the matter of Corbett sleeping in a tent beside a road that the man-eater apparently used on a regular basis. They were horrified at what they must have regarded as his carelessness and even though Corbett probably tried to explain that he was a very light sleeper and that he never slept without his rifle beside him, they insisted that he move into the forester's hut. To calm them and at the same time gain their cooperation, he moved his gear into the hut. Then he again sat down with them to talk about the man-eater and in the process learned something very interesting, which was that the animal moaned as it walked.

The villagers told Corbett that the big cat made moaning sounds when it was moving around at night, and that when it stopped the noises temporarily ceased. From this he surmised that the animal had a leg injury and also that this may have had something to do with its reasons for becoming a man-eater. He was also told that within the past months the tigress had been very active, to the point where they were all virtually living in terror, with the big cat killing as it pleased and no one knowing where or when it would strike next. Indeed, only three days before Corbett arrived, a local woman had been killed and taken away and eaten.

Corbett decided to bait the cat with *puda*s, and for this purpose he had already had two young buffaloes sent up from Ramnagar. The next day, after a night in the forester's hut, during which an animal came up to the back door and waked him but moved away too quickly for him to see it, he tied the buffaloes out. On one of them he hung a small bell.*

**Villagers hang bells on their cattle to help find them if they stray. Cattle killing carnivores, both leopard and tiger, learn to associate the sound of a bell with grazing animals and, when they are hunting, will often use the sound as a guide to home in for a kill. A bell hung on the neck of a bait buffalo serves the same purpose.*

He put one of the *pudas* near where the tigress' last victim had been killed and the other at a hairpin bend in the road where he found some pugmarks which were possibly those of the tigress. He spent a second night in the hut during which the baits remained untouched. The following night he changed the position of one of the buffaloes and tied it where a trail climbed up the north side of the hill to the top of the ridge, to where there was a pool of stagnant water.

For the next few days he established a pattern of visiting the animals morning and evening. His morning visits were part of the standard procedure used when baiting tiger in areas where there are villages and human movement, as a result of which they will usually hunt only at night. But a man-eater, fearless of human observation or interference, may also kill during the day, and so he made his visits to the baits a twice-daily routine.*

On the fourth evening, after checking on the buffaloes, Corbett was returning down the road to the forester's hut when he suddenly sensed danger. West of the hut the ridge road dropped off the top of the hill and ran below it, along its north face. Below the road was scrub jungle and brush and above it more brush and big jumbles of rocks, with single boulders as big as a large automobile. In one place, one of these rock masses came right down to the edge of the road itself and it was as he was approaching this that he suddenly sensed that the tigress might be close and, if so, that she could be stalking him.

**In areas where there are villages, with movement of people during the daylight hours, tiger will normally kill only after dark. If the human population is dense, this will usually be very late at night, or in the early hours of the morning, not long before dawn, when human movement will be minimal. But when a big cat is a man-eater, its psychology changes and it quickly puts aside the wariness that as a normal tiger it would have for man and, as a result, may hunt during the daylight hours, as many of Corbett's man-eaters did.*

Normal tigers will also hunt diurnally in areas where there are few or no people. An example of this can be found in the White Grass Plains Wildlife Reserve in south west Nepal where, with a minimal number of people moving about–and these mainly composed of the reserve's Wildlife Scouts or a few visitors-tigers can often be seen hunting during the day.

Alert to the danger, he stopped to study the rocks. But he saw nothing. He moved forward about ten feet, walking crabwise and staying along the outer edge of the road, facing the rocks, rifle at the ready. Again he saw nothing. He repeated the movement, another ten feet or so. Still nothing. Then, when he had passed the rock pile and was moving away from it, he heard a low growl and his intuition was confirmed.

The tigress, moving in the vicinity, must have seen him coming back down the road from where the bait was tied and had decided to have a go at him. She was probably lying in the brush on the upper side of the hill, above the rock pile when she spotted him. When she saw him, she slipped quickly down among the big boulders, close to the road, to lie in ambush. Only an inbuilt sixth sense, or Corbett's total alertness to the patterns of sound around him, and their subtle changes, plus his ability to analyze them, saved him from becoming another victim of the man-eater. When a Barking Deer called from nearby and two Sambhur started belling from the crest of the hill, alarm calls that indicated that the big cat had moved off in that direction, he knew that the tigress had left and that it was safe to continue on back to the hut.

CHAPTER TWO

The next day, after early morning rain, Corbett set out to check on his buff baits. Now aware, from his encounter of the previous day, that the man-eater was living and hunting in the immediate vicinity of Kartkanoula, he took along an old and trusted friend of many years, his D.B. 450/400 rifle.

He was probably pleased that it had rained in the night, because dirt, softened by rain, makes for easier tracking. Approaching the place where he had tied one of his baits he was surprised to see that it was missing. When tying out baits for tiger, unless there is a reason to the contrary, it is important to 'anchor' the bait, tying it securely with strong rope, or wire. If this is not done, the tiger, after the bait is killed, may pick it up and carry it away. Corbett had tied his *puda* very securely, with several lengths of strong rope twisted together. Now it was gone.

Making a careful approach to where the *puda* had been tied he found that the tigress had killed it and after killing it had gnawed through part of the rope and than snapped the remainder, something that tiger do not usually do. Then it had carried off the bait.

After carefully examining the ground for sign, Corbett, set out to track the cat. Tracking was not difficult, for the big cat had carried the *puda* by the neck, leaving its rear end to trail along the ground and leave a drag mark. A little later the tiger changed its hold on the animal, dropping it and then picking it up by the small of the back. Because this meant less of the *puda's* body touching the ground, and less ground sign, tracking was a little slower. Nevertheless Corbett soon found the kill.

He had stopped to rest on a big rock, one that, because of its elevation, gave him some protection against the possibility of the tiger stalking him, when, looking down, he saw what he thought was the cat, lying in a patch of thick brush, about fifty yards below him. What he saw was red and black, with vertical striping that looked exactly like the markings of a tiger's pelt. Wanting to make very sure, before he fired, that what he was looking at definitely was the tigress, he spent some time carefully studying the object before shooting.* As he did so, and as his eyes adjusted themselves to the light and shadow on and around the object, it seemed to change shape, to where he soon realized that what he was looking at was not the tiger at all, but the dead *puda*.

The black that he saw was the hide of the dead puda and the red was blood on its hide; the striping proved to be the animal's rib cage. The fact that he waited, that he did not fire the instant that he saw what at first truly appeared to be the big cat, is a mark of the man's professional cautiousness in the use of a heavy rifle.

A lot of people have been killed across the years, all over the world, by careless shooting. More often than not the shooter sees something that looks like his quarry and, without taking the time to properly identify it, takes a shot. I very nearly did it myself, years ago, hunting *murghi*—Indian Jungle Fowl—when I was a planter in North Bengal. I was out one morning with a fellow tea planter, Dick Sparke, (presently living in Vancouver, B.C., Canada). Armed with twelve gauge shotguns we were walking side by side through ten foot high brush on the bank of a jungle river. After a while we became separated. I heard Dick fire a shot and saw a nice fat *murghi*

Another reason why he withheld his fire in this case was probably that he was aware that the sound of his shot-in this case the thunderous blast of his big D.B.450/400-if it did not kill the cat might alarm it to where it would leave the vicinity. This would mean his having to start his searching and tracking all over again in another area, time consuming work in which he did not wish to be involved.

go curving down into the brush. Then I spotted one myself, sitting in a bush about five and half feet above the ground at a distance of about fifty feet. The winter sun, just rising, burnished its wings with red and I immediately slipped off the safety catch of my gun and raised it. But instead of shooting I waited; in the hunting fraternity to which I belonged it was not considered sporting to shoot a sitting bird. Wing shots were what counted and although the little Indian game hens we were after took off at great speed, it was not too difficult to put one down using Number Six Shot, or even Number Fours. And so, poised for my shot, on my toes, and ready to whip the gun to my shoulder and pull the trigger, I waited. And as I did so the object of my attention moved and turned towards me and I instantly saw, to my horror, that what I was looking at was not a *murghi* at all but the side of Dick's sunburned face. An unwritten sporting rule-wing shots only, gentlemen, if you please-saved him from a nasty accident, maybe even a fatal one.

In the excitement of a hunt, especially when the quarry is a big cat, it is all too easy to take a quick shot and hope for the best. It is even easier with a man-eater, where just about any kind of shot is justified; for a wounded man-eater is not a lot more dangerous than an unwounded one. In his fine book, THIRTY YEARS OF SHIKAR, published in 1855, Sir Edward Braddon, a renowned hunter of his day, tells about shooting a big striped animal, that he thought was a tiger, in a cave. The animal turned out to be a hyena. Again, a little later, in the excitement of a beat, a big black animal came bounding through the brush to the accompaniment of shouts from his beaters of *balu, balu*. He shot that also and the *balu,* which was supposed to be a bear, turned out to be a village buffalo.

CHAPTER THREE

When, after eating, a big cat covers up its kill with leaves or other matter, it may go off for a considerable distance to rest and digest its food. But when the kill is left uncovered, it is usually safe to presume that it will lie up not too far away, to protect it against scavengers, mainly vultures. Seeing that the kill had not been covered up, Corbett remained where he was for half an hour, watching for any movement on the part of the tiger and no doubt listening to the sounds of the forest and interpreting what they told him. He would also have watched and listened for flies.

It was May and even at this elevation in the hills, flies would have been quite prolific and, in the case of a kill, would have been attracted to it. The buzzing and whining of a swarm of flies on a kill makes quite a lot of noise; the sound can sometimes be heard from as far away as a hundred yards. After a tiger has eaten it often has blood on its paws and around its mouth and when it leaves the kill, and goes to lie up, swarms of flies will follow it. Big cats are bothered by flies to the point where they will sometimes get up and change position in the hope of getting rid of them. Sometimes they will actually go and lie in water. In this case Corbett hoped that flies from the kill might make the tiger get up and move, giving him a glimpse of it and the possibility of a shot. But the tigress, if it was close by, remained hidden and so after half an hour he left his observation point and went down to the kill.

Arriving at the kill Corbett noted that the tiger had eaten nearly half of it. With this considerable amount of meat in its belly he surmised the cat would not go very far and so he decided to try and follow it, and stalk it.

At the kill site he found what he called a confusion of pug marks. Ignoring these he circled until he found where they left the site. Then he set out to follow the tigress.

Corbett's method of picking up the prints of the tigress is a standard method used by professional hunters the world over; it is one that is even used today by police forces seeking suspects who may have fled on foot after a crime. As such it is worth a word of explanation.

In any kind of tracking the easiest way to pick up a line of prints, which it is necessary to do to commence a follow up, is not to spend time trying to analyze the meaning of a conglomeration of marks on the ground, but to start by circling them. Groups of prints, at a kill, of either tiger or leopard, will seldom indicate where the cat has come from, or to where it has gone. But by circling, one will, as it is professionally called, cut the sign, and then quickly ascertain both where the animal came from and, more important, the direction of its departure from the scene. The latter indication is what may then be used to follow up and stalk the animal in question.

Corbett tracked the tigress for about a hundred yards and then came to a small clearing. Here he found that the animal had lain down and when he saw a blade of grass spring up from the imprint of its body, where it had been lying, he knew that it had just been there.

Like Corbett, the tigress had come into the clearing from the east; arriving there it had lain down for a moment or two, most probably in the shade. Then the hot May sun had come flooding in, causing it to get up and move on, seeking a cooler place to rest. When Corbett, moving very carefully to the edge of the clearing, saw a big dead tree lying across its far end, he guessed that the cat might be lying behind it, sleeping in whatever shade it provided. He was right.

Now Corbett had to be very careful. His entry into the clearing and his examination of the place where the tigress had been lying in the grass, before it moved, had taken him to within ten feet of the fallen tree. This meant, though he did not know it yet, that he was now just ten feet from where the man-eater was lying.

His main concern now, in moving into a position from where he could see either over or around the fallen tree, was sound. With his ability to move quietly he would have had no trouble avoiding small sticks and dry leaves, thus eliminating the telltale sounds these make when crushed underfoot. But it was May and the short grass that covered the clearing, and through which he had to move, would have been very dry and brittle. The noise that he would make when walking on it, and how this could quickly alert the tigress to his presence, posed a serious threat to his hopes of getting close enough to see it and get a shot at it, as well as his personal safety.

When stalking an alert wild animal through dry grass, or other noise making ground cover, there is only one way to move without making any sound and that is, very, very slowly and within the pattern of a fixed procedure. The procedure is comparatively simple, but rigid in its rulings.

A route having been visually decided upon, the ground immediately ahead is scanned to determine what obstacles lie on it and how if possible they can be avoided, or negotiated. This done, forward movement begins. It starts with a raising of the first foot, elevating it high enough to clear whatever obstructions lie below it. The foot is then thrust slowly forward to the desired length of the step; this will be a distance that will enable the owner of the foot to retain perfect balance while standing on one leg. The foot is then lowered, down, down, very slowly, the forward outer edge of the sole of the foot leading, a quarter of an inch at a time, until this edge makes precise contact in the place in which it is intended to set it. When firm contact is made, then the remainder of the foot is laid down behind it, after which the weight of the body, nicely balanced, is slowly and carefully eased down on to it. The whole movement is then repeated with the next foot and the next step.

In stalking an animal on 'noisy' grounds, e.g., surfaces that have dried sticks or dead grass or other jungle debris lying on them, patience is essential because forward movement is going to be at the rate of a maximum of ten or twelve inches a minute. Impatience, usually generated by the thought that if the stalk is not completed quickly the quarry may get up and leave, can quickly shatter the best made plans. For Corbett, the ten feet between him and the fallen log must have taken at least ten minutes.

Corbett was within five feet of the fallen tree when he saw something yellow and black protruding around its end. It was the tip of the tigress' tail. For a moment he wondered if the cat had seen him coming and, like the Chowgarh tigress, was waiting for him, belly down, crouched behind the log, ready to attack. But moving a little closer he was able to see that the animal was lying on its back, sleeping, and this was confirmed when more of its body came into view and he could see its stomach rising up and down with its even breathing.

Moving the last few inches into a position for a shot, Corbett must have thanked the fates for what they had given him, a sleeping tiger at a range impossible to miss. But then its head came into view and he quickly saw that the remainder of the animal's body, stretched as it was away from his line of approach, lay behind and was blocked from his view by its head, and that to kill it he was going to have to take a head shot.

As has been discussed elsewhere, head shots on tiger are never advisable. But in this case there were two things that must have persuaded Corbett that he would have to take this shot. One was that the position of the big cat's body, lying head on towards him, allowed for no other shot. The other was that the only way to get a shot into its rib cage and heart, or even its lower neck, would mean shifting his position and moving slowly around the cat. In other words a continuation, if short, of his precarious stalk. This was not advisable. Sleeping tigers have a nasty habit of waking up very suddenly, with sometimes dire consequences to the person or persons foolish enough to disturb their slumbers. With the Mohan man-eater this could happen at any moment and, all things considered, he had been very lucky to get this far without the big cat even opening an eye.

So the head shot it had to be and he was about to align the sights of his big rifle on the animal's forehead and slide its butt into his shoulder and lean forward and shoot when he suddenly remembered that he had not yet cocked it. And to cock it he had to release the safety catch, which, like many an old fashioned rifle, indeed, like the Charles Osborne D.B.470 with which I did my first shooting in India, made a distinctive metallic click when released, one that in this case would awaken the big cat in a split second.

It was nine in the morning of a hot May day. No doubt there was bird song in the little clearing, and insect sound, as well as the distant murmur of the voices of villagers, back at Kartkanoula. Distinct and separate, nevertheless all these sounds contributed to an overall general pattern, one that would be sublimely registered on the sleeping tigress's semi-conscious mind. Any new sound would quickly awaken her. But she could be aroused equally quickly by any sudden change in the general pattern, something that could happen quite naturally, such as with a flight through the clearing of a flock of small birds. Even shifting patterns of light and shade that might allow hot sunlight to start creeping down behind the log, where she was sleeping, could disturb her.

Corbett, with all this obviously running through his mind, knew that whatever he did now he had better do it quickly. And so he did the only thing possible. He aligned the sights of his rifle on the cat's forehead, squeezed his forefinger down on the trigger and then pushed the safety catch forward. The very risky reverse firing procedure worked and to the echoing thunder of the big rifle, a first shot, and then a quick second for good measure, sent the Mohan man-eater into eternity.

The author at the pool in the Bulmaria khola into which the Muktesar man-eater fell when Corbett shot it.

Mr. And Mrs. Birendra Singh Negi, of Nanital, who helped the author in his research on the Muktesar man-eater.

Stone bust of Jim Corbett at the entrance to Corbett National Park.

In country where every inch of ground may be under cultivation, one camps wherever one can. Author and Forty Pound tent on the way to Kala Agar.

The guest book at the Kala Agar dak bungalow, eaten by insects and in a sad state of repair.

Faint with the passage of the years, Corbett's name, in his own handwriting, in the Kala Agar dak bungalow guest book.

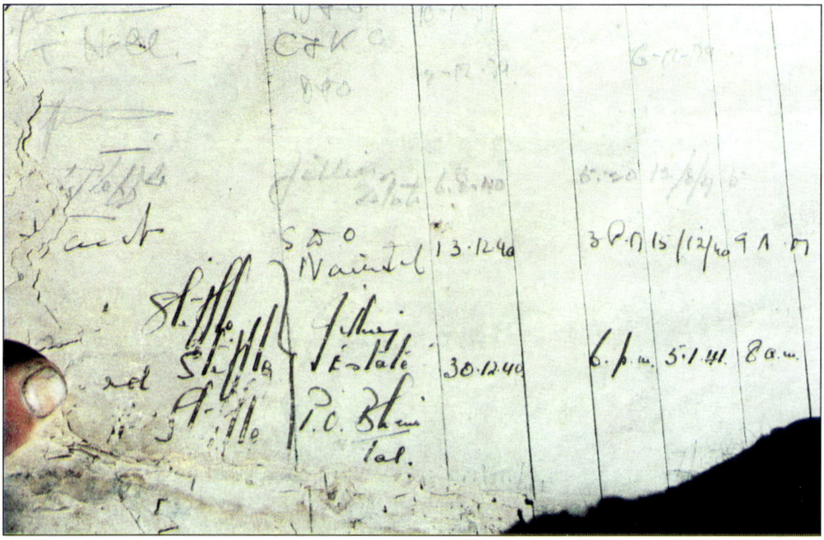

Other entries in the Kala Agar dak bungalow guest book include Stiffe, a friend of Corbett, who is mentioned in his writings.

A fine young Kumaoni hillman who was the author's energetic guide to the Kala Agar dak bungalow.

The Kala Agar dak bungalow where Corbett stayed during the hunt for the Chowgarh tigress.

The author stands by the huge leaning boulder down behind which the Chowgarh tigress stalked Corbett and his men.

The author in the exact place—at the lower end of the leaning rock slab—where the Chowgarh tigress sat, smiling, Corbett said, to ambush him and where, from a distance of 8 feet, he managed to shoot it.

Fly camp (temporary overnight camp) on the Bauni river in the SW Terai on a tiger hunt in the fifties.

Even when a man-eater menaces a district, people must leave their homes to work. Here village women carry fodder home for house-bound small animals like calves and lambs.

Vultures waiting at a kill. The fact that they are in the tree indicates that the cat, tiger or leopard, is lying up close by.

A proliferation of small, second rate hotels, all named after Corbett, line the highways in Kumaon and Gharwal. One doubts that the Corbett family has been consulted.

The road to Kartkanoula, where Corbett hunted the Mohan man-eater.

Garjia village, on the Kosi river, where Corbett spent a night while on the way to hunt the Mohan man-eater.

A Kartkanoula villager points to the place where the Mohan man-eater lay sleeping, behind a log, when Corbett stalked and shot it.

Tiger droppings, in Nepali "goo", from a big tiger.

Haldwani, also spelled Halduwani, south of Nanital, from where Corbett often took the train when setting out on his hunts.

Ramanagar railway station, from where Corbett, travelling from Nanital, disembarked for the Mohan man-eater hunt.

Sign on the wall of a dak bungalow in Kumaon.

Author on the porch of the Kanda dak bungalow during research on the Kanda man-eater.

Dense vegetation in the steep and rocky hill country around Kanda.

The Kanda man-eater. Corbett: "The ground in front of me was strewn with large smooth boulders...shod with the thinnest of rubber soled shoes, the going over these boulders was ideal for my purpose..."

Author on safari in the sixties in SW Nepal with basic tiger hunting gear; rope, flashlight, batteries, kukri (jungle knife), binoculars, .12 gauge shotgun, .375 rifle, sweater, sleeping bag, Jeep.

Author at the Kaladunga bungalow, on the Sarda river, north of Tanakpur, built by Collier, the British timber contractor and where he and his wife lived during his work in Nepal.

The dak bungalow at Tanakpur, where Corbett stayed from time to time.

The storekeeper at Chuka, from whom Corbett purchased supplies during his hunt with lbbotsen for the Chuka man-eater.

The rugged east side of the Sarda (also called the Mahakali) river gorge in the vicinity of Thak and Chuka.

The author with Sundar Singh, grandson of the immortal Dungar Singh, Corbett's guide in the shooting of the man-eater of Talla Des. Picture taken at Tula Kot, Kumaon, March 2002.

Mr. Lakshmi Dutt Sharma, 88 years of age in March 2002. In 1929, from the saddle below Tula Kot, he and other villagers watched Corbett track and shoot the man-eater of Talla Des.

The pass at the head of the Surya khola valley up which Corbett and his men struggled, on a long hot day in 1929, to reach the Talla Des district on the other side.

Jim Corbett's grave in Nyeri, Kenya, with the author, in 1965. He is buried between Matthew Leaky and Lord Baden Powell. The inscription, which is the same as that on his mother's grave in Nani Tal, reads: Till the day breaks and the shadows flee away.

The pine forest below Tula Kot, in the upper watershed of the Ladhya Khola. This is where Corbett tracked and shot the man-eater of Talla Des. Photograph taken in March 2002.

BOOK SEVEN

THE KANDA MAN-EATER.
1933

CHAPTER ONE

To get to Kanda nowadays one must travel by car through the Corbett National Park, at the main entry gate of which there is an imposing bust of the great *shikari sahib* himself. The route to the park is via Ramnagar, a bustling little city on the edge of the hills, one that can be reached by train from places like Pilibhit and Halduwani. But when, after getting permission to drive through the park, one arrives at Kanda, it will be to find that the village is long since gone and that all that remains of it now is a series of eroding terraces where once there were crops and, here and there, buried under brush, some small flat areas where perhaps village houses once stood. However, this does not matter too much because the man-eater that Corbett hunted and then shot here, was not actually shot at Kanda, but some distance away from it, closer to another village called Taria, the village which, though it is not named by him, is the one featured in his story of the Kanda man-eater.

Both Kanda and Taria lie on the top of a long, forested ridge; the distance between them is about three miles. And though Kanda is no more, there is a very comfortable *dak* bungalow there, close to where the village used to be and where, permission having been obtained from the park authorities, one can stay. This is where Corbett based, accompanied by his men, during his hunt for the man-eater and where I also stayed when carrying out my research on the story.

The country around Kanda, at the northern end of Corbett National Park, is composed of short, steep hills covered with *sal* forest and brush. The brush is thickest in the bottoms of the many ravines and it was in these that the Kanda man-eater made its home, presenting Corbett, on arrival in the area, with the very difficult task of finding it. In fact it was fifteen days before he even got wind of the animal and then, as is often the case, it was via village intelligence, a chance sighting of the big cat by a Taria villager.

Corbett got the news of the sighting late one evening; it was most probably brought to him by a party of men from Taria. Next morning, he set out for Taria to search for the tiger.

Arriving at the village, all of the inhabitants of which, on his instructions, were staying in their houses, he immediately put into effect a standard method of search, which is to take the place of the incident in question-in this case the place where the tiger had been seen-and then circle around it and, from whatever sign could be found, determine where it had come from and, more important, where it had gone. He spent a day doing this and looking for pug marks of the big cat but was unable to find any. In the evening he returned to the Kanda *dak* bungalow.

The following morning he set out for another day of searching. In the evening of this second day he found the tracks of a tiger in a field above Taria village. Telling the villagers that he would come back next morning he returned again to Kanda.

On the third day of his search, arriving at the village, he was told that a domestic buffalo had been killed during the night. The villagers quickly showed him where the buff carcass was and he saw at once that the animal had been killed by a tiger and that after downing it the tiger had dragged it along the ridge towards Kanda and then taken it down into a narrow, steep ravine on the north face of the hill.

To see into the ravine Corbett climbed up onto a rock, on the ridge above it. Noticing how dense it was, and how steep, he decided that it would be easier, and, in case the big cat was in it, probably safer, to enter it from its lower end. This is what he did, finding his way down the long, steep, north face of the Kanda-Taria ridge, his plan being to work his way back up to the ridge via the ravine.

In Corbett's day the mouth of the ravine in which the kill lay was wider than the remainder of its body, as it climbed the hill. It is the same today. From this mouth, and for a considerable way up, it is filled with big, smooth surfaced river rocks and on entering it Corbett made use of these to make a silent approach up towards where the kill lay and to where he hoped to find the tiger.

Corbett's use of the river rocks to make his approach up the ravine was a natural one. In my own experience there are few things quieter to walk on than the water worn surfaces of river stones.

He had climbed about three quarters of the way up the ravine when he found the kill, hidden in a bank of ferns. Believing that the tiger might be lying up close by, he selected a position and settled down to wait.

Corbett had excellent eyesight and what he hoped for was that the tiger would move and reveal its position, either to him, or to some animal or bird. He would very probably visually catch the movement himself and then of course take appropriate action. But if he missed it, then the animal or bird in question would call in alarm, alerting him to the movement and possibly giving him a chance of a shot at it.

For several minutes nothing happened and then, suddenly, he developed a very strong feeling that the tiger was close by and that it had detected him and was watching him. This was confirmed when the big cat, which had probably seen him coming up the ravine and which was now lying in the brush and watching him, suddenly became uneasy about his presence and broke cover and made a run for it up the steep hillside. The tiger was sixty yards away and high above him and going fast when he took a shot at it and it is a measure of his expertise with a rifle that he hit it, for any animal going fast in heavy brush is a formidable target for the best of hunters. The excellence of his shot is all the more emphasized when one realizes it was taken with a heavy rifle, in this case his D.B. 450/400, a weapon that is designed for steady, close quarter action and not for snap shooting at fast moving targets at ranges of sixty or more yards.

Unfortunately his shot was not a fatal one, or even a crippling one; the bullet hit the cat in the elbow joint of its left front leg and then, bouncing back off a rock, hit it again in the jaw. The big cat roared its displeasure and for a moment sounded as though it might be coming back down the hill to attack him. Then the roars ceased and the last that Corbett saw of it was as it went across the side of the hill, high above him, too far away for another shot.

CHAPTER TWO

Next morning Corbett again visited the kill and was pleased to see that the tiger had come back in the night and eaten some of it. Believing that the cat might come again, he thought about building a *machan* and sitting up for it. But there were no suitable trees in the ravine itself and while a younger Corbett might have elected to sit on the ground all night and just wait for the man-eater to come, an older and wiser Corbett, as he was now, decided against the idea.

Climbing to the top of the ravine, Corbett found a tree with a stout branch about eight feet above the ground and he was examining it, with an eye to spending a night in it, when he heard the tiger call from across the valley below him, the valley from which he had made his stalk up the ravine the previous day. This gave him the idea of attracting the tiger vocally, and with this in mind he started calling the big cat.

Tiger calling is an art and to successfully accomplish it takes years of practice. Corbett could do it and was adept at it. But my guess is that it must have taken him years of work, and much trial and error, because this is what it took me. Only in recent years have I been able to call up tigers and even now my successes are numbered on the fingers of one hand. Corbett was able to do it with considerable success and in one case, during the hunt for the Thak man-eater (see BOOK TEN) he was able to bring a big cat right in to within twenty feet and then shoot it. In my case, my purpose has of course been photography and on four occasions to date I have been able to successfully photograph big cats that I have called in. But it has not been an easy task as well as which, as it has to be done on foot, and on the ground, it is what might be called a somewhat hazardous form of sport.

The call that is used to attract tigers is the mating call of the male and the cats that will respond to this, if it is done in the right way, are, firstly, females looking for a mate and, secondly, males challenging the call of what they think is another male. In both cases there is considerable danger for the caller, especially if he is unarmed. In the case of a female, the cat is answering the call in the hope of mating with a male and when she finds out that the male she has been expecting to meet is not there, she is liable to get very angry, very quickly. In the case of a male answering the call the situation is similar. Answering the call of another male means that it is accepting its challenge and challenging it in return and, like the female, when it discovers that the source of the calling is a single man, alone in the forest and—in my case, these days—armed with nothing more than a camera, its reaction may generally be described as uncertain.

Adding to what is essentially an unpredictable situation is the fact that the caller is going to be on foot and on the ground. I have tried calling tiger from the comparative safety of small trees and have not been successful. I wondered why, until I was able to analyze the problem and find the answer, which comes in two parts.

One, tigers are not tree living or tree climbing animals. Two, they have a unique ability to pinpoint sound which includes, I believe, the competency to precisely determine both direction *and* elevation. The result of this natural endowment on the part of the big cats, when applied to my trying to call them from trees, was obvious. The tigers who heard me calling from my arboreal perches were able to determine the sound as coming from a place where no sensible tiger would ever be—up in a tree—and, clever and wary animals that they are, they were not about to be fooled by it. This discovery brought me back to earth, so to speak, to ground level, where tigers live and from where, as opportunity allows, I continue to engage in this very challenging and exciting sport.

****This book contains several pictures of tigers. The one on the front cover, of the tigress that killed and ate our safari camp cook in the White Grass Plains in 1999 (See BOOK TEN, Mangal, A Jungle Tragedy) was taken by me at night, using a motion sensor camera. The others, pictures of different animals, are of tigers that I called up myself.***

CHAPTER THREE

Corbett's calling of the man-eater on this occasion was unsuccessful. He called for an hour and the cat answered him. But very possibly because it had had a nasty experience the day before, from close to where he was calling-shot at and clipped on the elbow by the big slug of a DB 450/400 would be considered a nasty occurrence by any animal-it did not react to his calling, or show itself. And so he gave up for the moment and went back to Taria, where his servants cooked him a meal. After the meal he returned to the head of the ravine and there found a tree he considered suitable for a *machan*.

It was not the kind of tree that I would have chosen to sit for a man-eater.

Sometimes, looking at some of Corbett's actions, in some of his near incredible hunts, I wonder about what almost seems to be blatant insensitivity on his part to the dangers that surrounded him. To the real and horrible danger, for instance, of being caught by a man-eater and killed and eaten. Or, worse, being caught and dragged away and eaten while-for a short time anyway-still alive. Because some of the things he did are really quite extraordinary to the point where, being positive, one would describe them as acts of sublime courage, or, being negative, as downright foolhardy. One of these was what he did now, which was to climb into a tree to wait for a very dangerous and very alert man-eater and to do so from a single branch just eight feet above the ground.

The tree that Corbett chose for his sit was on the west side of the upper end of the ravine, and within a few feet of its actual rim. The side of the ravine that fell away behind the tree, to the north, was steep, indeed, near vertical, and the bed of the ravine itself, about thirty feet below, contained a number of small pools.

Corbett expected the man-eater to come up the ravine from where he had last heard it calling, from the north. At first, with this in mind, he probably considered sitting and facing in that direction, because if the cat came that way it would have to climb up the steep bank to get to his tree, in the process of which he believed he would hear it coming and get a shot at it. However, if he did face that way, and it came from the other direction, from the south, this would mean that he would have his back to it and while he does not say so, his perch on a single branch suggests to me that it would have been very difficult, if not impossible, for him to turn around to deal with an approach from this direction.

Again, if it came from the south, it was very important that he be facing it and in a position to get a shot at it before it got too close. Coming up the ravine, from the north, would mean that until it got close, the depth of the ravine would physically place the cat well below him. Whereas if it came from the south, even before it reached his tree, it was going to be very much closer. The reason for this was the general dimensions of the quite incredible perch that he had chosen for his sit.

The branch he had selected for his natural *machan* was eight feet above the ground. Allowing for the height of the big cat's head to be about three feet high, this would place the bulk of its body no more than five feet below his perch, a distance that an adult tiger can reach up, with either of its razor taloned front paws, with the greatest of ease. This thought is probably what decided him to take up a position facing south, rather than north. It was a thought which I believe saved his life.

Soon after Corbett climbed into his tree a Langur monkey called several times from a long way off, to the north, and Corbett surmised that it had seen him climbing into the tree and, at that distance, had possibly mistaken him for a leopard. He was wrong, as he was about to find out.

CHAPTER FOUR

Not long after Corbett got into the tree the sky reddened to the west and the sun sank quickly below the horizon. Night soon wrapped the forest in darkness through which he sat for several hours, peering into the gloom, listening, waiting for the big cat to appear. Then, suddenly, he heard it approaching, making the soft, telltale sounds that the pigs of a big cat make as it plodded though the debris on the ground below his tree. Envisioning this, we can imagine him tightening his grip on the big, double barreled rifle and tensing in anticipation of a shot. However, with the arrival of the big cat, far from getting a shot, he suddenly found himself in an extremely hazardous situation. Because, firstly, the tiger had arrived from behind him, from the direction of the ravine, and not in front of him as he had hoped. And secondly, it knew he was in the tree, waiting for it, and promptly advised him of this with a serious of deep throated growls.

Then, or a little later, Corbett remembered the Langur calling from the opposite side of the valley below him, the one that he thought had seen him and mistaken him for a leopard. Reassessing the reason for the monkey's alarm calls, he realized that the little simian may not have noticed him at all but had actually been watching the tiger, sitting in the brush, possibly in the upper part of the ravine from where the clever cat, in turn, had been watching Corbett climb into the tree. Now it was voicing its displeasure at his presence and with powerful and angry growls informing him of this;

and, no doubt, of the fact that, given an opportunity, it intended having him for dinner.

I think that on this occasion Corbett may have regretted sitting so low to the ground. As has been discussed, tigers seldom look above the level of their eyes and the singular advantage of hunting one from a tree *machan* is that its elevation raises the hunter above the contained area of the tiger's visual range. Movement of any kind will of course always catch a big cat's eye and even movement in a tree will attract its immediate attention. But if the hunter is aware of this and remains still, the big cat will not notice him unless, like the Kanda man-eater, an unusually wary animal, it has actually watched him getting into his tree and already knows he is there.

In the case of the Kanda cat this is what had happened. But whereas a normal tiger, having seen the hunter climb the tree, will almost always quickly leave the area in alarm, in this case the tiger was a man-eater and to its thinking, a man in a tree represented a meal. This nasty aspect of the situation is what Corbett must have been thinking about now, in the darkness, with a man-eating tiger moving around no more than four or five feet below his feet.

Corbett thought about firing a shot into the darkness to scare the tiger off. This might have worked. But it might also alarm the big cat and persuade it to leave the area, thus forcing Corbett to start his hunt for it all over again, in new terrain. So he refrained from doing this. However, to protect himself as best as he could against the tiger reaching up and trying to swat him off his branch, he took the 450/400 and pushed it down between his left arm and his side, at the same time cocking it and placing fingers on both of its triggers. And he kept it there until the tiger, deciding that buffalo meat would be a satisfactory enough meal this time, left him and went down the ravine to eat on its kill.

Corbett may have slept. He had a great ability to do this in places the extreme discomfort of which would send many a better man running for his bed. But when the sun rose out of the east he was wide awake and it was good that he was, for minutes after his men, no doubt bringing him his beloved tea, called to him from the ridge, he saw the tiger dashing across the hillside that composed the east side of the ravine, to his left. He does not say how far away the animal was and in the shallow light of the new day, with his eyes strained by a night of peering into the darkness, it represented only a fleeting target, one on which it was undoubtedly very difficult to align the sights of the big rifle. Nevertheless he unhesitatingly took a shot at it. When he did, the man-eater turned and with a mighty roar came straight for his tree.

When you are hunting a big cat and it comes at you, enraged and with the distinct intention of killing you, there are several things you can do. One, you can drop your rifle and turn and run. This is usually fatal. Two, you can start shooting the split second it commences its charge and keep shooting and give it everything you've got in the hope of putting it down before it closes with you. This too is often fatal. Or you can wait, on one knee if you are on the ground—something that will give you a flatter angle and a more killing shot—and withhold your shot until the animal is simply too close for you to miss. This method, requiring you to wait until the big cat is no more than ten feet away at the very most, requires a very cool head as well as absolute confidence in your ability, with whatever weapon you are using, to stop its onslaught. But it is, undoubtedly, the most appropriate one in the case of any, large, thoroughly provoked wild animal that has singled you out as the object of its savage intention. It is the one which, unless bad luck intervenes, such as a misfire, will allow you to enjoy a peg of whiskey at the campfire that evening, plus the pleasure of telling your friends the story of what happened, rather than having someone else tell it.

Corbett waited. He waited as he did in the charge of the Muktesar man-eater. He waited with the rigid discipline of the true hunter and, I feel, with the thrilling awareness of the fact that this, and little else, is the hunter's real moment of truth.

He ignored the big cat's roars, powerful sounds expressing the animal's rage that can often be fatally disconcerting to the object of its attention. He ignored the speed of the animal's charge, which was very fast and probably close to the limit of its ability. He ignored the fact that the tiger knew where he was and was coming directly at him. And no doubt he put out of his mind what would happen if he did not wait until it was close enough to be a positive target, what would happen if he missed his shot, or just wounded it, and failed to stop its charge. What it would do to him when it smashed itself in on top of him. What it would be like to be pulled from the tree and then subjected to the shocking savagery of an enraged big cat.

My guess is that Corbett waited until the tiger was no more than fifteen feet away. He said that he shot it the *second* time as it was in the act of springing upwards towards him and, coming as fast as it was, I feel that this is the distance it would have naturally selected to make the surging lunge that would carry it up to Corbett's perch. Which means, as shots from a double barreled rifle can be taken split seconds apart, or can even be instantaneous, that his first shot was taken as it gathered itself for this action, very probably at no more than fifteen feet and his second immediately after.

Corbett aimed for the very best target presented in a situation like this—a frontal charge—which was the broad expanse of the big cat's chest. The bullets from his heavy rifle would have been travelling at something close to maximum muzzle velocity at this range and no doubt would have raked the animal end to end. Nevertheless the momentum of its charge carried it forward and it actually crashed into the tree below him, spattering him with its blood. The tree deflected the impetus of its passage and it bounced off it and fell, head over heels, into the ravine.

From the tree to the floor of the ravine is a drop of some thirty feet. I mentioned earlier, in a description of the ravine, that its upper area contained a number of small pools. In Corbett's time there was one slightly larger than the others, directly below his tree. The tiger fell into this, no doubt with a mighty splash, and then, rather unbelievably, considering that it had just been shot twice at close range with a powerful rifle, got up and staggered out and lurched on down the ravine.

Corbett waited a moment, saw that the tiger had disappeared and then slid down the tree. After massaging his legs to bring back circulation—he had just spent fifteen hours sitting on a single branch—and reloading his rifle, he made his way cautiously down into the ravine to look for the tiger. He found the big cat a short distance away, lying in another small pool, quite dead.

tiger fell into this, no doubt with a mighty splash, and then, rather unbelievably, considering that it had just been shot twice at close range with a powerful rifle, got up and staggered out and limped off down the ravine.

Corbett waited a moment; saw that the tiger had disappeared and then slid down the tree, first massaging his legs to bring back circulation—he had just spent fifteen hours sitting on a single branch—and reloading his rifle he made his way cautiously down into the ravine to look for the tiger. He found the big cat a short distance away, lying in another small pool, quite dead.

BOOK EIGHT

THE MAN-EATER OF CHUKA.
1937.

CHAPTER ONE

Some years ago I owned a white water river running company in Nepal. I ran it for eight years and in the course of those years explored and did the first runs on three major Himalayan rivers and three minor ones. The big rivers were the Karnali, which took two attempts to complete, one of thirty-two days and one of ten days; the Tula Beri, which took a month to run; and the Sarda, also known as the Kali Gandaki, which required seventeen days.*

For the Sarda expedition I took a team of stalwart river runners by chartered bus to Dandeldura and from there we walked north for a week to the junction of the Sarda and the Chamlya. We put in at the junction of these two beautiful Himalayan rivers and then set off down the Sarda in two big, fourteen-foot Willawa inflatables, slowly and carefully scouting the unknown waters, all the way down to the dam at Banbasa, near Tanakpur, from where we were picked up by my safari camp partner, Colonel Bisht, and taken to Mahendranagar. From Mahendranagar we found our various ways back to Katmandu.

**Although it seems hardly relevant to a book about man-eaters, readers may be interested in knowing why an unexplored river may take a month or more to run. The reason is the very fact that it is unexplored and, as such, may contain unknown hazards, such as violent rapids, whirlpools and dangerous obstacles like huge, sub surface rocks, or tree jams. Because of these, every single stretch of the river has to be visually scouted and this of course will include every bend around which, not visible to approaching rafters, these dangers may lie. Scouting means stopping, pulling in and tying up the rafts and then sending someone on foot down the river bank to see what lies ahead. Scouting, a standard safety procedure on unknown rivers, may require hundreds of time-consuming stops and these, more than anything else, are what add up to the prolonged duration of exploratory runs.*

On the way down the river, as is the historical right of explorers who make the first footsteps in unknown country, we named all the big rapids, one by one. About four miles south of a village called Amora, the Sarda leaves its north to south course and, turning, flows due west, past the villages of Miuri and Kanai. After about another four miles it turns south again at the villages of Murgoan and Sem, where it picks up the waters of the lovely little hill river, the Ladhya.

A mile or so after the Ladhya junction, and just before the village of Chuka came into view on the west bank of the river, we came across a set of short, fast ferociously hazardous rapids. There were six of them, all in a line, a boiling, downhill run of furious white water studded with masses of broken rock, a Class 8 on the Himalayan White Water scale of 1/10. We studied them for a while to see if there was safe way through them. But there was none and so we were forced to portage around them. We did this on the Nepal side and we named the rapids the Chuka Man-Eaters.

CHAPTER TWO

Chuka is a Koumani village of about two hundred people lying on the west bank of the Sarda, just south of the its junction with the Ladhya river. In the winter of 1936 two men were attacked by a tiger, on two separate occasions, in the forest between the village of Chuka and the village that lies just above it, Thak. Both men managed to make their escape, one when the cat mistook a wooden plough and a bag of food, that the man was carrying on his back, for his body, and attacked it instead of the man; the other when the tiger grabbed a sack of *gur*, raw sugar, off his shoulders and got its teeth entangled in it. However, in the new year of 1937 the tiger changed its tactics and in June of that year took its first human victims.

One morning in June, the hot month that brings the monsoon to Kumaon, some men and boys were herding cattle in a field near the village of Thak. When some of the cattle began to stray towards the nearby jungle, one of the boys, a youngster of fourteen, was sent to drive them back. When he left to do this the men settled down to sleep through the heat of the day and it was not until several hours later, awakened by the calling of a Barking Deer, that they realized that the boy had not returned. A second boy was sent to find out where the first boy was and to bring the strayed cattle back out of the forest. This boy went into the forest and started to herd out the straying cattle. But as he was doing so, the cattle suddenly panicked and began to run for the village and as they did a tiger attacked one of them and pulled it down. In the confusion that followed more men and women came running from the village and it was soon determined that both of the boys who had been sent into the forest were missing.

Among the men and women who came from the village was the mother of one of the missing boys and with commendable courage she went straight into the forest to look for her son. She quickly found his remains; the tiger had killed him. Soon afterwards the parents of the other boy found their son, also killed by the tiger and, in this case, partially eaten.

One of the instances where a tiger can be dangerous, one of what is called The Instances Of Provocation, is when it is with its kill and either eating it, or about to eat it. Tigers survive by killing and eating other animals. But they only kill when they are hungry. Thus, when a tiger has its fresh kill in front of it and is just about to start eating it, it is hungry. And a hungry tiger is an animal that will not tolerate interference of any kind with its dinner plans.*

Anyone, or indeed any animal, that approaches a tiger on its freshly killed prey is, in the tiger's mind, someone or something that is coming to take its food away from it, something that a big cat, within the limits of its capabilities, will not tolerate. Approaching a big cat on its fresh kill is always dangerous and one does it at one's peril. This may be what both boys did, albeit by accident, for when their bodies were being recovered, the villagers found a freshly killed calf, on which the tiger may have been eating, close to where the first boy was killed. The second boy, blundering on the tiger while it was eating either the calf or the first boy, suffered the same fate. The partial eating of the body of one of the boys made the Chuka tiger a man-eater and marked the beginning of a period of fear for the villagers of both Chuka and Thak.

**The only animals that may succeed in separating a hungry tiger from its meal are, one, another tiger and, two, sometimes, a big bear. With tigers, the other animal will have to be bigger and stronger than the owner of the kill. With bears, the same applies, although a hungry bear can put up a fearful demonstration, together with the most awesome, screaming roars, when it challenges a tiger for food, to the point where a tiger will sometimes, though not always, back down.*

CHAPTER THREE

The Chuka man-eater's next victim was another boy, one of two orphans, cattle herders, also from the village of Thak. Again, as in the previous instance, the boys were tending cattle. Possibly because of the now prevailing fear of the man-eater, and with the knowledge of what happened to their other two friends firmly in their minds, the two boys stayed together for safety, and in the middle of an open field. But when a cow began to stray towards the edge of the forest, one of the boys got up to drive it back and when he did so the tiger, which must have been lying up in cover close by, watching them and waiting for a chance to take one of them, leapt on him and went charging off with him in its mouth.

In Corbett's writings the name of the Ibbotsens, "Ibby" as he was known to his friends and Jean, his wife, appears from time to time. Ibbotsen was Deputy Commissioner of the three districts of Naini Tal, Almora and Gharwal at this time and Corbett describes he and his wife Jean as great friends of his. More than this, although he does not dwell on it too much, Ibbotsen was one of the very few men that he would take hunting with him, one of the rare ones, in other words, that he trusted, obviously as far as the dangers of man-eater hunting were concerned, but also, as a hunting companion, with a rifle at close quarters. And so when he came to hunt the Chuka man-eater, in 1937, he brought them with him.

When people talk with me about my years as a professional hunter, they almost invariably ask what was the most dangerous aspect of my profession. When they do I tell them, unhesitatingly, that it was nervous and excitable clients and the rifles that they carried and what they were liable to do with them when they got agitated or, worse, when they panicked. From experience I know what that is.

I had a client, a young man from New York, with me on a Swamp Deer hunt. We were out in open country one morning looking for trophy animals and soon came across a group of big bucks feeding in a stand of thick, high grass. Looking for a suitable position from which to shoot, I was whispering to my client that the best thing to do would be to walk around to the other side of the grass, where the ground was a little higher, and take advantage of the elevation there for a shot. Suddenly, rifle in hand, he took off at a run, in a state of high excitement, into the thicket and the next thing I knew he was blasting away and there were bullets zipping out of the grass in all directions, not a few of them towards me and my gunbearer, both of us prone on the ground. The shots continued until he ran out of ammunition, when, with sighs of relief, we got back to our feet. The sound that a 30.06 bullet makes when it goes by you, an inch or so from your ear, is what might be called attention getting; one tries not to think of what it will do if it hits you.

On another occasion I had a lady on a tiger shoot. I had found a dead buffalo that a tiger had killed and I built a *machan* in a nearby tree and, together with my client, who was armed with a Winchester .375, sat in it until near dark. Just as the light was almost gone, the tiger appeared and she took a shot at it. It whirled around and was gone in a flash. After waiting for a while to see if there were any sounds that might indicate that it was wounded, or unwounded and returning to the kill, I climbed down from the tree and rifle in hand and as best as I could in the last of the light, did a careful search for blood sign. Doing this, I moved away from the tree that my client was sitting in and into some light scrub and I was moving slowly through this, stooping, going down on my hands and knees to look for sign on the ground when she suddenly screamed, "Look out!" and in a panic fired directly at me. I threw myself on the ground as three more shots whizzed over my head and then, thank the fates, she was out of ammunition. Later, asked what she had fired at, she said that she saw what she believed was the tiger—me on my hands and knees—and thought she should have another crack at it while it was still around. Fortunately for all concerned she was a very poor shot.

Provoked, or as a man-eater, the tiger is a very dangerous animal. But he comes in a poor second to the hunting safari client armed with a high powered rifle, one bullet from which will quickly send you to the happy hunting grounds.

CHAPTER FOUR

Corbett and the Ibbotsens traveled by bus from Naini Tal, via Halduwani, to Tanakpur. That they came in the hot month of April shows that they were well seasoned to India's sunny clime, as Kipling, with typical British understatement, used to call it, and that they came on an Indian bus, even if it was privately chartered, indicates a disregard for personal comfort which I find admirable.

They left the bus at the Boom, as the Sarda Canal Bifurcation operation was known in those days, below Tanakpur, and from there set out on foot for Chuka, up the Sarda gorge. They made their first camp at a place called Tuli Gadh, where a small river of that name flows into the Sarda from the Indian side, and spent the night there. Next day they marched on, eight miles, to Kaladunga, where they spent their second night in J.P. Collier's bungalow, high above the river.*

The hunting party, thirty-three in number-Corbett and the Ibbotsens plus thirty camp men-arrived at Chuka on the third day after leaving Naini Tal. I do not know where they made camp but my guess is that it would not have been close to the village but more

---

****In his writings Corbett speaks fondly of this lovely old bungalow, built in 1919, and the splendid view from its verandah across the river and into Nepal. The view that he mentions, of the Rangun Khola, in Nepal and where, at its lower end, it flows into the Sarda, is today as beautiful as ever. One can reach the upper Rangun by trekking down on foot, southwest, from the city of Dandeldura, which in turn can be reached by a motor road from the town of Ataria, on Nepal's East West highway, about one hour's drive, east, from Mahendranagar. (For an update on the present-2002-status and condition of Collier's bungalow, see, in the EPILOGUE, notes on the Talla Des man-eaters.)***

likely some distance away from it, probably at the confluence of the Sarda and the Ladhya. While the waters of the Sarda are often silted with glacial sand, the Ladhya almost always has the clear, clean water which they would have wanted for their camping needs. This is where I camped the last time I visited Chuka, on the Ladhya's southern bank, about two hundred yards back from Sarda.

CHAPTER FIVE

Five young buffaloes had been sent up from Tanakpur for Corbett to use as bait and these were now set out in the forests around Chuka in an effort to try and get a kill by the man-eater. Corbett believed that the tiger was still in the area, even though no human beings had been killed since the third boy was taken at Thak and so he and Ibbotsen designed their hunt around a baiting program, combined with local intelligence, for gathering of which latter they hiked back and forth to Thak, and other villagers.

Soon after the buffaloes were set out one went missing. Taking one of Ibbotsen's retainers, a man named Sham Singh, Corbett set off to try and trace the missing bovine and soon found where a tiger had killed it and taken it into a short, bottle-necked ravine that drained into the Ladhya. Not long after leaving the camp he was joined by three village men and rather than send them back, which was his immediate reaction, he somewhat reluctantly allowed them to come with him.

Accompanied by the four men, he approached the ravine and when he was within a short distance of its upper end, the tiger, lying in it, in a dense thicket, growled a warning. Corbett's immediate concern was for the men with him and what would happen if the tiger charged and so, keeping them all close together, he retreated from the ravine, walking backwards with them, very slowly, until he was well clear of it. Then, still worried about them but not wanting to lose this opportunity of getting a shot at the tiger, he kept them with him while he tried a flanking stalk of the tiger's position, one that eventually brought him to the upper end of the ravine, above where the tiger was lying with its kill.

With the men prone on the ground around him, Corbett carefully scanned the brush in the ravine. Suddenly one of the men whispered that he could see the tiger and when questioned by Corbett said that he could see its ears moving. The distance from where they were, to where they thought the tiger was lying, was fifty yards and for a while Corbett could see nothing. Then, when one of the men stood up to get a better view into the brush, the tiger, which had been lying watching them, suddenly appeared and, turning, started quickly up the hill behind the ravine. When its head showed, briefly, through the brush, Corbett took a quick shot at it, missing the big cat's body but slicing a little hair off the ruff of its neck. The cat then disappeared.

After the cat left, Corbett searched for the dead *puda* and found that the tiger had dropped it into a four foot deep pool in the ravine, no doubt to protect it from scavengers. Hiding the kill in this way was unusual. I once tracked a tiger that dragged a buffalo down a jungle stream, under water that was four feet deep, a depth that must have had the big cat holding its head high to be able to breath. But I have never seen a kill hidden like this, underwater.

While Corbett was camped at the Ladhya he was visited by a man named MacDonald, a Divisional Forest Officer. Corbett appears to have enjoyed his company and over the next few days allowed the man to accompany him on some of his scouting and intelligence gathering.

When he got back to camp from his first encounter with the tiger Corbett was told that a cow had been killed by a big cat and so accompanied by MacDonald, whom he called Mac, he set out to look for the kill. They found it with some difficulty, for even though the men who had discovered it earlier in the day had covered it up, the tiger had returned and picked it up and then carried it away without leaving any drag mark.

MacDonald helped Corbett build a small *machan* at the site of the kill and when Corbett had climbed into it and settled himself for his vigil, he went off and left him there. Corbett stayed all night, during which he watched another big cat, a tigress, with two cubs, come and eat at the kill. But the man-eater did not appear and in the morning he returned to camp.

CHAPTER SIX

Now another buffalo was killed at Thak, killed and carried away. Corbett, accompanied by Ibbotsen and two men, set out to find it. Their search for it was grueling for the tiger had carried it for more than two miles through very rough terrain.

At first they were not sure that the tiger that had made this kill was the man-eater.* But when they found the dead buffalo they were satisfied that it had been killed by the man-eater, for the villagers had told Corbett that the killer cat had a broken canine tooth, something they had been able to determine from teeth marks in the other kills it had made in the area. The same marks now showed in the throat of this most recent kill and seeing them, and also noticing that the tiger had not eaten any of the carcass, Corbett immediately looked around for a place of concealment to sit and wait for the big cat to come back. He soon found one in a big *ficus* tree, close to a small stream.

The giant *ficus* tree that Corbett selected for his sit for the man-eater was a mature tree in 1937. It was equally mature, healthy, bursting with greenery and trellis fronds, when I climbed it in 1983,

---

**In his writing about the Chuka man-eater Corbett states that when he saw that the tiger had not eaten any of this kill, which the big cat had made the previous night, he found this "disquieting". I find this statement subject to two interpretations. The first is, that as it had not eaten, it would now be hungry and thus more likely to return to the kill when it got dark. For Corbett this possibility should not have been disquieting; it should have been promising, for it would have meant the chance of getting a shot at the tiger. The second interpretation of why Corbett found the tiger's empty belly "disquieting" is that this indicated to him that it would be hungry, in which case its next kill might be human.*

on my first visit to Chuka. The big fork into which Corbett fitted himself, worrying about the possibility of snakes and scorpions in its dark recesses, was still there and sitting in it I could hear, just as Corbett did, the rush of the little stream on the hillside below.

As soon as Corbett had made himself comfortable in the giant *ficus* he signaled to Ibbotsen and when he did, his friend left with the two men who had come with them, all talking loudly in a effort to persuade the tiger, if it was lying up close by and listening to them, that whoever had been there was now leaving. Then, no doubt after carefully checking his 450/400 high velocity rifle, Corbett settled down to wait.

He did not have to wait long for about a quarter of an hour after Ibbotsen left, what Corbett said was a red monkey,* called in alarm from about four hundred yards away. Its alarm call indicated that it had seen either a leopard or a tiger; in this case what it saw, almost certainly, was the man-eater.

Corbett's immediate analysis of the calling of the monkey, and how it related to everything that had occurred within the preceding hour, can only be described as masterly; indeed it is a shining example of his superb knowledge of jungle lore.

First of all he noted that the monkey had not called previously. This meant that it had not seen the tiger until then and this in turn meant that the tiger, which must have been lying up close to the kill when Corbett and Ibbotsen got to the kill site and were examining it, had not moved. Had it moved, the Rhesus would have seen it and would have called. Now the big cat was on the move and the Rhesus, no doubt from some high, safe perch, had detected it and was calling in alarm. Again, Rhesus Macaques have excellent eyesight and although the monkey was calling from a quarter of a mile away, if the brush allowed the little simian to see it, the big cat it was watch-

---

**The monkey that Corbett refers to was most probably the Rhesus Macaque, (Macaca mulatta), a reddish brown monkey common to the Terai forests. Its alarm call is a single racking cough, repeated again and again until whatever has alarmed it disappears from view.*

ing could be up to a quarter of a mile away from it; in other words, quite close to where Corbett was. This, as it turned out, proved to be the case for not long after Ibbotsen and the men left, Corbett heard a twig snap and, turning slowly in his hide, he looked back and down to see the tiger approaching.

The tiger used all of a quarter of an hour to make its approach to the big *ficus* and only when it was completely satisfied that Ibbotsen and the men were gone, and that there was no one else in the vicinity, did it emerge from cover. When it did so, however, instead of going to the kill to eat, as Corbett had hoped, it lay down to rest. This was fine with Corbett for an immobile animal is a lot easier to shoot than one that is on the move. However, the place it chose for its siesta was right next to the bole of the *ficus* tree, too close for Corbett to see from his position in the fork. In fact he quickly found that even though he leaned out as far as he safely could without overbalancing, he could only see its tail and part of one hind leg. Which posed a dilemma.

Corbett noticed that the place where the tiger was lying was in shade, comfortable for the tiger in the hot April weather and from this concluded that the big cat might now go to sleep and lie there for several hours, possibly until dark. He decided therefore that it was imperative to take a shot at it while the light was good. The trouble was that a shot into its lower back, the only part of it that he could clearly see, would only disable it and cripple it and that was something that no true sportsman likes to do to a healthy animal.

But this was not a healthy animal. This was a man-eater and the code for shooting a man-eater allows for any kind of shot, even a crippling one that may condemn it to a slow and painful death. This is because it is already a man killer and, as such, is condemned by society to be disposed of in any way possible, regardless of whether the method is sporting, or humane, or not.

Looking at the angles of the shot, no doubt mentally speculating on how best to get his rifle aligned on the big cat, Corbett found that only by leaning far out of the fork could he get his rifle sights on the tiger, so far out that when he actually brought them to bear, the rifle was upside down. A rifle, of course, can be fired upside down as well as right side up and I have done this myself in a couple of difficult situations. But in Corbett's case he had to lean so far out that it was necessary for him to retain a hold on the trellis work of the *ficus,* with one hand, right up to the very last second before shooting, and then to release that hold, briefly, get the second hand onto his rifle and then squeeze the trigger. And so this is what he did.

His shot into the big cat's back probably partially paralyzed it. It lunged around in a single violent movement and then began to slide down the little slope of the glade under the tree. But quickly, before it could recover, knowing that big cats, incredibly, can sometimes come roaring back to life even after the shocking impact of a heavy bullet, he slammed another round into its chest and killed it.

When he was sure that the tiger was dead, Corbett climbed down from the tree, and started down the trail to Chuka. He soon met Ibbotsen, who had heard his shots and was coming up to meet him.

It is not difficult to imagine what Ibbotsen had to say to Corbett about his achievement when they met on the trail, or to envision the scene that night, at the campfire, as the two of them, with Jean, raised their glasses to each other in joyful toasts to their success. As sensitive, highly intelligent people, I feel they must have been very aware of the uniqueness of their lives at that moment, of the time, and the place, and, fleeting though the few days of the hunt had been, how for the rest of their lives it would cement the joyful and enduring bonds of their friendship. I also think that they may well have felt grateful, as I have, so many times, camping in the green mansions of the Terai, for the simple, delightful privilege of just being there.

BOOK NINE

THE MAN-EATER OF THAK.

CHAPTER ONE

Four months after Corbett and the Ibbotsens left the Ladhya valley, a young village girl was killed by a tiger in the area of the villages of Kot and Kindri, which, though named by Corbett as Kot Kindri, a single village, is actually two villages lying near each other on a ridge. The villages are about three miles due west of Thak and when a second victim was killed and eaten, a little later, presumably by the same big cat, at Sem, a little village just upstream from the confluence of the Ladhya and the Sarda, Corbett decided to go after the animal.

Corbett's easiest route from Naini Tal to the lower Ladhya valley was by train via Halduwani and Tanakpur, the route that he and the Ibbotsens had taken for their hunt for the Chuka man-eater. But now the month was September, when the anopheles mosquito rages through the Terai, inflicting and spreading malaria among its inhabitants and making it a dangerous time to be in the forests. So he decided to go due east from Naini Tal, straight across the hills, a pleasant enough, one hundred mile walk, through Almora and Mornaula, from where he would pick up what was called the Sherring road, and hike down it to Kot and Kindri.*

***I have been not been able to find out much about the Sherring Road. Presumably it was a road put in by the British to facilitate movement in the hills and named after some dignitary of the time. It may even have been planned as an early motor road. My old British maps from the geological surveys of the twenties show it marked-a thin red line-and so named and running roughly north-south from Almora, through Mornaula, to Chorgallia, on the edge of the plains. It is not shown as going east towards Kot and Kindri so presumably this section, that Corbett mentions, was built after the last printing of my maps, which was 1927. In 1938, when Corbett went to hunt the man-eater of Thak, he reported the road as abandoned.**

The second kill took place while Corbett was making his preparations to leave Naini Tal and when his friend Ibbotsen heard about it, he elected to go along. Corbett, to whom a hundred mile walk was nothing, allowed the Ibbotsens—for Ibbotsen's wife Jean was to accompany them—to persuade him to take a somewhat easier route, which was to start the journey by road—by vehicle one presumes—south from Naini Tal to Halduwani and from there, again by road, to the town of Chaurgallia, on the edge of the hills. From Chaurgallia they would walk up the valley of the Nandhour River to its upper basin, cross over the rim of the basin into the upper watershed of the Ladhya and then hike down the Ladhya to Sem.

Ibbotsen's group left Naini Tal on October 12th. Corbett in his writings stated that the monsoon rain, which can sometimes continue into late October, had already come to an end; I believe he mentions this as a factor to be taken into consideration by people planning to spend time in the open, and under canvas. Corbett met the group next day, the 13th, and then together they hiked for five days up the Nandhour to the high ridge that separates its watershed from that of the Ladhya.

Although Corbett does not say so, my guess is that they left the Nandhour at its tributary with another river, the Naulagaon Gad, and then went up the Naulagaon, a more suitably direct route, to the dividing ridge. On the fifth night they camped on the ridge at a village called Durga Pipal; I believe that the village shown on maps of the twenties as Pipal Kot, and known by that name today, is probably the same village. From there, next day, they hiked down into the splendid valley of the Ladhya and then, travelling via the villages of Chalti, Chanchri, Uparakot and Sera, arrived at Sem on the tenth day.

As at Chuka, Corbett and Ibbotsen designed their hunt for the new man-eater on a baiting program and for this purpose the Tahsildar of Tanakpur, at Corbett's request, had sent up four *puda*s to be used as bait. One of these died on the way up from Tanakpur but the other three arrived on the 24th. Just before Corbett's party arrived, MacDonald, the forester who had joined them briefly during the hunt for the Chuka man-eater, using a buffalo bait and in the company of a visiting British policeman, Gil Waddell, had tried unsuccessfully to bait the man-eater. Now they generously gave their single *puda* to the Ibbotsen group, thus providing Corbett with four baits for his program. Without delay these were tied out at different places around Sem.

As was his habit, soon after arrival, Corbett set out to look for sign of the man-eater and he soon found it in the form of pug marks of a big cat moving up and down the sandy, lower reaches of the Ladhya. The pugs were those of an adult tigress and Corbett guessed they belonged to the man-eater. Looking at them he wondered why she had become a man-eater and if there was a possibility that she had joined in eating the human kills of the Chuka man-eater, earlier in the year, from which she might have developed a taste for human flesh.

Once again the group camped at the Ladhya Sarda confluence. Three days after they had settled in, on the 27th, a group of men from Thak came to visit them. They were led by a man named Tewari, the brother of the headman of Thak and they came to inform Corbett and Ibbotsen that a man of their village was missing from the previous day. Apparently he had gone out of the village to check on his cattle and had not returned. Corbett made immediate preparations to go to Thak and as soon as he was ready set off for the village, accompanied by the Ibbotsens and the Thak village group.

The trail from Chuka to Thak, up which I have hiked several times, winds through dense *sal* forest* and is uphill all the way.

Corbett's party was within a short distance of Thak, on the trail coming in to the lower part of the village, when they heard a woman wailing. Corbett instantly recognized the crying as that of a woman who has lost her husband and soon they came upon a woman sitting

---

**The sal tree, Shorea robusta, is a hardwood common throughout the Terai.*

on the ground and surrounded by a group of villagers. She was the wife, and now, it was believed, the widow, of the missing man.

Making inquiries, Corbett was told by the villagers that from the houses above, from where there was a clear view down into the fields all the way to the edge of the forest below the village, something that looked like white clothing was visible. The villagers suspected that this was the clothing of the missing man and when Corbett learned this he immediately outlined a hunting plan. While Jean Ibbotsen took the weeping woman back to the village, he went down the hill, accompanied by Ibbotsen and Tewari, to investigate the clothing. When Tewari identified it as belonging to the missing villager, Corbett immediately decided to try and stalk the tiger.

There were signs of a struggle where the clothing lay, but there was no blood. This indicated that the tiger had picked up its victim and, retaining its original hold, had carried him off. A tiger's canine teeth will of course puncture muscle and tissue, whether the victim of its attack be human or animal, and cause blood to flow. But unless the teeth are relaxed, such as when the big cat changes the position of its hold, the canines will act as plugs in the holes that they make and bleeding may not take place. In this case, after killing the villager, probably with a single bite, the tiger appeared to have retained its original hold as it carried him off.

Accompanied by Ibbotsen and Tewari, with the villager immediately behind him and Ibbotsen following in the rear, Corbett tracked the tiger for two hours. Both he and Ibbotsen were armed and they had agreed that if they saw as much as a hair of the cat, they would shoot. In normal tiger hunting this is never justified, for snap shooting, as it is called, may create a wounded tiger and pose, for a conscientious hunter, the subsequent dangers and problems of following it up and disposing of it. But with a man-eater it is an accepted practice, for a wounded man-eater is not a lot more dangerous than an unwounded one.

Two hours into the search for the cat, the three men came to a huge rock slab lying across the top of a ridge that divided two valleys. It sloped away from them, arching into a big overhang, an ideal place for a tiger to lie up and one where Corbett felt he might find the man-eater. Light, thin-soled shoes and, in the case of Tewari, bare feet, enabled all three men to approach the rock silently and when they arrived at its base Corbett asked the others to wait for him while he climbed it and had a look over the top and into the overhang.

Here, with a little luck, Corbett might have been able to get a shot at the tigress and, being the excellent shot that he was, he would no doubt have put it down. But the tigress, possibly because of a life spent in forests where there was considerable movement of men and livestock, was a very alert animal and when Corbett, after inching himself soundlessly up the rock, was close to the top and ready to lean over and look into the overhang, the cat detected him and, silent as a shadow, slipped into the brush and disappeared.

One has to experience a tiger's movements in its natural habitat to really understand how they can, literally within seconds, seem to just disappear. Elsewhere I have talked about stalking a tiger with a safari client and having it move out of dense cover no more than twenty feet in front of us, without a sound, and with no more visible movement than the bending of a single blade of grass. On another occasion I have watched a tiger walk down a jungle trail that was covered with big, dry *sal* tree leaves and move between them and over them in total silence. Nature has taught the big cats how to do this, something essential to their ability to stalk their prey and thus a vital contribution to their survival. How they do it, however, is at times almost a mystery. On this occasion all that Corbett himself saw, to indicate that the tigress was there, was a single weed stalk springing upright after the big cat walked on it while it was leaving.

CHAPTER TWO

When the tigress left, Corbett came down from the rock and with the help of Ibbotsen and Tewari found the remains of the missing man. He and Ibbotsen then probably discussed a plan of action and the upshot of this was that they would build a *machan* in which Corbett would sit and wait, in the hope that the tigress would come back. For the *machan* however, they needed ropes and poles and so Ibbotsen volunteered to go back to Thak with Tewari, to collect these.

While he and Tewari were gone Corbett waited quietly to see if the big cat might return. It did. But it came with great stealth, saw Corbett waiting for it and silently disappeared again.

Ibbotsen was soon back and while Corbett rested he climbed into a tree to build the *machan*. Describing Ibbotsen's doing this, Corbett mentions it in a very matter of fact way. But the mention, when I saw it, caught my eye; not everyone has the ability to climb into a tree to build a *machan*-a task requiring considerable physical capability and skill-and the fact that Ibbotsen knew how to do this shows him to be more of an outdoors man than one might suspect of a high ranking British official. Further confirming his unusual abilities under rugged conditions was the fact that it was he who undertook the task of moving the body of the slain villager to where it could be firmly tied to a tree stump, a somewhat gruesome task that many a man might find too repulsive to undertake.

Tying to a tree a body that is being used as bait is an important part of the process of hunting a man-eater. For just as in baiting a tiger with a *puda*, it is imperative to anchor the kill by tying it to something solid. If this is not done the big cat may appear unexpectedly, come in fast and be gone with the kill before the hunter has a chance to get his rifle up for a shot.

A somewhat humorous example of this, a story based on the speed with which the big cats can move, is a tale of woe revolving around an American missionary whom I met in Delhi some years ago. He arrived in India with a 30.30 rifle with which, he told everyone who would listen, including myself, he could shoot the eye out of a squirrel at a hundred yards. He was, he said, an expert hunter; he had done his reading and there was little that he did not know about hunting. He planned, he said, to shoot a leopard. And then a tiger. And then whatever else was available.

For his leopard he chose a place in the hilly scrub country somewhere south of Delhi and, armed with his squirrel gun, drove out there one weekend after work and tried to buy a goat, to use as bait, from local villagers. The villagers, however, did not like his approach and refused to sell him one. When on a second weekend he again failed to obtain a goat his fellow missionaries told him that he should try and get a dog and use that. Leopards love to eat dogs, they said; dogs make great bait, better maybe than a goat. Again he approached the villagers, this time for a bait dog and again they would not work with him. In the end, in desperation he decided to use Fritzy, his wife's little Dachshund; he chose a time when his wife was out of town.

Returning to his chosen hunting area he managed to get a villager to build him a *machan* and when it was ready had the man tie the little dog to the branch of a small bush with its leather leash. Then he climbed into the *machan,* loaded and cocked his trusty 30.30, told the villager to take off and, finger on trigger, settled down to wait for a leopard to come along.

It was just about dark when Mr. Spots arrived. Describing the incident later, the squirrel hunter said that he heard absolutely nothing and that all he saw was a sort of lightening fast, black and yellow blur, after which little Fritzy, his wife's pride and joy, was gone. What he said to his wife when she got home and learned that little Fritzy had gone to doggy heaven, or rather what she said to him, is not recorded.

CHAPTER THREE

When all was ready Corbett climbed into the *machan* and when he had settled himself Ibbotsen and Tewari left, to head back to camp. Knowing now, from the tigress' behavior, that he was dealing with a very clever cat, Corbett would surely have warned Ibbotsen about being careful on the way back to Thak; and after that, as the shadows lengthened, even more so, when walking back down the trail to Chuka with Jean. If he did it would have been good advice, for, as the ground sign told them next day, the tigress followed the Ibbotsen's and Tewari all the way back to their camp on the Ladhya.* Fortunately, probably because of Corbett's warning, and Ibbotsen's wariness, it did not get an opportunity to attack them.

Corbett sat up all night, waiting for the tigress to come back. In the darkness two porcupines came by and inspected the dead man's remains and not long afterwards they were followed by a bear, either a Sloth or a Black. Corbett called it a Himalayan bear which means that it could have been either. The bear homed in on the scent of the decaying corpse and stayed around for a little while. But it did not touch it and after a few minutes, moved on.

If the scrub jungle at the Ladhya confluence was the same in Corbett's time as it is today, then it is a type of brush that lends itself perfectly to the needs of a stalking tiger. It stands about twelve feet high and its roof canopy is dense, shutting out much of the light. But, underneath, it contains dozens of tunnels, two to three feet wide and four to five feet in height. The ground surface in these tunnels is packed dirt, clean and clear of noise making debris, all of which would contribute perfectly to the fast and silent approach of an attacking tiger.

Not long after sunrise Ibbotsen came back with a group of villagers, bringing Corbett a hot drink, almost certainly the milky, sweetened tea that he enjoyed. Then they all left, the villagers carrying the dead man's remains down to the Sarda, where they would be cremated. The date was October 27th.

Over the next few days a series of incidents kept Corbett and Ibbotsen on their toes. Two of Ibbotsen's *dak wallahs,* his official government mail runners, were stalked by the tigress as they came through the scrub jungle near the camp, sending the hunters scrambling for rifles and running out to see if they could get a shot. They did not see the big cat.

Then, on the 29th, a buffalo was killed. The buffalo was a huge animal. Nevertheless, after being killed, it had been picked up and carried away. Corbett was not absolutely certain that the buffalo killer was the man-eater. But nevertheless he decided to sit up for it and when a small *machan* was made ready for him in a little tree—he describes it as a few strands of rope between two branches—he climbed into it and settled down to wait.

He waited for fourteen hours, right through to the following morning and while he does not complain any more than to say that the *machan*, with its few strands of rope, was uncomfortable, sitting like that for a period of fourteen hours is nothing if not praiseworthy.

But the tigress did not come. She may have been lying up close by while they were building the *machan*. If so she may even have seen Corbett climbing into it. In any case she stayed away. And so another day passed.

A couple of nights later one of the *puda*s was killed. Corbett went out to try and stalk the tigress at the kill but again she outwitted him. There being no suitable trees for a *machan*, he did not try another overnight sit and left the kill where it was.

That night the tigress came and picked up the kill and carried it away, climbing a thousand foot hill face with it, to hide it in a dense growth of young *sal* trees. Next day Corbett, accompanied by Ibbotsen, tracked the drag to where she had hidden it. The tigress was lying up not far from the kill and growled at them from a short distance away. Encouraged by this both men climbed into two small trees and sat for five hours, hoping that she might emerge and give them a chance of a shot at her. But she did not appear and so, with the shadows lengthening, and keeping a wary eye out for her, they returned to camp.

Then came a change of scene. Ibbotsen's official duties called him away and he and Jean, with their full entourage, folded their tents and left. Ibbotsen's work required him to go to Ascot, twelve days walk to the north, and after warning Corbett to be very careful, he and Jean set off, leaving Corbett with just two men in camp and with his *coolies*-his baggage carriers-in a room at the headman's house at Chuka.

Now, with a much smaller camp, Corbett felt that there was a chance that the tigress might come around at night in the hope of a meal. And so he had his men gather large quantities of firewood, bone dry driftwood from the bed of the Ladhya and the bank of the Sarda—which I also used when I camped there, and which burns well—to keep a fire going all night. The purpose of the campfire was not so much to keep the tigress out of the camp as to enable Corbett to see her if she came around in the dark, and enable him to get a shot at her.

For the next few days, as Corbett had done before in his hunting life, he played cat and mouse with the tigress. The cat in this

---

**In tiger hunter's jargon, an "educated" tiger, or leopard, is a big cat that has been shot at and injured. The shot will probably have been taken from the concealment of a machan and as in many cases the weapon used will have been inadequate, such as a .303 rifle, or something even lighter, or even a muzzle loader, the cat survives with a small bullet, or perhaps some lead pellets, in its hide. The result is what might be called instant education. The cat never forgets what happened, or the injury, and as a result will never again approach a kill site without visually checking out all of the surrounding places of possible concealment for a hunter, including trees. When it does this, even the most expertly built machan may fail to hide the waiting hunter from the big cat's intense and prolonged scrutiny.*

case was a very clever tigress, possibly an 'educated'* one and although Corbett got close to her on several occasions, he never saw as much as a hair of her. But the mouse, Corbett, was equally clever and although the tigress must have stalked him half a dozen times while he was in the forest looking for her, his superb knowledge of jungle lore—mainly his ability to analyze the warning calls of the jungle folk—prevented her from getting close enough to him for a charge and a kill.

Corbett continued to hunt right through to the 6th of November. Then, either his work, which in this case included moving his summer home in Naini Tal with all of its goods and chattels down to his winter home at Kaladungi, or the fact that he may have been tired, made him decide to terminate the hunt and leave. On the 7th of November, as he was loading his *coolies* for the march down to Tanakpur, a delegation of villagers came to see him, to plead with him not to desert them. He told them that he had to go, but that he would return.

Marching out of camp on the morning of the 7th, he caught the train at Tanakpur on the 8th and was back in Naini Tal on the 9th. Three days later, on the 12th, the tigress killed another man at Thak.

CHAPTER FOUR

Corbett came back to Chuka on the 24th of November, planning to spend another week after the Thak man-eater and then return home on December 1st.

When he returned I wonder if, like me when I go to the Terai in the winter, he rejoiced in the cool, clear air and the brilliant sunshine that is the gorgeous weather of the north Indian winter. There are very few places in the world that have weather like this; one of them is the Terai. The monsoon comes to an end in October and within a couple of days the heat goes out of the air and temperatures drop. Then, through November, December, January and February, weather in the Terai can only be described as perfect, with days in the open country, the grassland, in the F70s and nights down into the F40s. In the forest it is a little warmer at night and a little cooler during the day, than in the grassland. In March the temperatures increase but are still pleasant enough, with days in the F80s and nights in the mid F50s. In April the temperature rises again, with days in the F90s and in May the real heat comes, with daytime thermometer readings soaring over the hundred mark.

In June comes the rain, the southwest monsoon, sweeping up out of the Indian ocean, dropping the heat by ten degrees. But with it comes high humidity and all of the discomfort that this means for Terai dwellers. The monsoon is a time to leave the Terai and find somewhere else to spend the rains and wait, patiently, for the glorious North Indian winter to come again.

When he came back this time Corbett planned to make camp at Thak and use the village as a central place for the next phase of his hunt for the man-eater. But on arrival at Chuka he met the headman of Thak there, and was informed that the village was deserted, all of its inhabitants having fled in fear of the man-eater. When Corbett arrived, no one had lived in the village for twelve days.

In his account of the hunt Corbett does not go into detail about the fact of the Thak man-eater actually going into the village. But apparently it was doing this, at night, and when I visited Thak, years later, the headman told me that it began doing this while the people were still in the village. It did not try to get into any of the houses, as a man-eating leopard might do and as the Panar man-eater did-literally tearing down doors to get at its victims. It just padded silently through the village, no doubt hoping to find a lone man or woman out in the streets. At sunset of course every villager was behind closed doors and, because the big cat did not attempt to get at them while they were in their houses, relatively safe. But the cat was seen several times in the moonlight, silently winding its way up and down the stone flagged streets and in the end this was enough to send the whole village into panic, to where they abandoned their homes and, in a body, moved out.

This was very unusual behavior on the part of the tiger. Tigers do not normally come into villages, even at night. A leopard will, either a normal leopard, looking for a stray goat or a careless dog, or a man-eater looking for a human victim. But the tiger is a much more wary animal that the leopard. He will circle a village through the hours of darkness, hunting for a stray domestic animal like a cow or a pony, or he will lie up outside it, watching and waiting for a victim. But his psychology will not allow him to enter it. The Thak man-eater was an example of how the behavior patterns of the big cats, no matter how fixed, can sometimes change. (For more information on this aspect of tiger behavior, see, in my book, GONE ARE THE DAYS, the story of the Girwa-Kauriala man-eater.)

CHAPTER FIVE

Getting back to the hunt, Corbett once again brought in bait buffaloes and tied them out in different places. Two days later, on the 26th, he went to inspect one of the *puda*s and on the way was warned by the calling of two Blue Himalayan magpies—the same birds that had warned him, years before, of the approach of the Panar man-eater—that he had a kill. The Blue Himalayan magpie is a carrion eater and will often feed on the carcasses of tiger and leopard kills. Like the crow and the raven, it is, for the hunter, a bird that plays an important part in the detection of the kills of tiger and leopard.

In this case, however, the *puda* had not been killed by the tiger; it had been fatally bitten by a cobra, a Hamadryad. But the tiger, finding it lying dead on the jungle trail, took advantage of a ready meal and ate part of it. Then, being unable to break the rope with which the *puda* was tied to a stump, it partially covered it with leaves and left it.

Corbett states that tiger are not normally carrion eaters. This is true. But just like the pattern of behavior that prevents them from coming into a village at night can be broken, so it is with carrion eating. During one of my hunting safaris I and a client were out scouting for Cheetal—spotted deer—for camp meat, and when we came across a group of them I let him take a shot. We picked up the animal that he killed and took it back to camp to be butchered into steaks and chops by the camp cook. Next morning a Taru villager came into camp to tell us that there was a dead deer lying at the place where my client had taken his shot. What had happened was that the bullet from his high powered rifle had gone right through one animal and then killed another. But when we retrieved the second deer we found that a tiger had come across it in the night and had eaten all of the hind quarters.

Corbett put up a *machan* where the *puda* had been killed by the Hamadryad and sat for the tigress. But she failed to appear and Corbett spent another long, cold and uncomfortable night in vain. The big cat called a couple of times during the night. But that was the only sign she gave him that she was still in the vicinity.

Back in camp, just as Corbett was leaving to investigate a reported blood trail—which turned out to be the kill of a leopard—four men came in to tell him that they had just heard a tiger calling on the hill between Thak and Chuka. After quickly checking out the blood trail, Corbett returned to camp, had a meal and then, accompanied by the four men, set out for Thak to see if he could pinpoint the location of the tigress by her calls and perhaps get an opportunity to stalk her. But the animal did not call for long and after the few calls the men had heard, she was silent. Perhaps a little exasperated at this, and at the way the cat was continuing to outwit him, plus the fact that the time that he had allotted to this second phase of the hunt was now running out, Corbett decided to sit again over the *puda* that had been killed by the snake and from which the tigress had eaten. But again the tigress did not come and once more, with a chilling Himalayan wind whistling out of the Sarda gorge, he spent a long, cold night. This took him to his last day of the hunt, November 30th.

CHAPTER SIX

Corbett had purchased two goats* for the hunt but intended to use them only as a last resort. Tiger will not normally bother with a goat; even a large goat barely provides for a sufficient meal for the big cat. But with a man-eater there are some possibilities that a goat will be taken because a man-eater, usually incapacitated in some way and perhaps without the strength to take down a big *puda*, will instinctively know how easy it is to kill a goat. The average bait buffalo is usually about six to eight months old. At this age it will weigh three to four hundred pounds and have considerable strength. Some of the reluctant buffaloes that I used as bait for tiger when I was hunting took five or more men to get them into the forest and tie them up. A village goat will weigh twenty to thirty pounds and as far as a tiger is concerned, can be killed with a swat of the paw.

That the Chuka man-eater was quite capable of taking a *puda*, even a big one, was obvious, and so until now Corbett had not used the goats as bait. But the Chuka cat, for some reason, had bypassed his buffalo baits many times and now Corbett, at the insistence of

---

When tying out goats as bait (which can also be done nowadays for purposes of tiger or leopard photography) it is always better to use two of the animals and if possible to tie them within sight of each other. A single bait goat will sometimes, after being tied out, just lie down and go to sleep and as tigers and leopards hunt with their eyes and ears, and without using their limited sense of smell, either cat may walk right past the animal without detecting it. But two goats tied within sight of each other will call to each other and in the damp night air of the Terai forests, where sound carries a considerable distance, a big cat may hear their bawling from a mile away.

the villagers, who assured him that the tigress would take a goat, set out to bait the big cat with the ones he had purchased.

Leaving camp in the early afternoon, accompanied by a group of five men who came along to bring the goats and help him tie them out, Corbett headed up the trail to Thak. Not far below Thak, after selecting a couple of bait sites, he tied out the animals. This done he sent the men on up to Thak village, telling them to lock themselves in the headman's house and to stay there until he came for them. Then he returned to the bait site, where the goats, distressed at being separated, were bawling lustily to one another. Wasting no time, he climbed into a convenient tree to wait for the tiger, which, with a bit of luck, might home in on the goat calls.

In anticipation of having to take a long shot at the tiger, perhaps before it actually came in on the goats, Corbett had armed himself with a light rifle, in this case his .275 which I believe was a Rigby. But he also took along his 450/400, his big, double barreled rifle, a better weapon for close quarter shooting and one the heavy projectiles of which would stop a charging tiger, where a .275 might not. It was as well that he did this because before the day was out, he was going to find himself face to face with the Thak man-eater, within split seconds of being attacked and at a distance of less than twenty feet.

CHAPTER SEVEN

Corbett sat in the tree he had chosen, at the goat baited site, for about three hours. The weather was mild and the air temperature in the forest, at this time of year, was probably in the F60s. He apparently climbed into the tree at about one in the afternoon. About four, the sun sank into the western forests and soon after this a cold wind, no doubt pouring down out of the Sarda gorge, came sweeping through the trees. He was soon feeling very cold and when what might have been the first stages of hypothermia began to chill him, to the point where his hands may have started to shake, he gave up and came down from the tree and walked to the edge of the cultivated land of Thak to call his men.

His men quickly joined him, telling him that not long after he had left them they had heard the tigress calling in the forests below Thak. Corbett no doubt thanked them for the information and then had them untie the goats. Then, accompanied by the men, wearily, and with something like no more than half an hour of light left to get back to his camp, he started down the trail to Chuka. That he was dispirited was obvious; he says so in his writings. For this was the last day that he could give to the hunt for a very cunning killer cat that had outwitted him every step of the way since he started to hunt it. And now, with half an hour left before dark, time was fast running out.

What were Corbett's thoughts as he turned towards Chuka? That he had failed and that now, with night coming on, there was almost no hope of coming to grips with the man-eater? That at his age—he was now 63—his man-eater hunting career was obviously coming to an end, allowing him not much chance of a return engagement with the big cat? That his unbroken record of man-eater hunting victories, spread across thirty-two years, was about to be shattered? That by giving up he was leaving a killer cat on the loose, one that would kill more villagers, more women and children?

Whatever they were, they were strong enough, now, to force him to dig down into his inner resources, down where his Irish genes harbored ancient qualities of tenacity and fortitude. Because not long after they had started down the trail to Chuka he stopped, told the men he was going to give the hunt a last try and, cupping his hands to his mouth, called out a challenge to the lurking man-eater. The call was immediately answered by the tigress.

CHAPTER EIGHT

As soon as the tigress answered Corbett called again and over the course of several back and forth calls it quickly became apparent that she was coming his way. Tigers mate in November and what the tigress thought she was hearing, the call that Corbett was using, was the mating call of a male member of her species. Now she was homing in on the sound, expecting to find a male waiting for her, expecting to be able to mate.

The place that Corbett had chosen to call the tigress was a flat, rectangular shaped clearing through which ran the Thak to Chuka trail. It was partially overgrown with small trees and short, stunted brush. At its lower end was a big flat rock, about six feet in height and sloping downwards towards the center of the clearing. From the direction of the tigress' approach, which Corbett could now determine by her calls, he guessed that she would enter the clearing from the upper end and at first he planned to lie on the ground beside the rock and try and get a shot at her from a prone position. But now the light was fading fast and this, together with the fact that the short bushes that covered the clearing might allow her to get dangerously close to him before he could see her, persuaded him to change his mind and move quickly to a position behind the rock.

The rock itself was too high for him to stand behind it and shoot over it. But it had a small ledge, about three feet above the ground, and by sitting sideways on this, with one foot on the ground behind him to partially support his body weight and one hand, his left, holding on to the top of the rock, he had just enough elevation to see over it for a shot. It was an awkward position, one that required a certain amount of balancing and one of the things that worried him was the recoil of his big rifle when he fired it. For now, wisely, with the tigress heading directly towards him, her arrival imminent, he had put aside the .275 and replaced it with his D.B. 450/400.

The tigress now closed on Corbett's position. With the men huddled behind him, the goats in turn huddled with them, he waited until the tigress was close and then gave a last call. The big cat, which had pinpointed his position but misjudged the actual distance to it, answered from close by and Corbett sensed her frustration and, in the power and depth of her roars, her anger at not yet being able to find what she thought was a waiting mate.

Then, suddenly, with the light almost gone, Corbett heard her footsteps as she came padding through the brush to his right front. She stopped, moved forward again, gave a last mighty roar and then stepped forward and raised her head and looked Corbett directly in the face.

As has been previously discussed, experienced tiger hunters know that the one place you never shoot a tiger is in the head. But when the Thak man-eater came through the short brush of the clearing and stopped, right in front of Corbett, her head was the only part of her that he could clearly see. This, plus the fact that when she came to a halt she was looking directly into his face, plus the fading of the light, plus the clear knowledge that this was probably the very last chance he was going to get of putting her down, told him not to hesitate but to take the forbidden shot, the head shot, and hope for the best. This is what he did.

His first bullet took the big cat under the right eye and the second, fired while Corbett, lashed by the recoil of the big rifle, was actually beginning to slip over backwards, took her in the throat. The shot to the head might not have killed her though undoubtedly it would have wounded her badly. But the throat shot, the big bullet going into an area that in all animals contains so many vital parts, instantly put her down.

This was Corbett's last hunt. Once again, as in so many times in his man-eater hunting career, his life, when the Thak man-eater closed on him, hung by a thread. He took an enormous chance on the cat coming in from a direction that would place it in front of him. That it did this was a combination of good fortune and his superb understanding of the psychology of the big cats. If it had come from behind him, it could have been on him before he saw it, before he could get a shot at it. Again, if it had become in any way suspicious of the calls on which it was homing—Corbett's imitation of the mating call of a male tiger—it might have hesitated, or circled around. If it had done this, the fast ebbing daylight would have been gone and then not only would he have been unable to get in a killing shot, but he and his men could well have been at the tigress' mercy. For even if they had turned and left the area immediately, it would have had no difficulty in following them down the Chuka trail and then, from behind, or from an ambush up front, come at them like a bolt of lightening out of the darkness. The forest that borders the Thak to Chuka trail today is dense *sal* with thick, three foot high undergrowth. Corbett's descriptions of it tell us that it was very much the same when he was there...perfect cover for a stalking tiger.

And so Corbett's extraordinary hunting career came to an end, a career that has in time become a legend. A legend of great and unwavering courage, of unmatched hunting skills, of a phenomenal knowledge of jungle lore and the psychology of tigers and of love and affection for the simple people of the Kumaon and Gharwal hill country. Those who knew Corbett stood in awe of his hunting skills and his knowledge of nature. All, from the high ranking British rulers of his day to the lowliest villager, liked him. Many, I am sure, loved him.

Today, sadly, his name is fading among the hill people. Until the 1980s there were men and women in Thak and Chuka who remembered him, remembered the tall, thin man from Naini Tal coming up the trail from Tanakpur with his porters, making his camp on the bank of the little Ladhya and walking through the morning forests with a rifle on his shoulder. Today those people are all gone and now, and less certainly, it is only their children and grandchildren who can talk about the man-eaters that at one timer terrorized their villages. And among them only those who lost a family member can in any way mentally relate to the terror that the man-eaters imposed on the villagers of Thak, Chuka, Sem, Kot and Kindri.

The records of killer cats in India tell us that there were man-eating tigers and leopards in Kumaon and Gharwal long before Corbett's time. But oddly, when soon after his last hunt he left India to go and live in Kenya, it almost seems as though he took the scourge of the great killer cats with him. For since then, and to this day, there have been none in this part of North India.

Author in the giant ficus tree, near Chuka, from which Corbett shot the man-eater of Chuka. Picture taken in 1995.

A Chuka villager stands at the base of the giant ficus, where the man-eater of Chuka lay sleeping when Corbett shot it.

The little stream below the ficus tree, the sounds of which Corbett could hear from his perch in the tree fork.

A Chuka villager who helped Corbett build some of his machans during the hunt for the Chuka man-eater. He told the author that Corbett appeared to be deaf in one ear at this time.

Author at Thak village with the skull of the man-eater of Thak, in possession of the headman of Thak in 1995.

The village of Sem above and a little north of the Ladhya river.

A village poacher at Thak, a stupid and ignorant man who boasted that he had wounded two tigers with his muzzle loader; the kind of action that often turns a normal tiger into a man-eater.

An elderly lady of Sem who told the author that her sister had been carried away, screaming, by a tiger—possibly the man-eater of Chuka—and then killed and eaten.

Dense vegetation bordering the Chuka-Thak trail up and down which Corbett and Ibbotsen hiked many times during their two hunts in the area.

The author crouches where Corbett was when he shot the Thak man-eater. Corbett: "Protruding out of the rock, from the side opposite to that from which I expected the tiger to approach, was a narrow ledge."

A Village woman of Thak cutting barley in a field below the village.

Thak village fields, where the woman do most of the work, edged by the jungles that in Corbett's time harbored the dreaded man-eater.

The village of Thak.

The main street of Thak up and down which the Thak man-eater walked at night. Eventually, in terror, the whole population fled and only returned when Corbett killed the big cat.

The headman of Chuka who knew Corbett and helped him with his hunt for the Chuka Man-eater. Child is his daughter. Picture taken in 1995.

Corbett: "Berthoud, who was Deputy Commissioner of Naini Tal at this time and who after his tragic death now lies buried in an obscure grave in Haldwani, was a man loved and respected by all who knew him..."

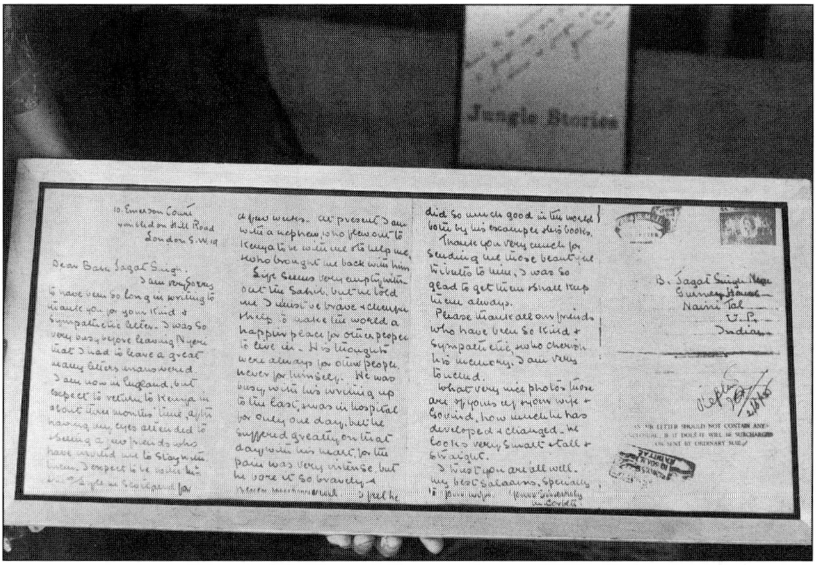

10 Emerson Court
Wimbledon Hill Road
London S.W.19

Dear Bam Jagat Singh,

I am very sorry to have been so long in writing to thank you for your kind & sympathetic letter. I was so very busy before leaving Nyeri that I had to leave a great many letters unanswered.

I am now in England, but expect to return to Kenya in about three months' time, after having my eyes attended to & seeing a few friends who have invited me to stay with them. I expect to be [illegible] in Scotland for a few weeks. At present I am with a nephew, who flew out to Kenya to be with me & to help me, & who brought me back with him.

Life seems very empty without the Sahib, but he told me I must be brave & cheerful & help to make the world a happier place for other people to live in. His thoughts were always for other people, never for himself. He was busy with his writing up to the last, & was in hospital for only one day, but he suffered greatly on that day with his heart, for the pain was very intense, but he bore it so bravely & [illegible]. I feel he did so much good in the world both by his example & his books.

Thank you very much for sending me those beautiful tributes to him, I was so glad to get them & shall keep them always.

Please thank all our friends who have been so kind & sympathetic, & who cherish his memory. I am very touched.

What very nice photos those are of yours, of your wife & Govind, how much he has developed & changed. He looks very smart & tall & straight.

I trust you are all well. My best salaams, specially to your wife.

Yours sincerely
M. Corbett

B. Jagat Singh Negi
Gurney House
Naini Tal
U.P.
India

Letter written by Corbett framed on the wall of his home in Kaladhunghi.

Gurney House, Corbett's home in Naini Tal.

Kaladhungi, Corbett's winter home in the Terai.

Sign at Kaladhungi.

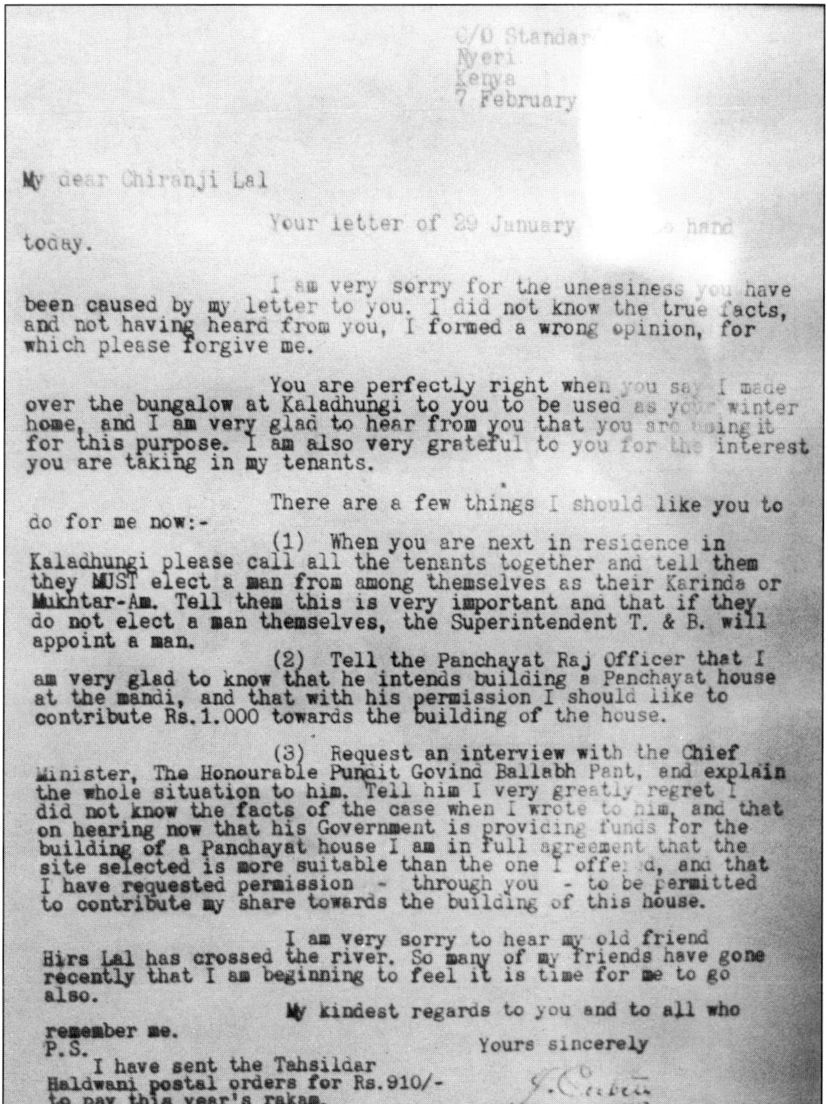

C/O Standar
Nyeri
Kenya
7 February

My dear Chiranji Lal

Your letter of 29 January [illegible] hand today.

I am very sorry for the uneasiness you have been caused by my letter to you. I did not know the true facts, and not having heard from you, I formed a wrong opinion, for which please forgive me.

You are perfectly right when you say I made over the bungalow at Kaladhungi to you to be used as your winter home, and I am very glad to hear from you that you are using it for this purpose. I am also very grateful to you for the interest you are taking in my tenants.

There are a few things I should like you to do for me now:-

(1) When you are next in residence in Kaladhungi please call all the tenants together and tell them they MUST elect a man from among themselves as their Karinda or Mukhtar-Am. Tell them this is very important and that if they do not elect a man themselves, the Superintendent T. & B. will appoint a man.

(2) Tell the Panchayat Raj Officer that I am very glad to know that he intends building a Panchayat house at the mandi, and that with his permission I should like to contribute Rs.1.000 towards the building of the house.

(3) Request an interview with the Chief Minister, The Honourable Pundit Govind Ballabh Pant, and explain the whole situation to him. Tell him I very greatly regret I did not know the facts of the case when I wrote to him, and that on hearing now that his Government is providing funds for the building of a Panchayat house I am in full agreement that the site selected is more suitable than the one I offered, and that I have requested permission - through you - to be permitted to contribute my share towards the building of this house.

I am very sorry to hear my old friend Hira Lal has crossed the river. So many of my friends have gone recently that I am beginning to feel it is time for me to go also.

My kindest regards to you and to all who remember me.

Yours sincerely

J. Corbett

(J.Corbett)

P.S.
I have sent the Tahsildar Haldwani postal orders for Rs.910/- to pay this year's rakam.

Letter written by Corbett framed on the wall of his house at Kaladhungi.

A very early picture of a very young Corbett framed on the wall of his home at Kaladhungi. The tiger is possibly the man-eater of Champawat and his retainer probably Sher Singh.

Another picture of Corbett, hanging in his house at Kaladhungi

Author skinning a cattle killer tiger after a hunt.

Standing, Corbett, while probably in his twenties. To his left, his sister Maggie. On his right, his mother and, sitting, possibly his brother.

A set of old British India advertisements from stores in Calcutta, which Corbett used, including the gun shop, Mantons, at One, Mangoe Lane, where he bought at least one of his rifles.

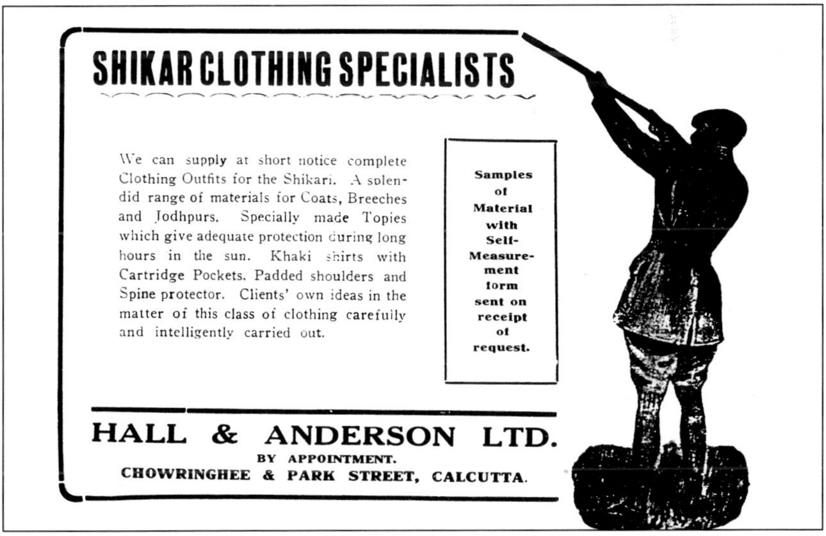

BOOK TEN

1

MANGAL, A JUNGLE TRAGEDY.

1

MANGAL, A JUNGLE TRAGEDY

Los Angeles International Airport. December 7th. 1999. In the bright sunshine of the southern Californian sky, the thunder of jet engines fills the air as huge planes land and take off. Inside the massive airport buildings the concourses throb with the movement of hundreds of people arriving and departing for destinations all over the world. Domestic arrival monitors list flights arriving from New York and New Orleans, San Francisco and San Jose, Anchorage and Atlanta. International monitors show flights scheduled for departure to exotic destinations that include Bangkok, Manila, Seoul, Tokyo and Singapore.

Under one of the glittering monitors my daughter Rara and I are checking the gate listing for Singapore Airlines flight number 11, one that will take us via Tokyo and Singapore to Katmandu, Nepal. I am going there for talks with the government about the planning of a rhinoceros relocation project, one that will transfer rhino from Chitwan National Park in central Nepal to Sukila Phanta, the White Grass Plains, in the far west, where they will be placed to establish a breeding herd. And Rara, sixteen and six feet of exuberant young womanhood, is coming with me to join Gilbert Henry and his wife, Susan Barksdale, good friends from Portland, Oregon, for a river run on the western Rapti river, an expedition that will conclude the first running of this beautiful Terai stream. She will then spend time in the White Grass Plains to continue studies that are part of her future plan to work as a naturalist in Nepal.

This will be her fourth visit to Nepal, her first being when she was four, when I was doing research on Tula Hatti, the great elephant of the WGP. Both of us, for we live apart, are looking forward to spending time together in the Terai forests, to seeing the wildlife and to visiting old friends, among them our Sherpa staff, including Pasang, my old gun bearer, and Jangbu, our cook, as well as the Bisht family of Mahendranagar, in western Nepal, who have adopted Rara as a much loved daughter. Also the staff of our tented safari camp which, pending the construction of a long anticipated safari lodge, Colonel Bisht and I run for guests in the WGP. The staff there, all Taru men carefully and patiently trained by us to cater for foreign guests, will include Mangal, the camp cook, a good man who has been employed by us and who has run the camp kitchen for eleven years and Rara is particularly looking forward to seeing him because he always has a friendly word for her and, unlike many a cook, does not mind having a curious child taking up his time and asking him questions when he is working in his kitchen.

At LAX we pass through security and then spend an hour waiting for our departure announcement. When it comes, we join the shuffling line climbing aboard the huge Boeing that within another twenty minutes will start its ascent to 38,000 feet and from there hurtle out across the Pacific at five hundred plus miles per hour for Narita, Japan, our first stop. Delightfully upgraded at the last minute, we settle into the luxurious comfort of Singapore Airlines Business Class seats, our thoughts on the month that lies ahead, the things we will do, the sights we will see, the friends we will meet. And only the fates know how what we anticipate will be shaped, and what strange twists it will take and how, sadly, on this trip, it will not include meeting our friend Mangal.

Because earlier on this morning-morning in Los Angeles and evening in the White Grass Plains-not long after we were up and I was drinking coffee and Rara was doing last minute packing, Mangal, twelve thousand miles away, had set out on his bicycle to ride from a Taru village on the edge of the WGP, back to our tented camp, where he worked. And unknown to him a big tigress, a killer that had already taken one man, is waiting for him. She is waiting for him with two hungry cubs. And her intention is to kill him and then eat him. Which, a little later, is what she and her cubs did.

Those of you who have read my book, GONE ARE THE DAYS, will remember another Mangal, a native *shikari*, who took me, as a young and inexperienced hunter, under his wing, many years ago, when I first went to live in north Bengal. A good man who in time introduced me to my first tiger. That Mangal died under the pounding feet of an elephant in *musth*, an enraged and vengeful animal that caught him as he walked back through the forest from a visit to friends in a jungle village, and killed him within seconds.

The death of Mangal, my *shikari*, was almost certainly quick. Those of us who knew the WGP Mangal can only hope that his death was equally swift. For whereas in a fatal attack by a large animal like an elephant, or a buffalo, or rhino, a man, dying, may yet, while he is still conscious, be aware that the intent of the animal in question is only to kill him. However, in a deliberate and unprovoked attack by a tiger, a man's last thoughts may dwell on something different, something much more terrifying, which is why he is being attacked, and what is going to happen to him next. In the case of Mangal we can only hope that his death was a matter of seconds, sparing him from the full realization of why the tiger attacked him, which in this case was to eat him.

Mangal of the WGP was an unusual man. A tall, long-faced Taru from the Girwa-Kauriala delta, far east of the WGP, he was possessed of a jovial personality and a ready wit, something not too common among the rather dour Taru. He had a keen sense of humor, something equally uncommon and on one of the last occasions that we talked, he provided me with a quick example of his ready wit.

It was morning and he was cooking pancakes in the tented camp kitchen. Just behind the kitchen was a huge old fig tree and high up in it was a dead branch with a big hole in its broken end. Sipping a mug of strong black coffee—Mangal knew how I liked my coffee—and warming myself beside Mangal's kitchen fire, I noticed the black, serpentine head of a huge Monitor lizard protruding from the hole, its neck curled towards us, its beady eyes looking down at us from fifty feet above. I pointed out the animal to Mangal and asked him if he knew about it. Deftly flipping a pancake in the air and without even turning to look up he replied, "Oh yes, Peter *sahib*. That's a friend of mine. Comes out every morning to watch me cook. Loves watching me do the pancakes. Makes him very happy."

Apart from his sense of humor, Mangal had other traits of character and personality that separated him from the average Taru and one of these was a complete lack of fear of the forest and its animals. Most Tarus have a great respect for the forest and for the larger animals that make their habitat in it, such as elephant and rhino and especially, of course, for the big cats, tiger and leopard. This respect, which probably has its basis in fear, dissuades them from travelling alone in the daytime forest and makes them stay completely out of it at night. To his credit, Mangal had no fear of the forest, day or night. Sadly, this is what contributed to his untimely end.

In the Nepalese afternoon of the 7th of December, whilst we slept soundly in our pre-dawn beds in Los Angeles, Mangal told the WGP tented camp staff that he was going to visit some friends in the village of Radapur, just outside the southeastern border of the reserve. He told them that he would be back in time to cook dinner and then jumped on his big, Indian made bicycle and rode out of camp, east, on the forest road that would take him to Radapur via the WGP guard post at Singpur. That was the last time any of the camp staff saw him.

In Radapur, Mangal had a few drinks with some of his friends, played with the village girls-which probably meant for the most part sitting and talking, for Taru village girls live within a fairly strict set of moral codes-and about nine o'clock, local time-and about the time that I was up and making coffee and thinking about waking Rara to get ready to go to the airport, set out to return to the camp.

He was in a good mood, one probably boosted by his alcoholic intake of the evening and the villagers heard him singing as he rode off into the darkening forest. The tigress that ended his life also heard him and when he came out of the forest and entered the open grassland that separates it from the Singpur guard post, she was aware of his approach.

About two thirds of a mile east of the guard post, where the jungle road runs close to the old bed of the Chaundar river, there is a shallow depression in the road. As Mangal cruised down into this, probably speeding up a little as he dropped into the incline, the tigress attacked. She came up behind him, very fast, pounced and, no doubt with her cubs dancing around her in anticipation of a meal, pulled him off his bicycle and bit him in the back of the head. She then picked him up and carried him into the thick, three-foot high grass on the south side of the road. Next to a small tree, a hundred yards in, she put him down. There she and the cubs started eating him.

Early next day a WGP Game Scout found Mangal's bicycle on the road and took it to the tented camp. Colonel Bisht was in the camp at the time and, recognizing the bicycle as Mangal's, went immediately by Jeep to the place where it had been found. Seeing blood on the road and guessing that Mangal had run into trouble of some kind, and being nervous about leaving the road and going into the grass on foot, he sent a man on a bicycle to the government elephant camp, on the western side of the park, to request a riding elephant. When this arrived he mounted it and, with its *mahout,* conducted a search.

Shortly afterwards, Mangal's remains were discovered in the grass close to the little tree. The body had been partially eaten, tissue being stripped by the tigress from the chest and buttocks.

One arm, his left arm, with his watch, had been cleanly snipped off above the elbow and bits and pieces of clothing lay scattered around, including one of his socks.

The body was picked up by the Mahendranagar city police and taken there for an autopsy. The findings of the autopsy were that Mangal had fallen off his bicycle and, assisted by his alcoholic intake, had gone to sleep on the road. There, the report stated, the tigress had found him and had attacked and killed him.

I disagree with these findings and my reasoning in this direction is based on my own experiences with tiger of some fifty years. I personally think that the tigress chased him while he was still riding—a short fast chase—and then attacked him and pulled him down. The bite marks in the top and back of his head support this; they are totally inconsistent with an attack on him while he was sleeping.

If the tigress had found him lying on the ground, and decided to attack him, she would almost certainly have gone for his throat, that singular part of all prey that tigers aim for in a killing attack. She would not have gone for the back of his head. If he had been lying face up, this is where she would have seized him. Even if he had been lying face down it is doubtful that she would have bitten him in the head. The bites in the top and back of his head were inflicted from the rear and are consistent with an attack from the rear, in other words an attack while he was still riding his bicycle.

Alas, poor Mangal, we knew him well, and, like Shakespeare's Yorick, this must be his epitaph. The little tree where the tigress and her cubs eat their grisly meal is his memorial. It stands a hundred yards back from the Singpur to Radapur road, on the south side of the road, about one mile east of the Singpur guard post. Whenever we pass it now, Rara and I are reminded of him.

The tigress, as of the winter of 2001-2002, still lives in the reserve, though her cubs will have left her by now. Tiger cubs stay with their mother until they are eighteen months old and then leave to fend for themselves. Estimated, from the size of their pug marks, to be about seven months old when their mother killed Mangal, by

December 2000 they would have been close to nineteen months of age and very possibly living on their own and fending for themselves.

Will the tigress' cubs become man-eaters, from the experience of having been with their mother at the kills of two men, and then taken part in eating them? I doubt it, just as I doubt that the mother is a dedicated man-eater. For as of the spring of 2002 she had not killed another human, which means that she must have recovered from whatever it was that incapacitated her and turned her to eating human prey, and regained the hunting capability needed to chase and kill wild game.

The fact that she killed two human beings is possibly nothing more than a tragic coincidence. Her first killing was the result of her finding a man in the grass on his hands and knees, a villager gathering herbs, a figure that could well have represented to her, by its shape and size, an animal such as a Hog Deer, or Barking Deer. I have several records of people being attacked by tiger when encountered by the big cats in this position and one of them is a cousin of Colonel Bisht's who was pounced on by a big, young tiger while crawling thorough high grass while stalking wild chicken. He escaped with a few scratches. Others have not. In addition, the second killing was a typical bicycle chase, something that, in spite of arguments to the contrary, tigers are traditionally known to practice.

The tigress returned to the scene of her kill the day after it happened. When she did a motion sensor camera had been placed there by Ube Raj Regmi, a young Nepalese heading a small University of Oslo sponsored tiger study team, working in the reserve. The camera recorded a picture of the big cat, though without her cubs.

I got to the White Grass Plains with Rara a week after Mangal was killed. Leaving Rara in camp, and to Colonel Bisht's dismay at what appeared to be a careless disregard for the danger presented by the presence of the tigress, I set off to examine, on foot, the scene of the tragedy armed, if that is the word, with a big Bowie knife I always carry with me in the Terai forest, and a camera.

Only someone with a clear understanding of the stalk and attack tactics of a dangerous tiger, that is to say one that is known to be dangerous to man—in this case one with the experience of taking down and killing at least two men—should attempt to move around on foot, in the known habitat of the cat, without a rifle. I have to admit that I would like to have had a high powered rifle with me when I went to the site of Mangal's death; but we have never kept weapons at the WGP tented safari camp and so I went without one.

As I mentioned, Colonel Bisht, whose experience with man-eaters is limited, was quite appalled, as were the camp men. But I depended on knowledge and experience to be my safeguard. In this case, this was a simple understanding of the strategy a dangerous cat will employ when stalking a man with the intention of killing him; using this knowledge I employed my own safety tactics which, I believe, kept me comparatively free from the danger of an attack. These included, one, facing whatever wind there was, however light, for tigers always stalk their prey upwind; keeping my face in this direction meant that I would have a fair chance of seeing the cat if it came at me and man-eaters will seldom approach an intended victim if they think they are going to be seen making the approach. Two, staying clear of dense thickets that would allow the cat to get close enough for a short, quick assault, which is the modus operandi of an attacking cat. And three, staying upright, which is to say, avoiding getting down on all fours.

I spent an hour at the place where Mangal was pulled from his bicycle and then another hour where he was partially eaten. Searching, I found some tiny pieces of bone and also some torn shreds of his shirt, a blue shirt that he was wearing when he was killed. With the shirt, what caught my eye was the many tiny holes in the fabric; these were from the teeth of the tigress' cubs and clearly indicated that they had joined her in her meal.

While doing my search I very carefully stayed away from a dense wall of grass that fringed a *nullah* that ran along behind the tree where the cats filled their bellies and although I found it necessary at times to bend over to look into the thick grass, I avoided getting down on my hand and knees. Only once did I think that the tigress might be around and that was just as I turned and started to walk out of the grass and back to the road, when I heard a low growl.

Was the big cat in there and had she been there all the time, watching me? Were she and the cubs hungry again and looking for a meal? Was that her growl I heard, a growl of frustration at being unable to get close enough to me, unseen, to launch a deadly assault? The jungle, as one learns, raises many questions which often remain unanswered. They also, when they harbor a big, dangerous cat, leave little room for carelessness, or mistakes.

Searching the general area next day, I determined that the most likely place for the tigress to be living was in the dense brush of the abandoned river bed of the Chaundari and after some searching there—rather dangerous work because the brush both in and bordering the old river bed is very thick—I found a fresh set of pugmarks of a tigress. Staying carefully away from thick stands of elephant grass and dense brush where the animal might be lying up, I managed to follow the prints for a mile and a half, northwest, to where they emerged on the Singpur to Rani Tal road. In the thick brown dust of the road edge I found several sets of pugs, old and new, which suggested that the big cat might now be using this road fairly regularly. Returning to camp I picked up a motion sensor camera and later in the day, this time, with the shadows lengthening, prudently using our old camp Jeep, I returned to the place and set up the camera.

Checking it next morning I saw that it had taken one picture. I also found the big cat's pugs again, this time fresh and winding down the road, right past my camera trap. Later, when I processed the film, I found to my delight that I had managed to get a picture of her.

As in Regmi's picture, she is without her cubs, travelling alone. She is a big cat, probably eight foot six and weighing, I would guess, from 375 to 400 pounds. She seems to have an unusually large head and the only thing that I can find physically wrong with her, as Regmi did, is what appears to be a twisted toe on her left front foot.

In the picture that I took, her eyes are frightening; they blaze with seemingly deadly intent in the reflection of the motion sensor flash. They make me think of Mangal's last moments, alone, helpless in the dark of the jungle night; moments which were, I hope, mercifully brief. And while the darkness allowed the big cat to come at him and close in on him and then pull him down off his bicycle and kill him, at least it would have saved him the horror of seeing those dreadful glaring eyes, the eyes of a killer cat intent on ending his life and then devouring him.

My picture of the killer tigress, a very rare picture of a big cat that has actually killed and eaten two human beings, is the one on the cover of this book.

2

THE BICYCLE QUESTION

Tigers will sometimes chase cyclists* riding through forests where they have their habitat, especially at night. There is some argument about whether this is factual or not among people who study tigers and in the case of Mangal, the official report, with which I do not agree, stated that he had been attacked while lying on the ground, and not chased. But I maintain that it happens and records that I have kept, from my hunting years, support this.

In 1952, when I worked as a planter on a tea estate in North Bengal, we had a company *dak wallah*, a mailman, who every day walked a fifteen mile round trip through the nearby Jaldaka forest to collect the mail. He had been with the company many years and was a trustworthy and reliable man. Some time in the winter of that year the estate manager, Benjy Llewelyn, decided, in view of the man's increasing age and as a reward for his long and faithful service, to give him a bicycle to use for the mail run.

**I almost began this story by saying that tigers chase people on bicycles. But then I remembered giving a talk to a group of law students in Sydney, Australia, many years ago where one wag, when question time came along, stood up and said, "So Mr. Byrne, you say that tigers chase people on bicycles?"*

"Yes," I said, foolishly opening myself up for his little sword thrust, which was, "And who teaches the tiger to ride the bicycle?"

"Alright, young man," I conceded, and to the sound of general laughter imparted the one about the regimental colonel who told people about how he got up late one night while in his hunting camp in north India and shot a tiger in his pajamas and who was subsequently asked how the tiger got into his pajamas.

The old man was delighted with the bicycle and started using it immediately and he used it, as far as I recall, for about six months. Then one afternoon he arrived at the company offices, back from his mail run, in what was obviously a state of considerable distress. He came in, wheeling the bicycle, saluted, parked the cycle against the office wall, gave us the mailbag and then walked away, leaving the cycle there.

Benjy and I were very surprised. The old man usually stopped to exchange a few words, and always took the bicycle, of which he was very proud, back to his house at night. This was unusual behavior. And so the next morning when he arrived at the office to pick up the mailbag we asked him what had happened. He told us.

"*Sahib*," he said, "a tiger chased me. It was very frightening. He came out of the bushes and rushed after me and I thought that I could outrun him but he came faster and faster, growling, with his mouth open. The trail is very narrow and so I had to look ahead to see where I was going and could not look back to see him or I might have fallen off. But I could hear him getting closer and closer."

"My God," said Benjy. "Then what happened."

The old man gave us a reproachful look, one that said that we ought to know what happened, without his telling us.

"I applied the brakes and stopped and got off the bicycle and turned to face him."

"And then?" I said.

This time the look was even more reproachful, clearly indicating that I, who am supposed to be something of a *shikari*, obviously knew nothing about tigers.

"Why then, *sahib*, he saw that I was a man and not an animal and stopped and looked at me and then walked away."

What a tiger sees when a man approaches on a bicycle is, quite simply, the possibility of prey. What suggests this to the cat is very probably the speed of the approaching entity, one in excess of the normal walking pace of a man or an animal. In addition, while a big cat will instantly recognize a human figure by its size, shape and upright stance, what it sees in the general configuration of a man on a bicycle is quite different. It does not differentiate between the man and the machine and see them as separate entities; it sees them as a single whole. It also sees that whole as a speeding object and this is exciting to it; in its mind a speeding object is one that is either fleeing from something or, in this case, attempting to flee from the tiger itself. Thus, in the tiger's mind, a fast moving object may be instantly regarded as a quarry, something to be chased and brought down.

Our old *dak wallah* did the most sensible thing a cyclist could do when chased by a tiger. He stopped, got off and identified himself as a man and when he did this the tiger, recognizing its mistake, called off the chase. The old man, incidentally, spent the remainder of his working days collecting the mail on foot.

My friend Bill Ryan, one of the great White Hunters of East Africa, discussing the enigma of big cats chasing people on bicycles with me, at his home at Malindi some years ago, told me something he had noticed with big game in Kenya, something which contributed to an explanation of the enigma.

This was a habit practiced by certain groups of African antelope that, until he found the reason for it, puzzled him for years. He noticed that when he passed a group of antelope out in the open plains, while speeding along in his Land Rover, that at first they all looked at the vehicle. But as he passed they would then turn their heads and look back towards where the vehicle had come from and eventually Bill surmised that what they were looking for was what was chasing the Land rover. To them, an object travelling at speed could only be something that was being chased by another animal, probably a predator, and the instant the vehicle had passed and indeed, he said, even as it was passing, they all looked back to see the predator they believed was coming up behind.

I believe that Bill's discovery is closely linked to the bicycle chase behavior of tiger. The tiger, being a predator, as opposed to an antelope, which is a herbivore, is not of course looking for a predator coming up behind. But in his mind he is looking at something being chased and so, ever an opportunist where food is concerned, fair game for a chase in turn by him.

The moral of all of this is of course that one should be wary of riding bicycles in tiger country. In lion country too, in Africa? Maybe. Although to date I have yet to find any instances of lions in Africa chasing people on bicycles. As my young Australian wag might have put it, for that I suppose we must wait for someone to teach Leo to ride.*

******My writings on the subject of tigers and leopards chasing people on bicycles have been challenged by others. But apart from myself I do not believe that anyone has done very much research on the question. Among the people I consulted was David Ommaney, the well known Kenyan White Hunter. Although he spent most of his life in Kenya, David was born in India and had some knowledge of tigers from his earlier life there. He told me that he had heard of the phenomenon of bicycle chasing but was not able to recall a particular instance. Now, as this book is going to press, my theory has received some support in the actions of a new man-eater, a tiger, operating in the Bardia district in far west Nepal. This animal is reported to have killed and eaten six villagers. But it has also attacked two motorcyclists travelling on the East-West highway, which runs along the edge of the reserve. Both were chased by the big cat. One was taken off his motorcycle and killed and dragged away to be eaten. The other escaped.*

3

SPEED AND THE ADRENALINE FACTOR

One of the most hair-raising things that can happen to a hunter is to be charged by a big cat. A number of big cats still live with us on our little blue planet. Among them the most powerful, and indeed the most aggressive, are the lion and the leopard in Africa, and tiger and the leopard in Asia. When any one of the these four big cats charges a hunter it is at a speed that can be both frightening and bewildering, one that, if the hunter is going to survive, will demand perfect reflexes and the ability to act on them instantly.

Some years ago I had a good safari season and about the time the Loo, the hot, Indian summer wind that heralds the monsoon, began to turn the Terai into its annual furnace, I thought it might be nice to spend the summer in Europe. For this I needed a car and so I cabled the Jaguar Company in Coventry, in the UK, and asked them for some details on their latest sports model. This turned out to be the E Type, also known as the XKE 120. The price was $10,000 and as the specs sounded exactly like what I wanted, and as the particular young lady I had waiting for me in England at the time just loved Jaguars, I cabled my bank in London and told them to mail a cashiers check for ten big ones to Coventry.

About a month later I landed at Heathrow Airport and within twenty-four hours was in Coventry picking up a brand new Jaguar

XKE—white, with red leather upholstery—at the offices of the Jaguar company factory. I signed a few pieces of paper and on a cool, June morning jumped in and drove what was essentially a beautiful piece of machinery straight out to the MI, England's main north-south freeway. There I put it though its paces.

I started by taking it up to 100 MPH and holding it at that for distances of ten miles at a time. Then I took it to 120, 130 and 140. It held the road well at 140 and up to 150. The only problem with this speed, even on a super highway, was that few other drivers seem to be able to anticipate it, and act accordingly, which made it dangerous to both them and myself.

I stopped a few times to test the acceleration and then ran it through the gears—45 MPH in first, 65 in second, 115 in third and then into fourth, with all of this under 7000 RPM on the dashboard rev counter. I found all of the specs promised by the makers to be impressive, especially the standing start, zero to 30 MPH, which, as was promised, was accomplished in 2.6 seconds.

In Africa a number of White Hunters have been killed by lions. This has more often than not been in a charge and the reason why they have been taken like this, unexpectedly, and suffered fatal consequences, is attributed to two things.

The first is the adrenaline factor in seriously wounded animals that in some cases seems to literally bring them back from the dead and that in a charge keeps them going, in spite of the pain and shock of fearful injuries, sometimes, in fact, in spite of being shot again and again with heavy rifles. The second is the speed of the charge, which in most cases gives the hunter time to get off no more than two aimed shots.

The African lion can charge at 45 MPH—a measured speed—in addition to which it is recorded as being able to reach this speed, from a standing start, in two bounds that together take less than a second. So it covers a hundred yards in 4.54 seconds. My XKE was fast and on the road, as I soon discovered, could outpace most other vehicles, especially, from a standing start. But, should the competition have arisen, Africa's big cat would have quickly shown my beautiful 0-to-30 MPH in 2.6 seconds Jaguar, taking as it did 14.6 seconds for a hundred yards, a clean pair of heels.

The leopard is faster. Like the lion, African and Asian leopards also achieve their top charging speed with a couple of powerful, accelerating bounds. This is 52.8 MPH, which means that Mr. Spots will cover his hundred-yard charge in 3 seconds. Three seconds that will give the hunter just enough time to mentally sum up the significance of what is happening—that a big cat is coming at him at high speed, intent on taking his life—to thumb off the safety catch of whatever rifle he is using, to take an aiming position, preferably from down on one knee, to sight in on the animal and then shoot. He will have time for two shots if he is using a double-barreled rifle, and two shots if his weapon is a double-barreled shotgun. But only one if the weapon is a bolt action rifle, or a sliding action shotgun, because, time wise, that is all the charge will allow. Regardless of the weapon, to prevent the animal coming all the way home, the shot must be taken while it is still outside of irreversible closing range. This means not less than ten yards away, which in turn means that the hunter has to be prepared to shoot, and must do so, no more than two seconds after it has launched its attack.

I mention that in accepting a charge the hunter should preferably be down on one knee. There are a number of significant reasons for this which I learned from my own experiences.

When tigers and leopards charge I have found that they seldom come at you, as one might expect, in a straight line. This is particularly true with leopards, which for some unknown reason are inclined to jink from side to side. Thus a better shot is obtained if the hunter shoots from a lower and flatter angle. Hence the one-knee-down position, which I have always used, a position that flattens the line of the shot and thus reduces the error factor. It is also a position which may contribute to keeping under control any tendency on the part of the hunter to turn and run. Because considering the time limitations involved, and the fact that one is dealing with a life and death situation that is being measured in split seconds, whereas a standing position may allow for considerations of flight, the one-knee-on-the-ground position, requiring as it will additional time to get to one's feet, straighten up, turn around and then take off, tends to make one think twice about running for cover.

I have no figures for the timing of the charge of a tiger. It is possibly as fast as that of a lion. It is certainly as determined and whereas the adrenaline factor in lions is one that literally seems to bring them back to life when they are down, shot to pieces and within seconds of death, in tigers it is one that equally stirs the big cat to use the last seconds of its life in savage retribution against the person or persons who have hurt it.

In the mid sixties I had a safari client from San Francisco named Frank Radelfinger. Frank was a nice young man and a keen hunter and he came with me for a single trophy, a tiger. South of the great swamp in the White Grass Plains, the two of us, cruising the grassland on an early morning scouting trip, came across a big male tiger moving slowly through the grass and no doubt on its way to its lair after a night's hunting. We got out of the Land Rover and watched it carefully and when it slipped behind a big termite mound Frank ran forward a few yards and waited for it to reappear. When it did, he fired and put a soft nosed slug from his .300 Weatherby magnum straight into its chest. The big cat gave a roar of rage and turned and came straight at us and it took two more shots from my own H&H .375, using 300 grain rounds, to put it down.

Later, skinning it, I was astounded to find that Frank's first shot had blown the animal's heart to pieces and that when the big cat came at us, covering a hundred roaring yards in spilt seconds, it had done so with its heart completely shattered, its central nervous system barely operative and its muscles working on nothing more than a powerful rush of adrenaline.

Provoked, a normal tiger will charge a hunter from distances of up to a hundred yards. It will come very fast and the charge, usually the result of some kind of provocation, such as a wounding, will, unless stopped, come all the way home.

But a man-eater is different. A man-eater is a tiger that does not need to be provoked to make an attack on a hunter; all it needs is to be hungry. It has already, for the very reasons why it became a man-eater, lost all of its instinctual wariness of man. Not its fear of man, for tigers fear nothing on the face of the earth, and probably man least of all. So whereas a normal tiger, attacking a man because it has been provoked, may charge from a hundred yards away, a man-eater, unless it is provoked by something like gunshot wounds-as in the case of both the Muktesar and Kanda cats-makes its attack charge from a much shorter distance. It does this because its method of hunting a man is based on either a carefully planned stalk, followed by a short, fast charge, or an ambush. Both strategies are designed to get it to within twenty or thirty feet of its victim, prior to the assault.

Twenty to thirty feet is the ideal distance for the silent, very fast, rushing attack that closes the big cat on its intended victim. Provoked, with something like gunshot wounds, a man-eater may extend this attack distance. But in an unprovoked state it will not and as long as a hunter on the trail of a man-eater stays away from any kind of cover that will allow the big cat to get within this short, striking distance, he is providing himself with reasonably effective measure of protection. If he is foolish enough to go too close to cover that may conceal a big killer cat, and make himself the target of this blindingly fast charge, then he is asking for trouble.

Wounded, a normal tiger may do the same thing and, its adrenaline pumping, may come all the way home, with results that will make it highly likely that as the sun goes down, someone else, glass in hand and feet to the campfire, will be telling the story of what happened.

4

ON BEING FIRST; A JUNGLE VIGNETTE

The White Grass Plains, in Far West Nepal, was where I based for much of the time during my research on man-eaters and on Jim Corbett and his great hunts. I stayed there for two reasons.

The first was that the WGP lies in the province of Kanchanpur, the farthest western province in Nepal and one that borders on to India, in this case Kumaon, thus allowing me easy access to Corbett's country.

The second was that in the WGP, being allowed by benign officialdom the freedom of the forests, I was able to base in the aforementioned commercial safari camp a half ownership of which I hold with my Nepalese partner, Lt. Colonel H.B. Bisht, Rt. and avail myself of all of its amenities. From the camp the Indian frontier was just twenty miles away and I could drive across the border and be in Kumaon in a matter of a couple of hours.

The camp was also a good place to write. Situated deep in the *sal* forest on a small hill just above the WGP's beautiful little jungle river, the Bauni, it was quiet and peaceful. And for me, since I first went there in 1953, the WGP has been a place where I have always felt at home and indeed, where I have truly spent the happiest days of my life.

A number of things contribute to making a place special. Among the most important of these, apart from the natural beauty of the surroundings, is undoubtedly one's companions and in recent years these have included, for me, a tall, dark haired, lovely woman from Georgia whom the Nepalese who know her, call Cathy Maya.

Soon after we met, common interests helped to develop a mutual affection and when we had been on safari a couple of times this quickly developed into an intimate and ongoing relationship. In turn my Nepalese friends, delighted to see the happiness she brought me, gave her the name of Cathy Maya, a title of great respect and affection in Nepal.

In the WGP, where this fine and beautiful woman and I spent many delightful days together, the best part of a safari day for us was driving back to camp in an open Land Rover, after time spent in the *phantas,* the central grasslands where the Swamp Deer live. This was usually at the end of the day, with the dark red orb of the sun sinking into the trees behind us and the soft evening light burnishing the golden stems of the *phanta* grass. After leaving the grasslands the road back to camp tunneled its way through little peninsulas of tall, canopied trees standing in light undergrowth, each thicket stretching its fingers south, down towards the Great Swamp, each one, as we entered it, darker than the one before it.

While we were still in the *phanta*s the light would be slowly fading and in the still air the yellow grass, awaiting the approach of night, would ripple gently in the wake of the passing Land Rover. Dark shapes, briefly seen, would be big wild boar standing belly deep in the grass, motionless on short, muscular legs, curved yellow tushes gleaming, watching us carefully, waiting for us to pass.

Once into the forest the light would quickly change. Dark pools of shadows, heralding the night, would be starting to form under the trees and sometimes we would see a tiger standing in one of them, watching the passing vehicle with knowing eyes, waiting for it to go by. And if we brought the vehicle to a halt, slowly, quietly, and then made no noise and kept very, very still, Mr. Stripes might just stand and look at us and let us look at him for a little while.

If one keeps quiet and still in a vehicle, even an open vehicle, it is sometimes possible to view a tiger at close quarters. This is because, as has already been explained, a big cat sees the mass of a vehicle as a single, large but harmless entity, something not necessarily associated with people. And unless it has been previously threatened in some way by the occupants of a vehicle, it may not look upon it as a cause of alarm. And sitting together, close, silent, I holding the steering wheel, Cathy with one slim brown hand gripping the panic bar of the passenger seat, the other holding mine, this is how we would look at Mr. Stripes, a normal, peaceful cat, one of Jim Corbett's gentlemen of the forest.

Of course the cat might be a man-eater. But apart from the fact that we have not had a man-eater in the WGP in many years—at least not until December, 1999, and then only briefly—if it was a man-eater then it is more than likely that we would have known about it. Because once a big cat starts killing and eating villagers, the word goes out across country very quickly indeed.

The singular problem, however, in this respect, as has been pointed out to me by not a few people, is that just as every journey has to begin with a first step, so every man-eater has to start its career with a first victim. And so although the big cat now standing watching us could have been on the verge of becoming a man-eater, until it made that first human kill, it had to be regarded as a normal tiger.

By the time we reached the forest through which the dark waters of the Bauni wove their sinuous way, the light would be fading rapidly and when we crossed the old wooden Bauni bridge, its aged timbers groaning in protest, and started up the little incline with the high sandy banks behind one of which a big dog leopard had its lair, and rolled up to the fork in the road and turned there and drove down to the camp, it would be almost gone.

This last, short stretch of road ran down an old elephant walk and now, with the air chilling and the first, slate-blue layers of mist beginning to form in the open spaces between the trees, the yellow glow of our campfire, which the camp men would stir up when they heard the Land Rover coming, was a welcoming beacon through the trees and the pressure lamp that the cook liked to keep going in the kitchen would wink at us as we turned in to the campground and, in a cloud of swirling brown dust, drew to a stop. The men would come quickly to take our gear, whatever we had with us, and then we would walk down across the flat, clean, beaten earth of the camp ground to our big safari tent and go in and put hats and binoculars and cameras on the metal tent table and take off our jackets and close the tent flaps against the evening chill and drop into waiting canvas chairs.

Within minutes one of the camp men would be at the tent flaps, coughing gently to announce his presence and then parting the flaps with one hand and balancing a wooden tray on the other. On the tray would be a big Stanley stainless steel thermos of hot water, a huge Nepali lemon, brown sugar, a bottle of Kukri rum, a tea spoon and two mugs, all of which the smiling Mangal, our good camp cook, would have sent over from the kitchen.

Then came the best part of the day, if there is such a thing on a Terai safari, where every hour of every day is better than the one before it. This was the comfort of the canvas chair, firm to the back, feet up, shoes falling off, the dark brown rum, hot and spiced with the lemon and brown sugar, trickling down the throat and then as quickly moving the mind into realms of reflection, of how good life was for us, and how fortunate we were to be able to enjoy it, together, in such a beautiful place. I in particular, to have been able to spend so many years in the gorgeous forests of the Terai and, now, to be able to do it in the loving company of this beautiful, mature and intelligent woman, in a place that meant more to me than anywhere else on earth.

After a while one of the men would come to tell us that dinner was ready and we would put our jackets back on against the night chill and take our drinks and walk up to the big, glowing, camp fire.

If there were guests in camp we would join them. If not, we ate alone. We would have soup at the fire in big earthenware bowls, hot, our hands cupped around the bowls to warm them. Then we would walk over to the mess tent and have dinner and talk about the big tiger we had seen.

Later, the day gone, the men sleeping and the camp closed down for the night, lying in the big double bed together, the kapok mattress hard to our backs, the flaps of the big Eureka Riverside safari tent open and moving gently in the night air, yellow tongues of light from the campfire flickering on the canvas walls, we would hold each other gently and listen to the night sounds; the wild braying of the Swamp Deer out in the *phantas*; the cackling laughter of a hyena. And, sometimes, from deep in the forest, the long, sad moan of a hunting tiger.

And after we had made love and before we went to sleep, and perhaps even after that and into our dreams, we would be thinking about the big cat we had seen standing in the ink dark pool in the peninsular forest, still as a stone statue, golden eyes burning bright, warily watching us pass. And, dreaming, we might wonder about where he was now, and if maybe he had followed us back to the camp, and was lying out there watching our tent from beyond the dark wall of the forest, just out of the reach of the camp fire glow. And if he was a normal healthy tiger and was just curious about us, and about the sights and sounds of our camp, to him a strange thing to find, away out here in the middle of his hunting territory. Or if perhaps he might be injured and hurt and, because of this, unable to kill and eat. And, if so, how long he might have been without food. Long enough to make him hungry? Or longer, to where the first driving pangs of starvation were slowly diminishing the innate wariness that kept him, as a normal big cat, away from us? To where only one thing mattered and that was survival, for which he needed food and for which, now, he was prepared to do what in his psychology had previously been unthinkable—to look for this in human form.

Drifting into sleep, a nagging thought was that if this were the case, then out of it arose the question of who was going to be the first fatality? And that somewhere out there, if the cat was a man-eater, or about to turn into one, was someone who was going to have to be its first victim. It was important, I felt, as a little wind rustled the canvas walls of the tent and the night grew colder and we moved closer together, to avoid being that first victim.

BOOK ELEVEN

EPILOGUE.

EPILOGUE

Research for this book, which included visits to all of the places of Corbett's great hunts, was spread across twenty years. The main reason for this extended period for the work was the problem of finding time to visit Corbett's hunting sites in Kumaon and Gharwal and then, when there, finding more time to search for some of the more remote sites, many of which, having no road access, required slow, prolonged hill country hiking.

Adding to this was the problem of finding villages the place names of many of which have been changed since Corbett's day and although I am fluent in Hindustani and was able to get directions from villagers, sometimes I found myself asking for a village the name of which they simply did not know. An example of this was Pali, where Corbett first hunted the man-eater of Champawat. Corbett described Pali as being fifteen miles due west of Champawat. Today there is a village called Pati in what appears to be the same place. Villagers there told me that they thought, but were not sure, that their village had at one time been called Pali. But they knew of no village named Pali when I was there.

Another problem I encountered when searching for a particular place was the similarity of names of hill villages. I hiked out of Almora and spent four days on foot looking for Sanouli, where the Panar man-eater was shot, constantly being directed to two other villages, Sangrowli and Sanwanouli. (I notice, from Corbett's account of the hunt for the Panar cat, that he too seems to have had a similar problem when searching for Sanouli and also spent several days trying to find it, probably for the same reason.)

Again, it was no use asking about Corbett in any of the villages adjacent to any of the actual sites of his hunts. It was difficult enough in the hunt areas themselves for the simple reason that most the men and women of his era are nearly all gone now. A few of the villagers who worked with him, particularly in his last hunts at Thak and Chuka, may still be living, as well as relations of some of the victims of the man-eaters he hunted. But they are all slowly but inevitably passing away and as we now cross into a new century, even among them, memories are beginning to fade.

<<< >>>

But if the march of time erases the men and women of Corbett's day, one by one, and then the memories of those that knew them, it takes much longer for it to eradicate the natural physical monuments of the great hunts.

At Champawat, the thick, black, flat topped, projecting rock where the Rupal Champawat man-eater stood at bay, and where she died, is still there. The Champa river continues to flow brisk and clear and one can still get across it by jumping from boulder to boulder, as Corbett did, as I did, and as the tigress did, just before he got the shot at her that put her down. Both the Champawat *dak* bungalow, in the city, and the old bungalow above the gorge, the Fungar bungalow, to where Corbett moved for the hunt, still stand.

The site of the hunt, where Corbett shot the man-eater, is about six miles from Champawat via the Talla Des road, a pleasant walk on a sunny hill day and there are still a few people in the city who know where it is and will take a visitor there, or find someone to help. Among them are two of the journalists working with a Champawat newspaper called the Amar Ujala; they are a Mr. Dinesh Joshi and a Mr. Mahesh Sharma.

But a guide is necessary, for at the site itself there is nothing to commemorate the extraordinary events that started Corbett on his remarkable career. In addition to this, the man who took me there, for a fee of two dollars, a villager named Gopal Singh Metha, pointed out that although the killer cat that Corbett shot was called the man-eater of Champawat, the area where the hunt took place is actually called Gouri, after a nearby village of that name.

<<◇>>

At Muktesar, when I went there, I was guided to where Corbett shot the tigress by the grandson of one of the beater's of that eventful day. In 1998 he worked as a custodian at the Muktesar *dak* bungalow and he corroborated Corbett's story, as told to him by his grandfather, to the letter. He said that his grandfather had helped to carry the tigress up to Badri Shah's orchard, where it was skinned.

It will be of interest to readers to notice the spelling of Muktesar, as used by Corbett, a spelling that was in use when he actually wrote the story of the hunt, more than forty years later, rather than when it took place. In the twenties, and possibly at the time that he shot the tigress, the name of the little hill town was spelled Mukteswar and it is thus shown on old British Survey of India maps of 1922 and 1927.

Nowadays there is a motor road from Naini Tal to Muktesar. Readers who might want to go there for a visit will find the people of the little township as warm and friendly as they were in Corbett's time. The beautiful old *dak* bungalow has been well preserved and one can have a cup of tea on the front porch and enjoy the truly magnificent view to the north, rolling hills that climb away to the mighty ramparts of the Himalaya.

In the gorge, where Corbett stood to the full charge of the man-eater, the pool into which the big cat fell is still there, with six inches of cold, clear water in it and from its position one can determine exactly where Corbett stood, on a narrow ledge, about thirty feet above it, when the man-eater came at him. The place itself is about one mile below the Muktesar *dak* bungalow, down a long winding trail through dense brush and the bungalow's caretaker is happy to take visitors there. The trail down was well signed with leopard pug marks and droppings when I visited there in 1998.

<<◇>>

The Panar man-eater, the deadly leopard that took so many of the villagers of the Panar river valley, was shot in one of the village fields close to and just below the village of Sanouli. Corbett mentions the unusually high terracing of these fields; they are the same today, with some of the packed dirt terraces six to eight feet in height. It was from behind one of these that the killer leopard came at Corbett after he wounded it, uttering the deep, savage grunts that only a leopard can make and sending Corbett's Sanouli village companions running for their lives.

When I was there the headman of Sanouli pointed out the oak tree where Corbett sat in wait for the man-eater. I found it hard to believe that it could be the same tree. But Himalayan oaks, I am told, grow to a hundred years or more and this tree, as seen in my pictures, is precisely where Corbett said his tree was, about three hundred yards below the lower village houses and growing out over the edge of one of the high terraces as he described it. In addition, it was the only tree there as well as which I was unable to find the stumps or roots of any other trees that might have preceded it.

Below it, in turn, two terraces down, is a stand of Blackthorn bushes, almost certainly the same stand from which Corbett's men cut the branches that he tied to the bole of the tree to stop the leopard climbing up to attack him.

On the way to Sanouli I had a strange experience. Leaving Almora on foot, with my cook, Jangbu, and three Nepali porters, young men from the Baitadi district in Nepal, I took the Pithoragarh road. I camped for the first night on the roadside about a mile beyond the Panwa Naula *dak* bungalow, where Corbett stayed on the way to Sanouli on his second visit. Next day I went on down the road for about a mile and then left it and, turning right, took a trail that led down into the Panar River valley. I hiked all day, a long, steep descent, all the way down to the Panar river and in the early afternoon made camp at the mouth of a small, brush choked ravine, close to the bank of the river.

The men helped to set up camp and we soon had three fires going with dead wood from the ravine. One was for them to cook their meal, one for Jangbu to cook my dinner and his, the third, a campfire for an old *shikari* who believes that no camp is complete without one.

After a quick wash in the river I set up my folding chair and sat with a glass of scotch to enjoy the scene, the river winding its way down through green, terraced hills that climbed up from it for thousands of feet on either side. Soon dinner was ready and after eating, with the shadows lengthening and the day dying, I told the men and Jangbu to sleep, and went into my tent. Jangbu had his own small tent and the men, who slept on the ground wrapped in a tarpaulin that I had bought for them in Almora, settled themselves down for the night at the mouth of the little ravine.

I had a last look at the ravine before I retired and thought to myself that it had good cover for a leopard and that these deep ravines were probably what the Panar man-eater used for his lairs. I undressed, got into my sleeping bag and stretched out on my camp cot and I was just composing myself for sleep when suddenly the silence of the evening was broken by the deep, powerful sawing of a leopard.

The sound, for those who are not familiar with it, is just like that made by a man sawing a hardwood log with a big handsaw; in this case it came directly from the ravine, immediately behind my tent. It was followed by the sound of running feet and shouts of alarm from the men and a call from Jangbu asking what was wrong. In seconds the men were at my tent. They were all very frightened and pleaded with me to allow them to come in and spend the night in the tent. I told them they could and after making sure that Jangbu was alright, we all settled down to sleep again, I on my camp cot and the three young Nepalis huddled together on the floor with the tarp wrapped around them. After about half an hour the leopard called again and when it did another leopard answered it from up the ravine. Then both leopards began to call, back and forth, and continued doing so, on and off, all though the night. The big cats did not bother us and, as far as I know, stayed out of my campsite. But with the Panar man-eater and its dreadful killing spree on my mind, even though it was something from many, many years before, I, and the men, spent a restless night listening to them.

Although I, and Corbett, had to hike many miles to find Sanouli, today, as I found out after I reached it, there is a motor road running within a quarter of a mile of the village. While I was there I saw a bus going by and the villagers told me that there are now bus services that connect many of the major towns of Kumaon and Gharwal. They also, with puzzled expressions on their faces, asked me why I was walking when I could be riding on a bus. I tried to explain that I enjoyed walking as well as that I was trying to follow in the footsteps of a man, a famous man, who came from Naini Tal, years ago, to rid them of a man-eater. But why anyone would walk when they could ride—particularly a *sahib* who could obviously afford the fare—was quite beyond their understanding. As to a man-eater? When was that? Where? Here?

If the man-eater had been named after Sanouli then perhaps today it might be better remembered in the village, for in '90s, when I was there for my research on the story, only one elderly woman recalled the animal, and the deaths, and the terror that it brought the region. And she, born in 1910, the year of Corbett's immortal hunt, and being eighty-nine years of age when I interviewed her, only remembered it from what her parents had told her. To the other men and women of the little hamlet, living their simple lives, busy with their crops and their cattle, getting married and having children and raising them and paying their taxes and growing old and dying, it was, sadly, just a old story from long ago. Too long ago for any of them to remember a tall, slim, sunburned young man who walked out of the hills one day with a shotgun on his shoulder and, within the space of thirty-six hours, rid them of a scourge that had terrorized them for a decade.

<<<◇>>>

At Kala Agar, one time stalking ground of the Chowgarh tigress, there is now a motor road running below and parallel to the great Kala Agar ridge. It does not go to the Kala Agar bungalow and thus the only way to get there is on foot, an uphill but pleasant enough three mile hike from the road. I drove to the area from Tanakpur, having reached there, from Nepal, via the Banbasa canal dam. From Tanakpur I had planned to take the forest road, the direct route west, via Halduwani. But it was closed due to rain and so my somewhat roundabout route was via Pilibhit.

Finding Kala Agar was a little difficult because the village itself, as mentioned, is not on the main road, in addition to which it is still quite small. I spent two nights on the way there, the first by the roadside north of Pilibhit and the second at a village called Sundarnagar. Here, because every inch of cultivatable land was under crops, I was forced to pitch my tent on the flat roof of a small house. My good man Jangbu, who accompanied me, served me dinner there and then himself slept in a room above a tea shop.

Next day, arriving close to the end of the motorable road below Kala Agar, I met a fine young hillman named Dewan Singh Rana Bista, from the village of Jargaon, who offered to be my guide to the Kala Agar *dak* bungalow, next morning.

Once again I pitched my tent in a tight space beside the road, next to an old water tank. Jangbu found some fire wood and made dinner and because, as at Sundarnagar, there was nowhere for him to pitch a second tent, he shared mine. I slept well, but had a strange and vivid dream. In it I was walking, alone, up the long winding trail to Kala Agar, when I saw a group of people approaching, a long line of them coming down the trail towards me. Leading them were a man and a woman, on ponies. Both were wearing solar topees, the old pith helmet of the days of the Raj, with long sleeved khaki jackets buttoned up the neck and jodhpur riding britches. I recognized them immediately as the Vivians and thought, how wonderful to meet them like this after all these years. Then I heard Mrs. Vivian say, leaning forward on the pony towards her husband so that she would not be overheard, "Look there, Ham. Some young whipper snapper coming up to the bungalow. Jim's not going to like that at all. You know how he likes to be by himself."

There the dream faded and ended.

The little bungalow itself was in fine condition when I got there next day (my last visit was in 1999) and from its front verandah, where the Vivians were sitting, having tea, when the Chowgarh tigress took a woman from right in front of them, there is a splendid view of the mountains to the north.

The old forest road that the Chowgarh tigers used, and where Corbett tied out some of his *puda* baits, still runs across the face of the hill and, as in his day, though almost wide enough for a vehicle, it is still just a foot road. About four hundred yards west of the bungalow is the ravine down which Corbett went to avoid the possibility of an ambush by the man-eater in the heavy scrub that bordered the road in those days. About a hundred feet down into the ravine itself is the big, smooth rock down which he and his men slid and down which I and my guides also slid to get into the little glade that is walled on the right by the huge leaning rock slab, from behind which the tigress stalked them. At the end of the slab is the little hollow where the man-eater lay in wait for them and I felt a cold chill come over me the day I stood there, measuring tape in hand, and envisioned the tigress, her powerfully muscled legs curled underneath her, her eyes locked on Corbett, ready to hurl herself on him from just eight feet away.

At Kala Agar Corbett was remembered, as were the details of the hunt for the Chowgarh tigers, and the place of its finale. The caretaker of the Kala Agar *dak* bungalow, as of 1999, was a very old man who said that his father had known Corbett. When I arrived at the bungalow, after my long climb up from the motor road, he smilingly gave me a cup of the best tea I have ever tasted; strong, black North Indian stuff, laced with brown sugar and cloves.

He then dug in an old, glass fronted bookcase and after rooting around among some ancient books—a novel called The Blue Peter, another called Irene Of The Ringlets and a third entitled Stay At Homes, dated October 10th 1903 and bearing the stamp of the Naini Tal Library Club and the name, Captain H.R. Palmer, R. A., Hon. Secretary—somewhat incredibly found the original, official, visitors book for 1930, the one that was in use when Corbett and the Vivians were there. It was sadly tattered and in some places eaten away by insects. But, faint through the passage of the years, barely legible, there they were, in their own handwriting, the names of Corbett and his friends.

There may have been an earlier book because this one was new in March, 1930. The name of the person who made the very first entry in the book is illegible. Whoever he was, his arrival date is noted for February 20th, 1930 and his departure date is given as the 22nd of the same month.

The next entry is by Ham Vivian and is written as 21/3/30, or March 21st, 1930. The next is for Corbett, dating this third visit to the area and his third attempt to come to grips with the man-eater and is for March 31st, 1930.

There is no entry in the book for the date of Corbett's arrival, which was March 24th. The reason why he did make an entry in the book then is that he did not actually move into the bungalow until the 31st, but slept behind it, in its little walled compound, in his tent.

He would have had two reasons for doing this. One no doubt was his love of sleeping in the open whenever he could and the other, most probably, his respect for the Vivian's privacy, the Kala Agar bungalow being quite small. Thus his arrival entry is noted as the 31st and his departure date, still visible in the tattered pages of the old book, is written as 13/3/30, or March 13th, 1930.

Corbett states, in his account of the hunt for the Chowgarh tigers, that the Vivians left Kala Agar on the 25th March. They actually left, according to Ham Vivian's handwritten entry in the old visitors book, on the 31st which is the day Corbett moved into the little *dak* bungalow. Corbett is to be forgiven the mistake. As far as we know he did not keep a journal—what a treasure that would have been! —and much of his writing about the great hunts, as I have stated previously, was done many years later.

After I had read and photographed the old book, the bungalow caretaker and a companion, a Kala Agar villager named Pan Singh Mewari, took me to where Corbett had his incredible face-to-face encounter with the tigress.

I spent a couple of hours there, photographing the little hollow and the huge leaning slab described by Corbett, and asking questions of my guides. When I was satisfied with their accounts of the story and had made all my notes, we walked back to the bungalow.

I would like to have been able to spend a night at the old *dak* bungalow. But I was unable to do so because these days permission for a stay has to be obtained from some obscure and no doubt difficult government office in Naini Tal. Corbett had the same problems even in his time; at Muktesar he received an official reprimand for having lunch at the public *dak* bungalow instead of the government one and at other times, in cold, wet weather when he probably would have been happy to get in out of the rain, he was unable to do so because he had not obtained official permission. So, in the evening,

I walked back down to the road and spent another night in my roadside camp there. Next day I left.

<<<>>>

One of the odd things about the Mohan man-eater was the fact that it made a strange moaning sound. When Corbett questioned Kartkanoula villagers about this they told him that it made the sound when it walked but that the sound ceased when it stopped, or lay down. From this Corbett deduced that the animal had a leg injury.

When he was skinning the tiger Corbett noticed hair missing from the inner side of the left foreleg and saw that the leg had a number of small holes from which pus was seeping. Exploring further he found what he was looking for and what he expected, a large number of porcupine quills, embedded deep in the flesh of the leg. These, and the damage that they had caused to the muscle and tissue they penetrated, were almost undoubtedly what turned the Mohan tiger into a man-eater, incapacitating it and depriving it of its ability to catch and kill other wild animals. It must also have been in great pain much of the time, which accounted for its moaning. Corbett said that he pulled about twenty-five quills out of the leg and that the villagers eagerly took them as souvenirs.

The clearing where Corbett shot the tigress, and that Corbett describes in his writings, is very much the same today as it was when he was there. My picture will show the reader its vegetation, short dry grass, stunted oak trees, light brush and here and there small stands of boulders. Like him, the sounds that I could hear when I was there, all of them contributing to a single pattern, were birdsong, the buzzing of insects and, from a distance, the voices of villagers back at Kartkanoula.

My picture of the clearing shows a fairly large black rock at its edge. The Kartkanoula villager who took me to the site told me that

Corbett used this for cover, approaching the tigress from behind it. But Corbett does not mention this in his account of the hunt and so whether he did or not must remain a matter of conjecture.

At Kartkanoula I asked about the porcupine quills that Corbett removed from the man-eater's body and that he said the villagers so eagerly took. But alas, no one had any, or for that matter could even remember having them or, if they did, what happened to them. So blow the winds of time in their endless passage.

<<◇>>

At the place where the Kanda man-eater was shot, villagers from Taria showed me a tree, which they said was the one in which Corbett sat for the man-eater, and from which he killed it. I doubted this because the tree they indicated just did not appear to be old enough. In the nineties, to be the same tree, it would have to have been over a hundred years old. All I can say for sure is that it was growing in the exact place described by Corbett in his story about the Kana man-eater, right on the edge of the ravine and directly above several pools. They also pointed out to me a big pool directly below the tree and said that this was the one into which the cat fell, when Corbett shot it.

Two of them came with me all the way down the ravine to just above where it flows into the Mandal River, to the point where Corbett entered it for his stalk of the man-eater. As he said, its bed was composed of flat, rounded river stones; walking on these with me, in their bare feet, the villagers who were my guides moved in silence. Later the same two men showed me a small field on the lower edge—the west side—of Taria vilage, which is where they said the man-eater was carried by the men of the village, to be skinned by Corbett.

<<◇>>

The victims of the Chuka Man-eater, an adult male tiger, totaled three, all young boys. The man-eater made its home in the forests between the village of Chuka and the village of Thak, which lies about three thousand feet above it. Because all of the Chuka man-eater's victims came from Thak, the big cat could have been named after that village. But Corbett's custom was normally—though not always—to name the man-eater in question after the village closest to where he shot it, in this case Chuka.

The Chuka cat was a male tiger in the prime of life. It measured—Corbett's estimate, made without a tape—nine foot six inches between pegs. It had a broken canine tooth in its lower right jaw and when skinning it Corbett found several rounds of buckshot lodged in its hide. In my opinion it was probably the broken canine that turned it into a man-eater. The loss of a single tooth may not seem much of an impediment to a tiger. But in this case the tooth was a canine, one of the four that a tiger has, all of which play a vital and essential part in the biting and killing, by strangulation, of its prey. A tiger's loss of a canine tooth can be compared to the loss of a thumb in a human being. It was principally this loss, I believe, that turned it into a man-eater.

Some confusion exists about the dates given by Corbett for the various incidents comprising the story of the Chuka Man-eater. In the opening part of his account of the hunt he states that the tiger's first attack, of the man with the plough on his back, took place 'in the winter of 1936.' The second attack, on the man with the sack of raw sugar on his back, happened 'a few weeks later.' Then came the killing of the two boys who went into the forest to look for missing cattle, in 'June, 1937,' followed by the killing of the orphan boy who was 'the Chuka man-eater's last human victim,' probably some weeks later.

Then Corbett opens up the story of the actual hunt by telling us that he and the Ibbotsens came down from Naini Tal 'on a sweltering hot day in April, 1937.' Obviously something is wrong with the dating of the sequence of events here and for a while I thought that Corbett might have made a mistake in setting the period of the hunt in April, 1938. Then I read the account of his next hunt in the same area, the hunt for the Thak man-eater, in the opening paragraphs of which we find him talking about the areas around Thak and Chuka and stating: 'It was in the valley between Kot Kindri and Thak that the Chuka man-eater had been shot the previous April.'

I think that this statement, about the date of the killing of the Chuka man-eater, fixes the correct period of the hunt, i.e., April, 1937. From this I deduct that the mistake that he makes is in the dating of the tiger's first attacks and that these took place, not in 1937, as he states, but in 1936, probably in the latter part of the winter of 1935-36, possibly in January or February. This would allow for and set the year of the killing of all of the tiger's first victims, the three boys, in 1936, not 1937.

When Corbett and the Ibbotsens arrived on the scene, in April 1937, it was probably close to ten months since the last fatality. Nevertheless, he was undoubtedly correct in stating that a reign of terror existed in the area, for the big cat, although it was not killing human beings, was still at large. It was this that brought he and the Ibbotsens to Chuka.

<<<>>>

Corbett's last hunt was at Thak, a prosperous little village high above the Sarda river that is home to the families of the priests of the Punagiri temple. The hunt was as dramatic and dangerous as any that he had until then and it ended when he called the big cat right up to him, and then shot it at very close range.

Things at Thak are very much the same today as they were when Corbett was there. The village remains unchanged. People still grow their crops around the little hamlet and right up to the edge of the forest. The spring at the mango tree below Thak still pulses with water that is clean and clear and good to drink. The big rock, set at the end of the forest clearing below Thak, on which Corbett balanced himself when calling in the man-eater, still dominates the little clearing where nature placed it and Thak villagers can point out exactly where Corbett stood.

When Corbett shot the man-eater there the big cat died, he said, with its head resting against the base of the rock. I neglected to measure the rock when I was there and can only guess, now, from memory, the actual distance, from where Corbett propped himself against it, to the place where the man-eater died. But I would say that it is about fifteen feet, much too close, in this case, in the fading light, for a tigress that was very angry at not being able to find the mate which had supposedly called her there and was on the verge of becoming angrier still, and deadly dangerous, if she had discovered that it was Corbett.

Today Corbett is remembered at Thak as he is at Chuka, which is to say, sadly, with memories fast fading with the years.

<<<◇>>>

Corbett shot one other big killer cat and this was the man-eating leopard of Rudraprayag. For part of that hunt his great friend Ibbotsen accompanied him and indeed, was with him on the night he shot it. This was a long and difficult hunt a description of which would take a book in itself. So I have not included it in my writings. Shooting this leopard, a very clever and tenacious animal, was a great achievement for Corbett so that whereas he wrote of his other great hunts as single stories within the confines of his separate books, he wrote a whole book, called The Man-eating Leopard of Rudraprayag, about the hunting of this extraordinary animal. It is published by and is obtainable from Oxford University Press, Great Clarendon Street, Oxford, England OX2 6DP.

<<◇>>

Lastly, there is the story of the Talla Des man-eaters and readers will probably notice that by placing it at the end of the Epilogue I have taken it out of the chronological sequence of the hunts, as Corbett carried them out, and as they appear in this book. There is a reason for this.

I began this book with the story of the man-eating tiger of Champawat and mentioned in my notes on that animal that it might well have been called the Rupal-Champawat man-eater, for it started its dreadful career around the village of Rupal, in the Dandeldura district of Western Nepal, before being driven into India, in a massive beat, by the people of that area.

As previously mentioned, because of the working schedules of the various occupations I have practiced during my life, time for research on Corbett's great hunts had to be taken as it became available. So it was that although the hunt for the Talla Des man-eater was not Corbett's last hunt, for me it just happened to be the last place that I visited for my final research for this book.

However, this is not why I have relegated it to the end of the Epilogue. There is another reason, an incident, which, with its timing, completed the cycle of my work by weaving its ending, quite perfectly, into its proper place within my twenty year pattern of research and by taking it, full circle, right back to where it began, which was with the story of the Champawat man-eater.

The very last phase of my writing research was on the Talla Des man-eater and I completed it in March 2002 by going to the Talla Des district and basing there at the village of Haram, where Corbett based during the hunt for the killer tigress and her cubs. I went to Talla Des by car from Nepal, crossing the Indian border at the Sarda Canal boom and then taking the Pithoragarh road, north, to Champawat. At Champawat I took the Talla Des road south and east, to the Talla Des district, and after some inquiry, eventually found the village that Corbett called Talla Kote. There was, however, a problem with the name of the village.

The village that I found, and where I was told Corbett had hunted the Talla Des man-eater, was called Tula Kot. Places names in rural Nepal, and India, may change with time and I believe I have given examples of this elsewhere. But in this case the villagers assured me that the village of Tula Kot had always been called by this name. Could Corbett have made a mistake about the name?

The hunt for the Talla Des man—eater took place in 1929 and Corbett wrote about it twenty—five years later, in 1954, actually at a time when I was in my second year of professional hunting, just fifty miles to the southeast, in Nepal. In this case, with his memory a little faded with time, I think that he did make a mistake, a forgivable one, just as, for example, when he was hunting in the Thak-Chuka area, he accidentally combined the names of the villages of Kot and Kindri, calling them Kot Kindri.

However, in the case of Tula Kot, another small problem arose, one that also puzzled me until I dug back into my own historical knowledge of the area and found the answer; this was in the name itself, which is not Indian, but Nepalese.

Tula is Nepalese and means big, large, or great. *Kot* is also Nepalese and means a fort. So what was an Indian village doing with a Nepalese name? Then I remembered that the Talla Des area and indeed land far to its west, had been part of Nepal until annexed by the British during and after the British Nepal wars. Hence the name Tula Kot and indeed the use of other Nepali names in India, such as the Tuli Gad river—where Corbett had an overnight camp with the Ibbotsens when on his way to hunt at Chuka—names that remained unchanged even after India became independent.

I arrived in the Talla Des district early on a March afternoon and after studying my map of the area and determining roughly where Tula Kot might be, stopped at a village called Haram. Leaving the car on the road with my driver, I walked in to the little village.

In the village I met a group of men who quickly pointed out where Tula Kot lay. One of them, a young man named Mahesh K. Sharma, who was visiting from Poona, where he lived, but who had been born in the Talla Des area and knew it well, offered to be my guide down to Tula Kot. With him, after waiting out a brief but heavy rain shower, I walked down to the village.

Tula Kot today is a village of probably a dozen houses clustered around a steep, conical shaped hill. It lies at an elevation of about 4500 feet at the end of a ridge and it is about a mile and a half from Haram and about a thousand feet below it. There is a saddle in the ridge below Haram, just before it climbs up to Tula Kot. The saddle had a small stand of massive, old pines, twisted and gnarled by the storms of the years; they were set in a little flat, covered with short green grass, one that caught my eye as a perfect camping place.

Arriving at the little hamlet, no bigger today than in Corbett's time, I was greeted by two elderly villagers. One of them brought out a thick brown blanket which he placed on a stone wall for me to sit on. The other, with true Indian village hospitality, offered me tea.

We sat down together and talked. It was a beautiful day, the air clean and clear after the rain. To the north the Himalaya gleamed softly and to the east the great rolling hills of Dandeldura rose out of the depths of the Sarda gorge.

Yes, they said, this is where *Carpet sahib*, as they called him, came to hunt the tigress. They pointed back to the saddle, over which I had just hiked, so meticulously described by Corbett as the apex to two great valleys, one taking its waters down to the Ladhya *khola,* the other dropping away, thousands of feet, to the Sarda river.

"Down there, *sahib*," they said, pointing to the east side of the ridge, "is where he shot the cubs, there, where that dry field is. And over the other side," pointing to the west, "is where he shot the tigress. The big trees that were down there in his time have all been cut now and so you cannot see the place for the new, young trees."

Corbett talked of huge pines down the slope on the west side; where they once stood is a forest of young pines, probably thirty to forty years old. The villagers told me that the old ones, having matured, were cut down.

While we were talking we were joined by another man. He was about fifty years of age, thin faced, with a bad cough and a pleasant smile. His name was Sundar Singh and after greeting me he listened to us talking for a while and then said, quietly, pointing down below the east side of the ridge, "That is where the tigress took a woman, its last victim. She was my great great grandmother."

I thanked him for the information and started to say something to one of the other men when a thought struck me. The man-eater's last victim? A woman? But the last victim of the Talla Des man-eater was the mother of the very brave young boy, Dungar Singh, who stepped out of the ranks of the villagers when Corbett arrived and courageously volunteered to act as his guide. If that was the case then the man in front of must be related to Dungar Singh.

And so it proved. He was Dungar Singh's grandson, the boy immortalized by Corbett in his story of the hunt. The boy who, with his father, was later taken to Almora where, in a public ceremony, the British Deputy Commissioner, Bill Baines, awarded he and his father a brand new rifle and a bag containing six hundred rupees, about twelve US dollars in today's currency, but of course worth a lot more than that in 1929.

I asked Sundar Singh if he still had the rifle. He said that yes, it was legally his. But it was in police custody in Champawat, all the guns and rifles of the villages of Talla Des having been collected by the police some years ago.

Before I left, Sundar Singh showed me the place where the tigress was brought when she was carried up to the village and where she was laid out for the villagers to see. No, she was not skinned there, he said. She was taken up to Haram, where Corbett's men skinned her. Haram was where Corbett based for the hunt, camping in a corn field just below the village, and where I stayed while I was there.

Walking back up the hill young Sharma said to me, "It is a pity you could not meet my grandfather. He is eighty-eight and was here in Corbett's time and saw him shoot the tigress. Unfortunately he lives quite far away from here."

But when we got back to Haram we found his grandfather there, visiting, and he quickly introduced me.

The old man's name was Lakshmi Dutt Sharma, a tall, thin, fine featured man, alert and intelligent. He had lost an eye some years before but otherwise appeared to be in very good health.

The old man told me, over a cup of tea, that he had not taken part in the hunt. However, when Corbett tracked and closed in on the man-eater, a thousand feet below the saddle, on the west side, he had stood with the whole population of the village and watched him. There were two shots, he said, and then he joined in the shouts and cheers of the villagers when Corbett, dressed in khaki shirt and khaki shorts and a felt *sahib's* hat, walked up to the tigress and sat down beside it to smoke a cigarette.

When my research was completed, I sent my car back and walked the roughly thirty-five miles from Tula Kot back to Tanakpur. I did this because I wanted to retrace Corbett's route when he came into Talla Des. In the process I found out what *talla* means. It means steep and indeed, that hill country there, high above the Sarda, is the most precipitous that I have encountered in years of hiking in the Himalaya.

I did the hike back in one and a half days, starting at Tula Kot and then leaving the area there via the pass in the ridge below which Corbett and his men spent a night, a saddle that lies roughly half way between Haram and Tamali. From there I hiked alone down the very steep trail that drops into the valley of the Surya Khola, a drop of about 3000 feet. The Surya, I was interested to note, is a stream shown on my old 1927 British maps as going dry about half way down its course. The accuracy of those old maps is a credit to the hard working and conscientious British cartographers of the Raj; the Surya is the same today, disappearing underground, about half way down the valley.

Coming down into the Surya valley, below the escarpment behind which lies the Talla Des district, I hiked south and east on good trails via the villages of Badar and Mooktan and Sem. I crossed the Ladhya Khola at Sem and then passed through Chuka, where I learned that the great fig tree from which Corbett shot the Chuka man-eater had at last fallen. From Chuka I went on south along the river via Kaladunga, where I found Colliers one time beautiful bungalow—its windows smashed and its roof rusting and leaking—slowly sinking into ruin, and eventually reached Tanakpur, from where I took a Jeep taxi to Banbasa and the Sarda Canal boom, where I crossed back into Nepal.

It was before I left the Talla Des district, however, that the incident—the milestone I would call it—that caused me to place the story of the Talla Des man-eater last among my stories, took place, the occurrence that knitted together all of my research, taking it, in this case in a few words from an old man, right back to were it started, twenty years before, at Champawat.

On my last morning at Haram I woke up a little before five and, keen to see the dawn in the hills of Nepal, went outside and sat on the stone wall that surrounded the little compound of the farmers house where I was staying. The air was cool, probably in the fifties, but I was comfortable in cotton pajamas, slippers and a robe.

A little after five, although the deep valley of the Sarda below me was still in total darkness, the light began to grow behind the Nepal hills. It was very faint and not much brighter than that of the brilliant starlight that bathed the little courtyard and the lush fields of oats and barley that surrounded it. Then it faded. This was the false dawn.

About half an hour later the light began to grow again and the real dawn slowly spread its exquisite mantle, in delicate shades of violet and rose pink, across the hills. As it did so the dawn wind blew for a minute or two, rustling the barley stalks, and then ceased. The scene was very lovely and I was completed engrossed in watching it when a figure appeared out of the gloom beside me. It was old Mr. Sharma and after a brief morning greeting, "*Ram, Ram, sahib*" he joined me on the stone wall and said that he had told a girl to bring tea.

We sat for a while in silence, both of us watching the growing day and after a while a little girl appeared with two metal glasses of hot, sweet, milky tea, the kind that Corbett used to love. We sipped the tea together and watched the great, rolling hills of Nepal slowly fill with light. When we had finished the tea, and the valleys and hills of the little kingdom across the river were distinct enough to separately identify, the old man leaned forward and pointed.

"You see that great hill there, *sahib,* with the little white houses lying across its front. Those are the houses of the village of Rupal. That's where another *badmass* tiger (an evil tiger) came from, many years ago. It was driven out of there, across the river, below us, by the villagers, in a great beat, and when it came here it went to live at Champawat. That is where your friend *Carpet Sahib* shot it. He was a very brave man."

<<< >>>

We know a great deal about tigers now, thanks to studies that have been conducted over the years by people dedicated to their survival. Sadly, however, there are still many people who look upon the big cats as savage animals; for this, irresponsible writers and film makers are often to blame. The man-eating tiger is a menace, true, and when one starts its depredations it must be put down. But when this happens we are nearly always dealing with an animal the bad habits and intentions of which we ourselves have created. When he is not a man-eater and is not molested, the tiger is as peaceful and harmless as any other forest dwelling animal, living with and adhering to a very simple code of ethics known as the jungle law. This commands him to respect man and this is what he does. In return, all he asks is, leave me alone to live my life. Give me a little space and some food, water and cover. Do this and in turn, when you come into my forest kingdom, I will leave you alone. More than that, when I meet you on one of my forest trails I will greet you as one forest dweller does another, with respect and courtesy and as one who obeys the jungle law.

The tiger is a noble beast. By the end of this century he will be gone from the wild, driven into extinction by the inexorable march of civilization, itself fed by the uncontrollable increase of human populations. When that happens the world will be a sadder and, for me, a less interesting place.

I personally cannot imagine the great forests of North India and the Terai of Southern Nepal without the great cats. I cannot conceive sitting at a campfire deep in the heart of somewhere like the White Grass Plains Wildlife Reserve of Nepal's far west, listening for the long sad call of a hunting tiger, and not hearing it, and knowing that I am not going to hear it, because the last one is gone. And yet that time is coming, for as I write, poaching of the tiger in India, which began seriously when the British Raj came to an end and when its protective wildlife laws were virtually abandoned, is operating on a massive scale.

Fed by the apathy and corruption of government officials and the greed and ruthlessness of a sophisticated poaching mafia, the Indian tiger, the great Bengal tiger of legend, is being devastated. Well organized gangs, using traps, automatic weapons and poison, have already made huge inroads into what may now be the last few thousand tigers left in the sub continent. The spur for the gangs is the money to be made in the bone trade, a huge market based on the ignorance of people who think that ground-up tiger bone has miraculous qualities. The result is a market that begins with the poacher getting, if he is lucky, $50 or less, for a tiger's carcass and ends with his gang bosses selling it on the street for as much as $100,000.

In Nepal, thanks to wise conservation methods and conscientious administrators, as well as a tough, shoot-to-kill attitude towards poachers, the tiger is still holding his ground. But in India the tiger, the big cat the British lovingly called Mr. Stripes, will soon disappear into the mists of time. Speeding him on his way are two things. One, the need to house and feed the one billion plus and ever growing Indian population, for which purpose more and more land must be cleared, land that in many areas is both the habitat and the last stronghold of the tiger. Two, the poacher rings, daily growing bolder and soon, many of us feel, when the Indian tiger is gone, ready to turn their eyes north, towards Nepal.

I consider myself fortunate, nay, privileged, to have known the big cats as I have done, to have been allowed by them to live among them and even today, spending winters in Nepal, to enjoy the company of the last of them. Tingeing my appreciation, however, is sorrow at knowing what is going to happen to them and, additionally, I must admit, sympathy for those who will come after me and for whom, one day soon, it will be too late to see one of the great animals in its natural habitat. I am not sure that I want to be here when that time comes. The tiger is a noble beast and when he is gone the world will be a sadder place, one which I believe I will be content to leave to others.

<<< >>>

Today, in the year 2002, for anyone who wants to visit Corbett's country of Kumaon and Gharwal and any of the sites of his great hunts, it is worth mentioning that as this book is going to print, a new safari lodge is being built by the author in Kanchanpur, in Western Nepal, from where access to Kumaon and Gharwal can be made in a few hours. The lodge will be situated on the edge of the White Grass Plains Wildlife reserve and will be called The White Grass Plains Safari Lodge.

It will be a five star, luxury establishment that will cater to paying guests, offering them wildlife observation and eco tours in the forests and grasslands of the WGP, on foot, from four-wheel-drive specially built safari vehicles, from silent electric vehicles and from elephant back. To this extent the new lodge will be like other safari lodges in other parts of the world. However, there the comparison will end.

For this lodge is planned as something completely different. It is designed and will have a charter to operate as a not-for-profit enterprise, with all of its net income to be directed into wildlife conservation and protection programs within the WGP, as well as wildlife education in the villages surrounding it. The lodge owners, headed by the author, will design and operate these programs. However, they will also welcome projects from registered scientific institutions in the US and elsewhere, as well as student study programs from universities and established schools, on an international basis. To this end, one of the buildings included in the lodge complex will be a Science House; it will contain a small laboratory and accommodation for accredited visitors.

The lodge is being built under the auspices of the International Wildlife Conservation Society Inc, a US registered not-for-profit society with 501 (c) (3) tax status and as such it will be a first for Nepal and, indeed, a first for Asia. (As of now, as far as is known, only one other similar nonprofit lodge exists, in South Africa.)

It will be built as a complex surrounding a spacious, centrally located, rondaval type building which will contain a bar, dining area, lounge, gift shop and library. Guests will be limited to twenty persons and these will be housed in luxuriously appointed, elevated, air-conditioned houses separate from but close to the lodge central building.

Each house will have a name and these will be for persons or entities associated, across the years, with the general area of Western Nepal, and of Kumaon and Gharwal, the hills of which are visible from the WGP. Among these will be a Baden-Powell House, after Sir Robert Baden-Powell, founder of the Boy Scouts, who hunted in the WGP in 1895. A Smythies House, after an immortal English lady of Raj days, Olive Smythies, who had the unique experience of having a tiger come up a tree and attack her in her hunting *machan*, in the Indian forests just west of the WGP. A Champawat House, after the incredible man-eater of Champawat. A Rara Lake house, after the beautiful Himalayan lake which lies to the north of the WGP and the lovely name of which is now incorporated into the author's family. A Tula Hatti house, after the great elephant of the WGP that is the subject of one the author's other books, TULA HATTI, THE LAST GREAT ELEPHANT, (Faber & Faber, 1998). And of course a Jim Corbett House.

In addition to the lodge itself, guests will also be able to spend a night deep in the heart of the reserve in a tented safari camp. Situated on an the site of one of the author's old, big game hunting camps, accommodation will be in spacious, wooden floored and netted safari tents; there will also be a mess tent, with appropriate dining facilities. A full, tented camp staff will attend to visitors, ensuring that good food and hot showers are available at all times.

The White Grass Plains park consists of 180,000 acres of pristine, old growth forest, grassland and wetlands. It is home to a twenty-five member wild elephant herd, rhino, tiger, leopard, five species of deer, wild boar, crocodile and many smaller and exotic animals such as jackal, hyena, porcupine and pangolin, or anteater. Its beautiful, slow moving and mysterious jungle river, and its single lake, contain between twenty-seven species of fish and to date three hundred and fifty species of birds have been identified in the reserve.

Tours that will be offered to guests will include viewing of the park's exotic wildlife in the wetlands and on the jungle river by canoe, in the grasslands—which contain the last great herd of Swamp Deer left in Asia, two thousand animals—by four wheel drive vehicle and in the forest from elephant back. Fishing for the mighty mahseer, the great sporting fish of British days, will be available on a nearby mountain river and in the forest itself a keen angler can try his luck, with lure or fly, for the many jungle river species available. Visitors with archeological interest can explore the ruins of the ancient fort of a minor king, the Singpal Raja, who lived deep in the forest at the edge of the WGP grasslands; to date the fort has not been studied or excavated.

Special tours will be arranged for visits to Jim Corbett's old hunting sites in Kumaon. Both Champawat and Talla Des are a day's drive and comfortable overnight safari fly camps will be set up for visitors. Also within a day's drive is the memorial stone and the site of the extraordinary 1925 experience of Olive Smythies, at Jaulasal. Host at the lodge will be the author

For more information on the this unique and beautiful new safari lodge, and on the International Wildlife Conservation Society, see the society's web site, which is www internationalwildlife.org and its quarterly newsletter, or write to the society at P.O. Box 34, Pacific Palisades, California, 90272.

For details on how to find Peter Byrne's other books, (both published and pending) including TULA HATTI, THE LAST GREAT ELEPHANT, the story of his discovery of the largest elephant in Asia, and GONE ARE THE DAYS, a stirring account of his hunting years and safari life in the great forests of north India and Nepal and of his eventual transition from hunter to conservationist, send a brief email inquiry marked Book Sales to the author.

Peter Byrne.
Katmandu, Nepal, and Los Angeles, California.
Autumn, 2002.

MAPS

MAPS, INCLUDING A MAP OF PART OF WESTERN NEPAL SHOWING RUPAL, WHERE THE MAN-EATER OF CHAMPAWAT BEGAN ITS CAREER.

BIBLIOGRAPHY

Corbett, Jim. *Man-eaters of Kumaon*,

——*The Temple Tiger and Other* Man-eaters,

——*The Man-eating Leopard of Rudraprayag*,

——*Jungle Lore, My India*, all published in many editions and available from Oxford University Press, New York, USA, and London, England.

Carrington Turner, J.E. (Indian Forest Service) *Man-eaters and Memories*, Published by Robert Hale, Lt., 63 Old Brompton Rd., London, England, in 1959.

Hodges-Hill, Edward. (editor) *Man-eater, Tales of Lion and Tiger Encounters*, Published by Cockbird Press, Ltd., PO Box 356, Heathfield, East Sussex, England, in 1992.

Montgomery (Sir). *Spell of the Tiger, The Man-eaters of the Sunderbunds*, Published by Houghton Mifflin Company, Boston and New York, in 1995.

Braddon, Edward (Sir). *Thirty Years of Shikar*. , K.C.M.G., published by William Blackwood and Sons, Edinburgh, Scotland, and London, England, 1855.

Hewett, John (Sir). *Jungle Trails in Northern India*, Published by Methuen and Company Ltd, 36 Essex Street, London, England.

Byrne, Peter. *Gone Are The Days*. A Limited Edition, 1000 copies, published by Safari Press, Huntington Beach, California, 2001.

——*Tula Hatti, the last great elephant*. Published by Faber & Faber, Manchester, New Hampshire, 1995.

——*The Wildlife of the White Grass Plains*. A complete description of the mammals, birds, reptiles and fishes of Sukila Phanta, the White Grass Plains Wildlife Reserve, of South West Nepal. Publication planned for the fall of 2002.

Jaleel, Jerry. *Under the Shadow of Man-eaters*. Published by the Jim Corbett Foundation, 1306-39, Street, Edmonton, Alberta, Canada, T6L 2M7.

Booth, Martin. *Carpet Sahib, A life of Jim Corbett*, Published by Constable & Company, England, in 1986.

Singh, Arjun (Billy). *Tiger Haven*, Published by Macmillan London Ltd., London, England, in 1973.

Prater, S.H. (C.M.Z.S). *The Book of Indian Animals*, Published by the Bombay Natural History Society and Oxford University Press, in 1948.

Ali, Salim. *Indian Hill Birds*, Published by Oxford University Press, Delhi, Bombay, Calcutta, Madras, India, in 1949.

Grimmett, Richard; & Inskipp, Tim and Carol. *Birds of Nepal*, Published by Prakash Books, M-86, Connaught Circus, New Delhi, India 11001, in 2000.

Fleming, Robert L., Sr., Fleming, Robert L., Jr., and Bangdel, Lain Singh. *Birds of Nepal*, Published by Robert Fleming Sr., and Jr., in 1976.

Woodcock, Martin. *Birds of the Indian Sub Continent*, Published by William Collins and Son, Grafton Street, London, England, in 1980.

Daniel, J.C. *The Book of Indian Reptiles*, Published by the Bombay Natural History Society and Oxford University Press, Walton Street, Oxford, England, in 1983.

Williams, J.H. *Elephant Bill*, Published by The Country Life Press, Garden City, New York, in 1950.

Baden-Powell, Robert (Sir). *Indian Memories*, Published by Herbert Jenkins Ltd., 12 Arundel Place, London, S.W., England, in 1915.

Delort, Robert. *The Life and Lore of The Elephant*, Published by Harry N. Abrams Inc., in 1990.

Mountfort, Guy. *So Small a World*, Published by Hutchinson of London, England, in 1974.

Symington, John M.D. *In a Bengal Jungle*, Published by Chapel Hill, the University of North Carolina University Press, Chapel Hill, North Carolina, USA, in 1955.

Thomas, Henry Sullivan. *The Rod in India*, Published by Natraj Publishers, 17 Rajpur Road, Dehra Dun, India 248001, in 1984.

Shrestha, (Mrs.) Jiwan, Dr. *Fishes, Fishing Implements & Methods of Nepal*. Published by Smt. M.D. Gupta, Lalitpur Colony, Lashkar (Gwalior) India, in 1994.

Fuchs, Stephen. *The Aboriginal Tribes of India*. Published by St. Martin's Press, New York, USA in 1973.

Burrard, Sir Gerald, (Major) Bt., D.S.O., R.F.A (Retired). *Notes on Sporting Rifles*, Published by Edward Arnold and Company, London, England, in 1920.

Yule, Henry and Burnell, A.C. *Hobson-Jobson, The Anglo-Indian Dictionary*, Published by Wordsworth Reference, in 1886, and republished by Wordsworth Editions Ltd., Cumberland House, Crib Street, Ware, Hertfordshire, England in 1996.